Why Are we Here?

The Scientific Answer To This Age-Old Question
(that you don't need to be a scientist to understand)

By
Dennis Marcellino

Lighthouse Publishing
PO Box 40 - B
Gladstone, Oregon 97027
(503) 557-2277
(503) 557-2278 Fax
E-mail: Light3740@aol.com

Why Are We Here?

The Scientific Answer To This Age-Old Question

(that you don't need to be a scientist to understand)

Published By

Lighthouse Publishing
PO Box 40 - B
Gladstone, Oregon   97027
(503) 557-2277
(503) 557-2278 Fax
E-mail: Light3740@aol.com

Copyright © 1996 by Dennis Marcellino
Printed in the United States of America

Library of Congress Cataloging-in-Publication Data

Marcellino, Dennis, 1948-
    Why Are We Here? : the scientific answer to this
    age-old question / by Dennis Marcellino.
            p.   cm.
    Includes bibliographical references and index.
    ISBN 0-945272-10-3
        1. Apologetics. 2. Bible--Evidences, authority, etc.
    3. Religion and science.   I. Title.
    BT1102.M325   1996
    239--dc20   96-9440 CIP

Table Of Contents

This book is dedicated
to all the hungry hearts and minds
who sincerely love
and earnestly seek
The Truth

Introduction

An Overview Of This Book

<u>From "Star Trek - The Movie" (1979)</u>:

<u>Mr. Spock</u> (with tears streaming from his eyes):

"I weep for V'ger as I would a brother. As I was when I came aboard, so is V'ger now. Empty, incomplete, and searching. .

Each of us, at some time in our lives, turns to someone....a father, a brother, a God...and asks: <u>Why am I here?</u> What was I meant to be? V'ger hopes to touch its Creator ...to find its answers."

<u>Captain Kirk</u> (poignantly quoting):

"Is this all that I am? Is there nothing more?"

This book, *Why Are We Here?*, has the answers to these questions. And it gives them with such logic and feeling that even Mr. Spock would be very pleased. It also shows you how to "touch your Creator".

Life is not as complicated as many make it out to be. It becomes complicated only when a person doesn't know the simple answers to its basic questions, and then fishes for them through many semi-true and untrue answers. The *science of logic* tells us there is only one simple answer for every simple question (e.g., in base 10: 1+1= [only] 2). And this includes the questions: Is there a God?, Is there an afterlife? and Why are we here? Many may not know these answers, but God, the author of them, obviously does. And if He were to be asked these questions, He wouldn't pop into the sky with long dissertations. He would simply say: "Yes", "yes", and "to try to become eligible for and prepare for a greater existence: heaven." (Of course this last answer brings up an even bigger question: How do we become eligible - or ineligible - for heaven? This question will be answered in great detail in this book. A note for now though: Christians, don't be too sure that you know the answer to this one).

But God is not presently offering verbal answers from heaven. And many people (especially in the media and science community) will not just accept the above simple answers without proof. These answers might not be obvious or visible, but they are scientifically provable. That is a big part of what this book is about. Besides proving the answers to these questions, this book also proves that God authored the Bible, and shows the logic behind His ways in creation and throughout history (His-story). Its purpose also is to show the surpassing beauty and practicality of His ways, and to show our role in His plan (collectively and individually).

Simple answers, once proven, are very valuable because: the simpler the truth is explained, the easier it is to deal with (and less are the chances of having problems with it). And when things are operated simply and correctly (in this case, life and our beings), greater is the possibility of enjoying them.

Christianity is usually presented with emotional appeals, e.g. 'freedom from guilt through repentance of sin', 'God loves you', 'Jesus died for your sins', 'hope for a good life', 'hope for prosperity', 'the end is coming soon', 'hope for freedom from life's problems', etc.

But how many really understand what these short phrases mean? Or...how many conversions were just the result of people being hyped up to an emotional response (which was fueled by their emptiness, pain and need)? Without a strong, simple, logical understanding of Christianity, themselves and this life, these people will often end up having serious difficulties with their faith at some point, or even be completely pulled away by 'the world', other non-religious people, a false or immature religious group, or their own minds.

Fortunately, Christianity is also the most intellectually satisfying way-of-life, story-of-human-history, explanation-of-life, and philosophy that exists. And, there is a great deal of evidence that can move a person's faith more and more out of the area of *believing* and into the area of scientifically *knowing*.

If a person chooses Christianity based on an initial emotional experience, when this experience wears off and it is realized that there will be some element of struggle, the person will need to have a strong and complete intellectual foundation to repeatedly explain to them, in the midst of their struggles, why they should press on in a Christian way......and how they should go about doing so. (Read Matthew 13:1-23, then know that reading "Why Are We Here?" will show you how to have those "roots").

'Knowing and understanding all of the logical answers' is taking the pig-with-the-brick-house's approach to life. This book contains these answers and tries to present them and their proofs in the simplest ways possible. But in fact, it is so simple that it all can be boiled down to one easy-to-understand sociological principle. And this principle appeals strictly to a person's sense of reason, not their emotion. (However, once understood and applied, it can unlock a wealth of good emotions....as well as stave off a lot of bad ones).

This principal also explains why God had to make this life exactly as it is.

It shows what the single purpose of our entire life is, as well as the purpose in each moment of our lives.

It would be easy for me to at this point tell you what this principle is. But if you want to build a permanent, solid, brick-like spiritual structure that will have the power to give you high purpose and strengthen you for your entire lifetime, you should start by laying a strong foundation first.

The way that this book builds this foundation is to first give the most extensive scientific and logical proof ever given that God does exist. And this proof can stand up to the most thorough scientist's scrutiny.

Next, it is proven that the Bible was authored by God, and the reader is shown how to *physically* prove this over and over to his or her self.

Then God's motive for making this world and all that is in it is examined.

Next, the viewpoint is taken of 'a Creator making this life' as being very similar to 'an inventor making a television'. That is, there are 'nuts and bolts' decisions that need to be made with both. For example: Why even make it?, Why design it in a specific way?, What are the inherent problems in the design?, and How do you solve these problems?

Then the aforementioned 'principle' is presented, which is the bottom-line idea behind the reason for this life.

Chapters 5 through 11 are devoted to looking at all of human history through the eyes of this principle. Finally, in Chapter 12 it is shown that by applying it, every moment of every life can have great purpose and deep fulfillment.

Preface

Why I Wrote This Book

"I once was lost....but now I'm found,
was blind........but now I see."

What a great statement to be able to make. I too was once blind, which brought suffering, both to myself and others. But now I can really see, which gives me a deep satisfaction, peace, purpose and security.

And what is it that I now see that I didn't see before? On the one hand I see an extremely beautiful Kingdom of God. On the other hand I see a world that is to a large degree lost, blind and suffering needlessly because of these conditions. I say "needlessly" because if people were to understand why we are here, and understand God's love and holiness, they would suffer much less. And if everyone understood these things, no one would suffer at all (this is the premise for heaven). I am very grateful that I can "see" these things. So my greatest desire now is to try to pass this vision on with this book. Why? Because it is very beautiful, and it is exciting to share with others the great things we discover....especially when we see how much it could benefit them. This vision contains the most beautiful, functional, clear, purposeful, fulfilling and peaceful way to see and approach this life.

In 2Cor. 4, St. Paul expressed the same feeling and vision I've expressed here: *"...by the <u>open declaration of the truth</u> we commend ourselves <u>to everyone's conscience in the sight of God</u>. And even though our <u>gospel is veiled</u>, it is veiled for <u>those who are perishing</u>, in whose case <u>the god of this age</u> has <u>blinded the minds</u> of the unbelievers, so that <u>they may not see</u> the light of the gospel. For God who · said, "Let light shine out of darkness," has <u>shone in our hearts</u> to <u>bring to light the knowledge of the glory of God</u>..."*

Many Christians *know* that they are living in the best of all possible worlds here on earth - the Kingdom of God - and that they have aligned with the best of all possible philosophies.

But there still is a huge gap between Christians and non-believers...between Christians and "the world" (the media, government, medical and psychology community, education system, intelligentsia, entertainment industry, etc.). And the Christian community has had a difficult time communicating what it *knows* across this gap.

Why? One reason is because many of the most vocal among those who call themselves Christians use short clichés to communicate (e.g. "Jesus died for your sins", "God loves you", "you are a sinner", "Jesus saves", etc.). And because these clichés are rarely fully-explained in the public forum, the world doesn't understand the perfect logic and beauty they contain. And because they are often presented in a finger-pointing, unloving and even hostile way, "the world", in turn, is hostile toward them and Christianity. They've become *sound-bytes* that push buttons and draw angry and cynical canned responses.

But this is a shame, because Christianity is exactly what humanity so desperately needs right now. This is because: within Christianity is the highest wisdom, the greatest beauty, and a perfect, practical set of standards for living a joyful, meaningful, functional and fulfilling life. And having this inner fulfillment is what prevents people from entering into very painful, dangerous and damaging pitfalls in life (and after this life). The extremes of these pitfalls presently inundate the daily news. But for every disastrous story on the news, there are a <u>tremendous number</u> of stories of suffering that go on without public recognition. This is evidenced by the very high rates of: divorce, suicide, child abuse, spouse abuse, addiction, etc. It is also evidenced by how the entertainment industry is mostly filled with negative feelings. Music, movies, and television are filled with anger, tragedy, violence and pain. And, in the entertainment industry, the accepted basic experiential norm is an unconnected spirit of *hyper-jivyness* (as opposed to God's spirit of love, which is: peace, patience, gentleness, etc.). And this hyper-jivyness is used to avoid and sweep under the rug the emotional repercussions of modern living (with 'the rug' being a forced sense of frivolity, delivered by <u>act</u>ors, who themselves are running from broken lives and/or are so desperate for work and attention that they'll do almost anything). It is also used as an energy boost, in an attempt to feel good in spite of the tragedies.

But the most tragic part here is that the only solution to our problems: God (with His love and holiness), is also being swept under the rug and banned from public life under the clever atheistic ploy that says: "You can't mention <u>any</u> religion because it would be offensive to the other religions". So now we've become a non-religious society. We and our children are being forced to live in a world which has as its basic philosophy a set of humanistic standards that are far more offensive to any truly religious person than any other God-centered religion could possibly be. (All religions...recognize this and unite against it!)

My feeling is that if people really <u>understood</u> the importance of holiness, and really <u>knew</u> the greatness and beauty of God, His standards and His love, they would institute these as THE standards and spirit of life and living (as much of the world did for many centuries). Therefore, it is my desire to spread this <u>understanding</u> and <u>knowing</u>. Whether this can be accomplished for society as a whole is debatable (and would require inspired efforts from a lot of people. Nevertheless, we should never cease trying.)

But it certainly can be accomplished in individual lives. One way of doing this is by reading this book and understanding its principles, then embracing the Bible and God's Spirit as that which is closest to us, and that which we revere, cherish and look up to above all else. My life is just one of many testimonies that says that God and His Bible can transform a life that was drowning in the quicksand of modern ways to a life that has great fulfillment, inspiration, guidance and purpose. I'll tell some of this story throughout the book.

So one of the main reasons I wrote *Why Are We Here?* was out of a desire to bridge the gap between Christianity and non-believers.....between the Church and the world, and to try to slow down the wave of dysfunction that liberalism has been inundating our society with. My efforts are not just for the sake of 'Christians being able to live and raise their children in a holier world', but they are also out of compassion for the many people who have become (and are becoming) suffering victims because they have been coerced into unholiness by the liberal-humanistic dominated secular church: television. My efforts are also out of compassion for the many innocent victims that we see on the news who, along with their families, suffer because of the crimes and dysfunctions of others.

But, if this world is going to change, it needs to be given a very solid *logical* argument as to why it should abandon worshipping its idols (sports, vanity, entertainment, media "stars", violence, sex, drugs, rebelliousness, hyperness, money, ego, desires, etc.), and why the God of the Bible is the only One truly worthy of our worship.

And this is a vitally important argument that needs to be made at this time because people are continually being hypnotized by the media into dysfunction and harmful, peace-robbing behavior. And if people are never exposed to the perfect logic, functional sanity and beauty of God and His Bible, they will never experience the deep peace, love and joy that happens when we focus on them. They'll never even know that these great possibilities exist, and therefore, they'll never be inspired to pursue them.

In this light, the secular media is not only flawed by what it <u>puts out</u>, but also by what it <u>leaves out</u>. How can anyone make good philosophical choices in life without having the logic and beauty of the only perfect philosophy (Christianity) presented to them *often and with equal time* (a la advertising theory)?

Right now, many people are sinking deeper and deeper into the quicksands of: 'dysfunction (from wrong living and wrong focusing)', and 'desperately reaching for new ways to cope with the painful experiences that result from this dysfunctional living and focusing'. I believe that the main reason for this is: the media *diet* that they are being fed is heavily overloaded with *junk*, and critically devoid of *nutrition*. The spirit of rebellion and jivyness that started in the mid-'50s has been like a spiritual cancer, working hard to kill off the social structures that preserve normalcy and keep dysfunction in check (mainly: religion, wise media, *natural* romance, and the family). But we still do have some things that can spare us from all of this and give us <u>perfect</u> guidance: the Bible and God's Spirit.

Actually, the Bible contains the highest wisdom available (and this is not just a blind belief or knee-jerk opinion. It is a statement backed by a 28 year scientific study, which I'm using this book to prove and present). But does the world believe this? The 'latest trends in government policies' and 'what is being glorified in the *mainstream* media' says that people (especially many of those in positions of power) don't really believe that this is true.

In order to prove that 'following God' is the most *beauti*ful approach to life, His followers would have to exhibit an experience of *beauty* (love). Do they? Not most who are held up in the media as representing Him.

Christians are being portrayed as being just as sinful as everyone else. And instead of gentle, humble love, and calm, intelligent reasoning...the "fruits" usually exhibited by those in the media who *claim to* represent Christianity are: hyper-salesmanship, vanity, self-glorification and angry condemnation. It's no wonder then that Christianity has been greatly devalued in public opinion.

In order to prove that the Bible contains the highest wisdom and the most functional approach to living, this argument must be made with very convincing, calm, intelligent reasoning and love. Is this what is being done? No. Hyper-emotionalism is what is too often being used to try to bring people to Christianity. It is too frequently presented by <u>'used-car salesman' types pressing for the quick sale</u>. But this cheapens the ultimate greatness of God, and doesn't convey the <u>invaluable</u> experiential highness, peace and love He offers (as well as perfect logic and practical wisdom). It actually conveys just the opposite because: people don't see God, they just see the messengers.

Therefore, a hope of this book is to start *from ground zero* in rebuilding God's credibility in the public forums. And the first step in this process is to give a solidly logical argument as to why God and His Bible should be elevated to the top of what we revere and follow - in spite of the current media's negative image of Christianity.

Destructive and irresponsible approaches to life can be seen as such only when they are held up next to the light of a *proven* perfect standard (the Bible). People, due to the current policies of the media and education systems, are very underexposed to this perfect standard (and why it is the perfect standard). A hope of this book is to help change that. How? By putting forth a pro-God, pro-Bible picture of this life that is so logically and scientifically solid that it can handle any non-Christian's questions and arguments (and, in my experience, I don't see how a person could satisfactorily live this life without this knowledge).

My background in logic, and how it applies here

Even though many people can be *emotionally snagged* by the media (and even by some religious groups), *logic* must ultimately be satisfied for them to give their heart and allegiance in a deep and lasting way. Logic also must be thoroughly satisfied for the world's systems of authority to give their endorsement, and for them to be reclaimed from their current liberal influences.

My functioning, involvements and philosophies have always had to answer (internally) to intense logical scrutiny. Why? Because as an engineering student, I was trained to be microscopically analytical. And anyone who has dealt with advanced science, math or engineering problems in college textbooks knows that if you want to come up with the correct answers (which are located in the back of these books), you have to develop a 'leave no stone unturned' approach to looking at problems. You have to carefully scrutinize the subject being studied for every possible flaw or contradiction. And, you must try to look at it from all possible viewpoints. Also, you must learn to dig with a fine tooth comb so as to uncover all of the pertinent evidence that there is.

When I later delved into philosophy, psychology, spirituality and religion, I didn't brush this training in analysis aside. When I was involved in a certain philosophy, method or religion, my mind would bring up to me any flaws or contradictions it would spot. Then I would have to deal with them, either by satisfactorily answering them, or by moving on to the next philosophy, method or religion. (Unfortunately, many people try to fight off and sweep under the rug the flaws that their minds spot. But this keeps them stuck in flawed philosophies and methods).

To make a long story short, after 14 years of searching, I ended up in Christianity, where I've been for 14 years now. The result of my studies and searching is that I have found the Bible to be a scientifically perfect document. It is the 'back of the book' for life, living, psychology, philosophy, spirituality, law and sociology. And it is the only perfect complete-document-about-life on the planet. This conclusion has been arrived at after 14 years of Bible study, based on my training at Logos Bible College. Also included in this conclusion are my 14 pre-Christian years of study, in which I had deep and continual involvement in most of the major philosophies and methods of personal growth in this world, including: most of the major and experimental forms of psychology (Freudian analysis, Transactional Analysis, hypnosis, psychodrama, Primal Therapy, Rolfing, drug therapy, wholistic psychotherapy, etc.), meditation (chanting, the Word, light and music), eastern religion (Indian), Utopianism, various 'new age' involvements, Scientology and secular-humanism. My involvement in Christianity has included: Protestant Fundamentalism, Catholicism, and a thorough knowledge of the Charismatic movement.

I don't just blindly accept things. I must be thoroughly and logically convinced. And because of this, I feel like I've formulated arguments that can be very convincing to a logic-oriented world, (as well as being able to handle any doubts that might arise in a Christian's mind).

The logical mind is the safeguard of the heart. But once logic has been satisfied and we let go to God, many wonderful things happen in our hearts. But the only proofs we have to offer that these things happen are our testimonies, our fruit, and our changed lives. We can't give someone a magic pill. We can only encourage people to try what we've tried. So one of my purposes with this book is to help a person let their logical guard down (by answering their logic questions) so they then can <u>experience the heart magic of God</u> for themselves.

Christians are eager to share the greatness that has saved our lives, given us clear vision and good purpose, and filled our hearts. "Why Are We Here?" has valuable tools that can help us do this.

I also wrote this book because, having been a Catholic, a Protestant, a new-age person, a secular-humanist, a liberal, and a conservative - and each for many years - I know that all of these groups could greatly benefit from wisdoms in the others. I present these wisdoms at various points throughout this book.

Although parts of this book contain scientific proofs,
it was attempted to use as little science-speak as possible.
Rather, the intention of this book is to be
reader-friendly,
and for everyone.

Chapter 1

Is There A God?

Is there a God? What do you think? In your heart of hearts, what do you feel? If you believe that there is, you are in agreement with 96% of all Americans, according to a December 1994 CNN/USA Today/Gallup Poll. Does this figure surprise you? It should, because if you look at television and most of the other "mainstream" media offerings in this country, there rarely is even a mention of God.

If you do believe there is a God, how sure are you in that belief? Is there anything that someone else could say to you that could shake your belief? And if you were to stop and really dwell on this question, do you think your belief would get stronger...or weaker? How strong would your defense be if someone, who either wasn't sure - or who felt very strongly that there isn't a God - was to ask you to give one?

Although God can't be seen by our eyes (which would be absolute proof), science offers many ways to prove the existence of things that aren't visible (that is, that can't be proven by our eyes).

The scientific evidence for the existence of God is even stronger than the evidence for the existence of the atom (which also has never been seen or photographed). Yet when the <u>theories</u> based on the <u>assumed</u> existence and properties of the atom are <u>applied</u> (in science and manufacturing), they <u>work extremely well</u>.

Similarly, when Bible <u>theories</u> are <u>applied</u> (to how we should think and live), they also <u>work extremely well</u>.

But there is a lot more evidence for the existence of God and the perfectness of the Bible than just the positive results we get when we apply the Bible's principles to our lives (although for many, this is proof enough). There is much evidence from physics, logic, history, personal experience, sociology, archaeology, botany, astronomy and psychology. This evidence will be presented in the first two chapters of this book.

Later in this chapter, from the fields of philosophy and logic, the arguments that have been considered to be the greatest in history, both for and against the existence of God, will be presented. I'll then argue against the 'against' arguments, as well as present some 'for' arguments of my own. I believe that when all has been said, it will be clear that the evidence is overwhelmingly in favor of the existence of God, even to the most scrutinizing mind.

Why scrutinize?

If you have any *skeleton questions* in your *logic closet* you've been avoiding, good things will happen to you as you read this book and get answers to them. You'll experience more strength, clarity, sureness, security and relief (from the subconscious tension that happens when we avoid these questions and doubts). This then would inspire you to do the things that will move you closer to God..and strengthen you to move away from pressures (inner and outer) that try to push you to do things you *deep down* don't really want to do. Plus, our ability to present and defend God increases tremendously if we are able to answer the logical questions people use to keep themselves from fully accepting God and the Bible (or that we might be using to keep ourselves from fully accepting God and the Bible).

Also, Christians are told (in 1 Peter 3:15) to always be ready to give a <u>reason</u> for their faith. And, Jesus said that all of God's laws can be summed up in 2 commandments, one of which includes that we love God with all our <u>mind</u>. Therefore, to not scrutinize is to not have a full Christian experience.

<u>Famous scientists who believed in God</u>

Even though the general public perception paints *science* and *religion* as being incompatible, they definitely aren't. A testimony to this fact is that most of the greatest scientists in history have said they believed in God.

For example, Albert Einstein, who is considered by many to have had one of the best scientific minds of all time, said he believed in God with the following statement: "My religion consists of a humble admiration of the illimitable superior Spirit who reveals Himself in the slight details we are able to perceive with our frail and feeble minds. That deeply emotional conviction of the presence of a superior reasoning power, which is revealed in the incomprehensible universe, forms my idea of God."

And Einstein is not the only scientist who felt this way. Most of the greatest scientists in history have been Christians, including: Leonardo Da Vinci, Louis Pasteur, Lord William Kelvin, Samuel F.B. Morse, Lord Francis Bacon, James Joule, Robert Boyle, Blaise Pascal, Michael Faraday and Sir Isaac Newton.

This shows that, contrary to what some believe, it is not necessary to be overcome-by-blind-emotion-and-then-check-your-brain-in-at-the-church-door in order to take a religious viewpoint. Obviously, all of these men had very high capabilities in analysis, which they didn't abandon when confronted with the basic questions about life.

The fact that most of the greatest thinkers throughout history believed in God and the Bible shows that Christianity is palatable to the highest degree of intelligence. One of my goals with this book is to show that taking the Christian viewpoint is not only the highest *experiential* approach in this life, but it is also the highest and most complete *intellectual* approach.

During my own experience, education and training in science, it was easy for me to gain an awe and appreciation for the Creator, just from looking very closely at the ingenious details of what He[1] created. This is what a lot of the activity of science is. Nothing is really being invented. Scientists merely experiment in manipulating and practically applying what God has already invented....and, often modeling their new inventions after His creations, for example: brain/computer, airplanes/birds, electrical wiring/nervous system, gas engine/digestive system, etc.

---

[1] I'm using the conventional 'He' here (the Jews and Jesus called God: Father, and referred to God as "He"). But God, being a spirit, obviously does not have a gender. This convention was probably chosen because a lot of His relationship to us parallels the positive spiritual aspects of an <u>earthly father's natural relationship with his children.</u>

Also, many scientists who have set out to disprove the existence of God, have ended up becoming very religious. And some of them were so impressed with what they found, they wrote books in support of the Bible.

In the fields of social, political and legal science, nearly all of the founding fathers of this nation (whose writings we still base our government on) were very religious. (By the way 'freedom of religion' was not meant to be 'freedom from religion'. The first amendment was made to protect the church from the state, not the state from the church). There are great books by legal scholars who have become Christians, such as Dr. John W. Montgomery.

Leonardo Da Vinci, considered by many to be the greatest genius in human history (accepting that Jesus was both human and divine) expressed how he felt about God by honoring Him with his best artwork (such as *The Last Supper*). He also had this to say about where his inspiration and guidance came from: "Where the Spirit does not work with the hand, there is no art."

How we get our opinions:
    finding-out-for-ourselves vs. trusting-others

I bring up all these scientists not as proof, but as credible testimonies. Many people have become intellectually lazy and just parrot 'opinion phrases' that they've heard on TV as their own opinions. And they often do so with emotionalism (which is usually a giveaway that reason has been abandoned). But then when asked to substantiate 'their' opinions, they can't adequately do so. At this point they often try to get out of this predicament by hyping the emotion even more (how many intellectually frustrating times have we seen this happen on talk shows and in news footage?). Whereas, a scientist's opinion can be generally seen as having a higher-than-normal microscopic, leave-no-stone-unturned scrutiny behind it. This is because this analytical trait is the most important one that is needed by a scientist and that is developed in their schooling and training. (And once again, most of the greatest scientists throughout history have been religious.)

Given that we are exposed to many conflicting positions in short sound-bytes and incomplete treatises from *supposed* authorities, what it comes down to for many is: who do you trust? But we shouldn't base our lives on trusting what others say. We should form our own opinions based on being exposed to as much pertinent information as possible. Therefore, one of the purposes of this book is to expose the reader to the basic questions of life, then give them a lot of data in regards to these questions, and then let the reader discern for his or her self what the answers are.

The logic

Contrary to the general *public perception*, there is a lot of real data that can give us clues as to the truths about this life and our place in it. And this data can be found both outside of us and inside us. First, let's start with a few points of logic. Let's examine the theory that says: there has to be a power/intelligence/being outside of human beings and planet earth.

There has to be an intelligence

There has to be another (other than human) *intelligence* because human beings don't possess the degree of intelligence necessary to be able to create this universe and the life in it. That is, a highly intelligent design (which this universe is) implicitly says that there must have been a highly intelligent designer.

A few other thoughts supporting the conclusion that this universe is an intelligent design, not a random evolvement: (1)If the first atom was unintelligent and spontaneously-generated, why did all other basic matter follow the same complex path that the matter which formed into the first atom followed? The odds of this randomly happening are virtually impossible. (2)Furthermore we know that the first atom didn't reproduce itself into zillions of atoms, because atoms don't have reproductive ability. (3)So then, did the first atom call a meeting with all other basic matter and say "form yourself into atoms"? But how could it if it were unintelligent? This points to an intelligence guiding the process. (4)Finally, why would basic matter make its first evolutionary jump to such a complex entity as the atom? An evolution process (e.g. first a proton, then a neutron, then an electron, then coordination into an atom, then more atoms, etc.) can't be thought of as applying here, because in order to have evolution, there has to be *reproductive ability* (which atoms don't have). And even if an atom did spontaneously generate, it has been calculated that the odds of a chance formulation of even just a typical protein molecule, made up of 3,000 atoms, is of the order of one out of 2.02×10^{231}.

These points show that it is almost infinitely more logical to conclude that there was an organized, intelligent effort at the beginning of atomic structure.

There has to be a being

There has to be a being, because the fact that there is an intelligent creation says that there has to have been a creator. That is, there had to have been a 'first mover' to design and initiate the intelligent design, and then see that it was carried out. If you're saying "Well then who initiated God?", the answer is: God is not an 'intelligent physical design' and therefore didn't need to be initiated. God is a being, and just is. (These points will be further supported later in this chapter.)

The 'atheistic random-evolvement' model (which is what is mainly taught in America's current education system) is also incomplete because it lacks an answer for the question: Where did the space for matter to randomly evolve in come from? Also, this *popular* 'random theory' (which says that all things evolved from random interactions of atoms, which themselves evolved from random interaction of basic matter) can't exist without there having been a creator because: where did the initial matter that randomly evolved come from? Plus, implicit in the word 'evolved' is the idea that something had to be there in the first place to evolve <u>from</u>. 'Evolved' does not include 'originated'. Therefore, there has to have been an originator, hence a creator, hence a being. I mean, atheists do cross the barrier of assuming something as being *eternally existent* (space and matter). So they really have no valid argument for not extending this to a spiritual being also.

Theology does have answers for the above two questions (which will be given later), while *modern** science does not (*but, as I pointed out before, most of the great scientists throughout history agreed with the Bible).

<u>There has to be a power</u>

There has to be an incredible power behind the universe because there is so much power in the universe, and humanity can't even come close to matching an iota of it.

And even though human beings can control things that are much more powerful than they are (which suggests this possibility for God), they did not originate the materials that innately carry this power, as God had to. That is, humans can't create power. They can only utilize and amplify power that already exists. Also, the Bible says that God is omnipotent (I'm not offering this as evidence at this point, just mentioning it).

If you want to get a feel for the awesomeness of the size and power of the universe, in comparison to human beings' size and power, here are a few statistics.

Size of the universe:

Size of the sun: 1,300,000 earths could fit in it.

The largest *known* star in the universe, Epsilon, could hold 27,000,000 of our suns.

Distance to the sun: 93,000,000 miles (this is like driving cross country 31,000 times). At the speed of light, which is 186,000 miles per <u>second</u>, it would take 8 1/3 <u>minutes</u> to get from the earth to the sun.

Now, traveling at that speed it would take 4 1/3 years to get to the nearest star which is Alpha Centauri (1 light year = 6,000,000,000,000 miles).

Well, in our galaxy, the Milky Way, which is 100,000 light years in diameter, there are 100,000,000 stars.

And, so far, we know of 100,000,000,000 galaxies.

When dwelling on these numbers and the unfathomable size of the universe, don't you get a feeling of awe? But let's bring this closer to home. Are you aware of where you physically are right now? Do you realize that you are standing on a 6,600,000,000,000,000,000,000 ton ball that somehow just hangs in space, sitting on nothing?

The Bible describes the earth as being a sphere

One point that gives the Bible credibility is the fact that over 3000 years before Columbus it describes the earth as a sphere that is suspended in space. In Job 26:7 it says that God *"suspends the earth over nothing at all"*. And this description was there in the Bible during times when people believed the earth was flat and sitting on pillars.

The verse that describes the roundness is Job 26:10 *"He has inscribed a <u>circle</u> on the surface of the waters, <u>at</u> the <u>boundary</u> of light and darkness"*. (The following page gives a geometric proof of this. You might want to skip it if you're not familiar with analytical geometry.)

The "at" and "boundary" clarify that it is the xy plane (see figure 1) and not the xz plane (see figure 2) that is being referred to. If it was the xz plane it would say "on the surface between here and the boundary of light (or some other point)". Plus, there aren't any circles on the faces of the bodies of water on earth.

It also verifies that the Bible is saying that the earth is a sphere, and not a finite rod. This is because this circle could be viewed from any point on earth, thus extending the curvature to being: all circles which would now include the z axis. And these all would pivot around an *origin* (x=0,y=0,z=0) at the center of the earth, because if there was no origin, there would be dents all over the earth where the descending points of the curvatures intersect each other. And obviously there are no dents. Therefore, when many of these circles are drawn, it can be seen that a sphere is formed (see figure 3).

Plus, it is not called a curve at the horizon, it is called a circle. This means that the curve does extend full circle (see figure 4).

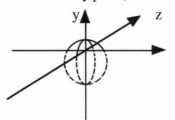

Figure 1: a circle on the surface of the waters at the boundary of light and darkness (i.e. the horizon is not a straight line on the x axis, but rather it is a curve on the xy plane).

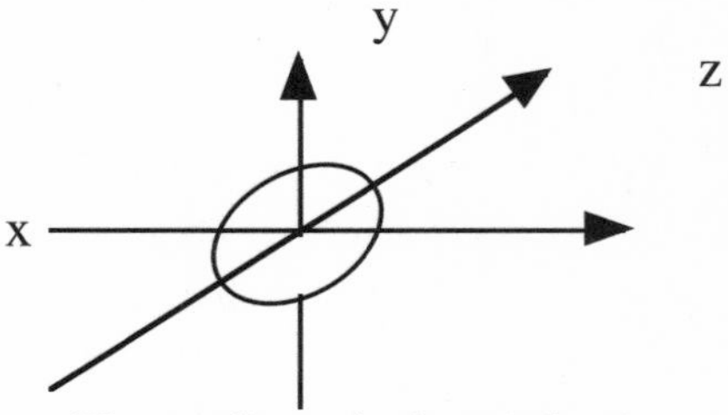

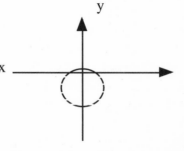

Figure 2: a circle on the surface of the waters not at the boundary of light and darkness

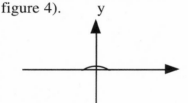

Figure 3: the horizon shifts as the viewpoint on the earth moves

Figure 4: a circle, not a curve

Columbus said that he was inspired by God

Christopher Columbus said that he was inspired and reassured by God (who <u>knew</u> the earth was round) to make his voyage. Also, one of his and Queen Isabella's main motivations for making and financing this voyage was to bring Christianity to new peoples.

Other facts that show that Columbus was religious: he approached the launching scene with his friend, a monk; everyone there got on their knees and prayed; Columbus' last words were "<u>In the name of God</u>, let go!" (By the way, I got these facts from a 5th grade, <u>public</u> school social studies textbook: "Exploring Our Country", published by the California State Department of Education in 1956. This shows how this nation's policy of not acknowledging God is just a recent phenomena in our history.) There are other books that quote Columbus' journals showing how inspired and assured from God he was about his voyage.

Our continual high-speed movement on this planet

Right now, we are continually traveling at 1000 miles per hour. This is how fast the earth is spinning. Also, we are simultaneously traveling through space at the rate of 67,000 mph around the sun. And, this path is continual and perfect. One slight gyration and we would have catastrophes on this planet that would destroy all human life.

What incredible power holds all of this so perfectly in place, and keeps it continually going? Doesn't this give you an appreciation for the awesomeness of where you physically are...and of the fact that behind all of this power that we can observe, there has to have been a tremendous power to originate it, and now keep it together?

How do we lose sight of this?

Still, some people are so blinded and hypnotized by

the media, and so shortsightedly focused in just their own lives, that they put all this data into a mental box, label it "unimportant" and put it into deep storage, where they lose sight of it.

But we are not just *mental* beings. We also are *experiential* beings. And because people are often smug, trivial, mental, stubborn, and shortsighted, the power of the universe has to give them an occasional <u>experiential</u> reminder that it exists and how great its power is and how fragile we are, e.g. earthquakes, tornadoes, hurricanes, etc.

Other ways that God gets our attention is through fragilities that He built into us. That is, He gave us a fragile heart (emotional upsets, broken hearts, etc.), a fragile body (disease, pain, etc.), and a hungry spirit (to know perfection, to grow, for things to be right, to know the truth, etc.).

Who made God?

A seeming problem in our discussion here is: if we claim that the God *of the Bible* is the power/being/intelligence behind this existence——it says *in the Bible* that He made us in His image. Therefore, He has an image, therefore a design. So then, who designed Him? Also, who created Him? In other words, who was the power/being/intelligence behind God?

A couple of points here: the image of God (which is human), could be just one of many images that He has. As a matter of fact, we would have to conclude that this is the case, because not inherent in the human image is the ability to make this universe.

Another point here is that maybe we are just being anthropomorphic and *projecting* two aspects of *our* reality onto God. Those being: <u>time</u> (because we are born, grow old and die), and <u>space</u> (because we have 3 dimensions).

But God, being a spirit, not a physical being, doesn't have to be limited by these.

In regards to *time*, we were born with no previous (remembered) history. Therefore, we <u>feel</u> like God would have to have been born at one time with no previous history. But this feeling is anthropomorphic, i.e. imposing a human limitation on a being that obviously exceeds human bounds in many ways. Besides, our human sense wouldn't be able to tolerate the opposite argument (which says: there has to have been a beginning) because it leads to the question: then what came before that?

In regards to *space*, once again we are trying to project onto God a limit of physical matter. But God not being physical would not be bound by the physical limitation of space. And being that <u>a universe can't be created from within a universe that doesn't yet exist</u>, we would have to conclude that either (1)God resides in another dimension, which exists parallel to this universe but that we can't see, or (2)our universe is eternally existent and is the only universe, it's just that all spiritual activity is invisible to us.

<u>Can 'infinite time' and 'infinite space' exist without human beings being able to conceive of them?</u>

Well, can a tree grasp comedy? Can a blind person grasp color? Can an amoeba grasp romance? No. Yet, all 3 of these phenomenae really do exist. Therefore, things can exist even though some lifeforms are unable to grasp them.

I mean, there is a tremendous amount of activity in this physical universe that is invisible to us, but that we know exists. And we know where and when it exists (e.g. radio waves, ultraviolet waves, gravity, infrared waves, X-rays, magnetism, etc.). We know these things exist because we've developed scientific instruments that can cause these phenomena to move physical parts of these instruments, which our senses can then detect. What great number of scientific instruments are yet undeveloped that could show us undiscovered phenomena in this universe (perhaps: a spirit world, parallel universes, or other dimensions)?

<u>Scientific proof that there has to be a God, and that the universe had to have a beginning</u>

In physics, the 'Second Law of Thermodynamics' (entropy) says that in a closed physical system, the amount of available energy is continually decreasing. For example, the sun is dying, it is not rejuvenating itself, or even staying at the same energy level. Why? Because its energy is being <u>spent</u> in the forms of light and heat.

Similarly, all physical bodies in the universe and on earth (including our own) are expending their own energy (life forms on earth also expend the energy absorbed from other life forms). If no energy was spent, everything would relax to the no-energy state of -273°C (i.e. 'absolute zero' temperature). Therefore, energy is continually being spent creating heat just to keep the *body* temperature up.

Another physics principle, the Law of Conservation of Energy, says that "energy cannot be created." Therefore, when you put this principle together with the second law of thermodynamics, it becomes clear that all energy in the universe will eventually be spent. (The universe as a whole does qualify to be classified as a closed system, which makes it subject to entropy. This is because: no process has ever been observed where energy is being fed into it, being created in it, or spontaneously combusting in it.)

Now if the universe and its matter have <u>always</u> just been here, as atheists claim (otherwise there would have to have been a God to start it up, and atheists by definition claim that there is no God), the universe's energy should have been completely depleted by now. And if we're looking back at an infinite past (as atheists claim), this would be true no matter how slow the rate of energy loss is.

Therefore, being that entropy is true, and being that energy has never been observed to pop out of a vacuum, there has to have been a beginning to the universe. And, there had to be a beginner. Once again, if you say "Well then who began God?" the answer is: God is not a physical being and therefore is not bound by laws of physics, which 'Entropy' and 'the Law of Conservation of Energy' are. So, the same rationale here would not apply to God.

So, with two laws of physics, we not only have proven that there was a beginning to the universe, but we also have proven that there had to be someone to start this universe (i.e. to create the initial amount of energy, design it, and implement this intelligent design) who is not bound by the laws of physics (but who actually invented and created *physics* itself). This last thought also means that this someone can be invisible to the physical universe.

So, science and physics don't disprove God and aren't at odds with religion, as many think. Rather, they prove God.

In short, what's been proven here is: the universe was created by something non-physical. And, as we proved earlier, this something was an intelligent being. Therefore, our theorem can be modified to say: This universe was created by a non-physical, intelligent being.

Can the Bible be included in our investigation?
The way that the God of the Bible answers the question of whether anything existed before Him is to say

that He is the only uncreated being, and that there was nothing before Him.

Because of these statements from the Bible, as a part of our investigation we will look to see if the Bible has any scientific credibility. And, if so, to what degree? But the argument in this chapter is not <u>dependent</u> on whether the Bible was authored by the Creator of the universe. However, if the Bible can be proven to have 100% scientific credibility (which will be done in the next chapter), then its statements just add more support and clarity to the arguments stated in this chapter.

<u>Having a complete argument</u>

Having been trained as a leave-no-stone-unturned scientist, I could not satisfy my mind with just faith. It needs facts. And it needs to question and test these facts. And it is continually on the alert for any flaws....even microscopic ones.

In the process of doing this I found that: the more a person faces 'the inner questions' and gets answers for them, the stronger their inner foundation and experience becomes. If we don't face these questions, we are implicitly saying that we're afraid we might find that what we are basing our life on is wrong. Or, a person might be afraid that even though they're sure enough for themselves about what they believe, if they ask questions, they'll be left hanging without answers, which is an unsettling feeling.

But, if you want to be able to communicate to others <u>why</u> they should believe in the God of the Bible (or whatever philosophy you believe in), they'll probably have 'logical' questions, and therefore you should have logical answers to give them (in addition to your experience and Biblical knowledge). And if you haven't turned every logical stone and gotten answers, the conversation could end up at: "Well that's your opinion and what you believe in." The discussion will hit a dead end and be unfinished because your presentation was incomplete. One of the purposes of this chapter is to turn over the pertinent stones and answer the questions under them...at least enough to prove there is a God. Let's see how the most highly acknowledged philosophers in history have done in this regard.

The main arguments from philosophy, throughout history, for and against the existence of God

One of the main focuses in philosophy is whether or not God exists. Another is: how God's existence (or non-existence) impacts us. Therefore, I consider "Why Are We Here?" to essentially be a philosophy book. But how have the greatest philosophers in history fared with these questions. In regards to the first question, I now will present (to borrow a term from the music industry) philosophy's greatest hits. First I'll present the main 'proofs for God's existence'. Following these are the main 'arguments against God's existence'. After the 'arguments against God's existence', I'll show how these are taking too narrow a view and why they are not able to prove the points they are trying to make.

Proofs for God's existence

In 1265, St. Thomas Aquinas offered five ways in which God's existence could be proven philosophically:

(1) Movement. Everything that is moving was propelled by something else. And that something else was also propelled by something other than itself. As we keep going back, in order to avoid infinity, there had to have been an initial mover (what Aristotle called "the unmoved mover").

(2) Creation. Everything was created by something else. And that something else was created by another something else. Once again, if we're going to avoid infinity, there had to have been an initial Creator.

(3) Necessity. Once again, everything physical was created by something else. And all everythings and something elses will at one point cease to exist (even our solar system). But because time is infinite, there had to be a time when nothing that exists now existed. But because something can't emerge out of nothing, there always had to be at least one something. And that something is God.

(4) Degrees of perfection. Degrees can only be determined if there is a perfect standard to compare to. And that standard is God.

(5) Order in nature. Everything in nature is *equip*ped to harmonize with its environment. There had to be an intelligent organizer of this order and designer of the *equip*ment, which is God.

Arguments against God's existence

One of the main points made against the God of the Bible being a reality is that the Bible claims that God is omnipotent and all-loving. Yet, evil exists. So then, if He's omnipotent and all-loving, wouldn't it be logical to conclude that He would stop evil from happening? He therefore can't simultaneously be omnipotent and all-loving. And also therefore, the Bible cannot be considered to be an all-true document.

A contradiction is also pointed out regarding freewill and God's omniscience. If God knows exactly what a person is going to do, then how can it be concluded that the person committed their actions out of their own free will? And therefore, how can they be held accountable?

Scottish philosopher David Hume criticized St. Thomas Aquinas' 3rd point when he said "Whatever we can conceive as existent, we can also conceive as nonexistent." He also asked why the ultimate source of the universe couldn't be the entire universe itself, eternal and uncaused, without a God? He also posed other possibilities, saying that this earthly world could have been made by an extra-terrestrial joint effort, and that it might even be a failed one of many experiments. Or, this planet and the life on it could have been made by "an infant deity who afterwards abandoned it, ashamed of his lame performance."

My arguments against the 'Arguments against God's existence'

My argument against the first point ("God can't simultaneously be omnipotent and all-loving if He allows evil") is: it doesn't understand how 'God allowing evil' is a more loving act than 'God not allowing evil'. The key here is free will. Evil is just an ugly byproduct of free will. In giving us free will, God also gave us the freedom to ignore Him and His standards of civility and perfect function.

Therefore, if we are to deem 'free will' as being desirable, then we must also accept that evil will occur. Human history, not God, has chosen to make this theorem a reality.

Also, inherent in giving someone free will is the negative possibility that they will reject you, and even hurt you (especially if you are spiritually attached to them). The fact that God is willing to suffer like this for us is a loving act. Only someone who loves another is willing to suffer for them. An unloving God would just have chosen to withhold free will from us, which would prevent evil. But then He would not have accomplished the plan he set for us and Him, <u>which will benefit both of us</u> in the long run (this plan will be discussed later). <u>Mutual suffering</u> for <u>mutual benefit</u> is an act of <u>love</u>. It is loving for a more powerful being to be gracious and show mercy to a less powerful being....especially when the more powerful being doesn't really need the less powerful one.

Therefore the first point in the 'arguments against...' is incorrect, because (1)God didn't intend to prevent evil. By allowing free will, He just created the *possibility* for the free will beings to create evil, and (2)allowing evil, and He Himself having to experience the grievous repercussions of it (through the torturous death of Jesus; and, because He is bonded to every heart in love, having to experience grief from our individual and collective evil), is a more loving act than not allowing it. God doesn't intend to prevent evil (at least for now).

By the way, as to how potent we are: God only gave us *limited free will*. He gave us just enough free will to prove that we can't handle having free will, but still enough for us to be able to have a relationship with Him.

Limited free will means that 100% of our actions are not controlled by God (nor are they controlled by us). Still, we <u>are</u> *somewhat* moved by God. This is so God can achieve His basic purposes, and also so He can protect whom He chooses to protect, without free-willed selfishness going completely rampant and creating a lot of harm.

To prove to yourself that we have *limited* free will, start making deep inner observations as to what percent of your words, thoughts and deeds are purely self-willed (i.e. self-originated), and how much of them are just <u>re</u>actions to other natural forces within you.

Hume's two points (no deity; infant deity) are speculative, and can only be refuted by proving the greater likelihood of the Bible's accounts being true....which means: proving the Bible's credibility (next chapter).

The emotional aspect of presenting a philosophy

One type of occurrence that often brings out the dysfunctional and self-centered sides of human nature is: a discussion about philosophy or religion.

Philosophy and religion are attractive to those who are inclined to be arrogant, sovereign, self-righteous and looked-up-to because these realms aren't absolutely regulated by obvious truth. That is, they are open to debate.

A person can claim his or her own private variation on the truth, and can build a following just on how loud and strong his or her persuasive and coercive *abilities* are.

But note how Jesus has been able to build the largest following in history, and yet is very soft-spoken. This is because He spoke the truth, very calmly, very deeply and very clearly. And the truth, on its own power, resonates in our hearts and is very attractive. It doesn't need to be hyped to be appealing. Unlike many of today's preachers, Jesus didn't need to resort to using emotionalism to try to persuade people. Actually, one of the most appealing things about the truth is that it makes us calm, and often gives us a warm, full feeling in our heart.

These facts make you have to question the motivations of many of today's preachers. But every once in a while, a scandal will surface from their private lives to confirm the suspicions that there must be something dramatically wrong in their hearts for them to have such dramatically unpeaceful and uncalm emotions.

It is frustrating to see preachers *adamantly* present and defend *their* personal doctrines of life, in the name of the Bible, in such an unpeaceful way. Especially in this day and age when the Bible has little credibility in the public forums, and yet it's what the public so desperately needs.

But even though these preachers speak as if there is absolutely no doubt that everything they say is true, their *fruit* gives them away. They often get wide-eyed and pushy, or they raise their eyebrows (body language: fear of getting caught), or they get glossy-eyed with a stiff mask, or they lose their temper, or they're too caved-in, or they get syrupy, or they yell and scream, etc. This exaggerated body language suggests that they themselves aren't sure (either consciously or subconsciously) that what they are saying is as true as they are presenting it. But they *push* forward with emotional energy probably because they are *attached* to keeping their authoritative position. (Have you ever caught yourself doing any of these things?) The truth, when really understood, is powerful enough on its own and doesn't need to be emotionally hyped.

The sad part here is that because of their pushiness and hyper-unconnected-to-God-salesmanship, a lot of these squeaky wheels get the grease, i.e. the television air time. This is frustrating because they, by their bad fruit, end up discrediting the Bible and Christianity. They give a false impression of Christianity. People who observe them often say "If this is the *fruit* of someone who is into Christianity, there must be something wrong with the *tree*". Many tele-vangelists are very *advanced* marketing, entertainment and sales people, but not very advanced spiritual people.

Why talk about Christianity in a science/philosophy chapter

In this chapter, besides giving a logical and scientific foundation that supports Christianity, I'm also addressing the common criticisms that are labeled against Christianity (which many people parrot without careful examination and use as reasons to avoid Christianity...and many times only because they don't want to have to deal with criticism by their 'friends', or be out of step with the 'mainstream' - as it is perceived in the media).

Some have told me that I should leave these 'defenses of Christianity', 'criticisms of those who *claim* to speak for Christianity', and 'evangelical asides' out of this chapter, and that I should make this be just a science/philosophy book. Perhaps in other centuries this would be the right approach. But in this time, when this nation's media, government and education system all have an atheistic muzzle on them, I feel that I must do all that I can to wipe away any and all negative stigmas on Christianity (besides spelling out the positives). Why? Because Christianity objectively stands at the pinnacle of this life. It stands alone as the only perfect jewel in this life. And what this time needs more than anything is Christianity (both on the individual and collective levels). Christianity could solve all personal and societal problems if people would just submit themselves to it. My heart is very much filled with the desire to give this message and explain the specifics of why this is true. This is why I couldn't leave a message so important as this out of this (or any) book.

Also, in this chapter, I deal with a lot of peripheral factors (like arguments against some Christians' behavior) to try to anticipate anything about this subject that might come up in the reader's heart or mind. I try to look at all of the questions that would arise out of a *complete* examination of the question "Is there a God?". Right now in this chapter, we're in the middle of examining 'the credibility of human testimony and opinion'. Throughout the chapter I will be showing the errors of both extremes on this issue: the atheist, and the falsely religious.

The *exclusive* religions

    Logic tells us that there is <u>only one</u> true, complete answer to any specific question. Yet, there are so many conflicting answers in the world to the basic philosophical and religious questions. And they all are presented as if they're true. Obviously (and logically), they can't all be right. As a matter of fact, there are only three possibilities: one of them is right; none of them are right; or one or more of them are partially right. Yet, so many speak as if they've got the complete truth and no one else does. And a number of these people and organizations spend a lot of effort trying to disprove the other guys. But there's a good phrase in the Bible, which I've already alluded to, that can help out here: *"You will know them by their fruits"* (Matt 7:20).

    All of the bad physical manifestations that I've been describing are examples of bad fruit, which are signs that the tree is bad (with 'the tree' being: the basic state of a person's mind, heart, will, and 'slant on the truth').

    In this light, many preachers, philosophers and public personalities have a credibility problem. If they were <u>secure</u> in their knowledge of the truth, they wouldn't <u>act</u> the way they do. They would be more calm and peaceful.

    It would be better if they would just be honest and share what they do know, instead of feeling the pressure to come off as absolute authorities about everything. If they just shared what they knew well, and did so with a gentle love for God, a deep respect for His truth, and a humble reflection on their own imperfectness, this experience would be infectious, and would be very uplifting and edifying to people...as well as glorifying to God. Bad fruit is not only unnecessary, but it is anti-Bible. Even the well-intentioned are gently rebuked in Rom. 10:2: *"they are zealous for God, though their zeal is unenlightened"*.

There are even religious practices in the *"other"* religions and denominations, that are holier and more Biblical than what many of the critical, "I'm-in-with-the-in-crowd" denominations do.

So then, being that all people *intuitively*[2] know what good fruit is, those who speak without it somewhat discredit themselves and that of which they speak.

([2] In Romans 2:14-16 it says that *"God will judge the secrets of people"* because His Law is *"written in their hearts, their conscience bearing witness."* He also goes on to say that His Law is instinctive in people.)

There is value in pointing out the errors in one another because it eliminates confusions and it sharpens our philosophies and methods. But being that none of us is perfect, it is wrong to label and then totally discredit a person....especially since most people in all religious groups and denominations have good intentions, are at least somewhat respectful of God, and want to grow and do good. These are the reasons why most people get involved in religion in the first place. Religious people should be seen as flowers that are growing. We should water each other, and help each other pull weeds. But we should never pull flowers. That's not our domain. That is only God's domain.

It is morbidly comical that many of the critical religious groups simultaneously claim that their way is the only way. Yet, they often show worse fruit than those whom they claim are not "truly" connected to God.

'Good fruit' can be encapsulated into one word: love. 1 Corinthians 13:2 says that without *love* we are nothing. This *love* (agape), which is the fruit of a person whose heart is connected to God, is defined in 1 Cor 13:4-8, Galatians 5:19-26 and Matthew 5:3-16. In secular terms, agape is 'sane, rational, loving, calm, peaceful behavior'.

I've been speaking mostly about emotional fruits here, but there are also the fruits of a person's actions.

Bad-fruit preachers: an example of the evils of using 'emotionalism' to present a philosophy

Bad-fruit preachers can attract people because they have *some* semblance of the truth, and the truth *on its own* is attractive. People often come to them because they don't know about anything higher, and yet want to satisfy their natural need to be connected to and involved in something high. Also, the faults of these preachers will often be overlooked by people who either are in pain and needy, or who are blindly traditional to the church and/or denomination of their parents and friends. Peer pressure is even stronger for those who are emotionally needy.

It's a shame that so many preachers feel as though they have to put on a *performance* when they preach. Can you picture Jesus, whom they claim to want to emulate, acting like they do?

The peace, love, and inspired feeling that I get from hearing a *calm** pastor teach God's word is <u>very</u> entertaining and pleasurable. (*I don't mean *sedate*, because an inspired speaker will naturally have energy peaks and valleys. But they won't lose their connection, centeredness or love.) Also, the joy and inspiration that I experience from getting new insights into God and life is very pleasurable. Emotionalism not only is not needed, but it just gets in the way, even <u>preventing</u> feelings of peace and love.

Having been in the entertainment industry, I realized that in an optimum entertainment situation, the audience is *submissive* (that is, not judging, thinking or resisting....just surrendering to and going with the experience). And the reason that the audience responds like this is because there is peace and pleasure in submission. And because the audience is submitting, this allows the entertainer (or movie) to hypnotize them into an experiential journey. In the case of music, each song is usually centered around just one particular emotion. Preachers, as entertainers, should limit their emotional *range* and basically only hypnotize their audience into agape (because without agape [love] we are nothing - 1 Corinthians 13).

In defense of an often-criticized aspect of some of the calmer religions (such as the Catholic mass, and eastern meditation), what is 'ritual' to some, is to others: meditative; peace-and-love creating; and it stops their busy, chattering, critical, evaluative mind, and focuses them in on drawing closer to God. A person that is too mental, hyperactive, or problemated in their mind, will find it difficult to submit to the beauty of God's calm in their spirit.

So then why do yelling preachers take the unpeaceful, unagapelike approach that they do? One possible reason is that they probably are quick-tempered to begin with. On the positive side, their anger could be fueled by the rampant unholiness in the world, and their desire to forcibly cling to God. But another reason could be that, as spiritual leaders, they feel that they must come off as absolute authorities. Now if they really were absolute authorities, there would be a calmness in their spirit as they presented the beauty of the truth. Being that they don't have this peace naturally, they then have to hype their message (a la a salesman who is just trying to pull the wool over your eyes and hurry you on to the sale lest you resist). Given all of this, it is obviously more important then to yelling preachers for them to be able to *claim* that they know the truth, than to *actually know* the truth. That is, it is more important for them to be able to continue their *act* (just like an entertainer has an *act*), which <u>they feel</u> is dependent on them being able to claim that they possess the whole truth, than to <u>really</u> know and be one with THE truth. Otherwise they would be honest about what they really do know and what they really don't know, and then would humbly and purposefully share what they do know (and seek the answers to what they don't know). A false claimer shows bad fruit, whereas a sincere seeker shows a humble desire to know.

For some false claimers it might be very hard for them to admit that they might be wrong or missing something because this would be inconsistent with their claim, and might threaten their *high position in their church.* Does this sound familiar? It sounds like the Pharisees who plotted Jesus' death, because Jesus criticized many of them for this exact thing. Does this mean then that a lot of today's preachers are actually false teachers? Well, Jesus did say that many will prophesy, cast out demons and perform miracles in His name, but that He never knew them (Matt. 7:22,23). Aren't these activities some of the ones that only the bad fruit preachers are involved in?

The Bible that they claim to be into says: *"In <u>quietness</u> and <u>confidence</u> shall be your strength"* (Is 30:15).

1 Corinthians 13 says that love is not boisterous, is not quick-tempered, does not act unbecomingly, does not brag, is not arrogant and is patient.

I point these things out so that people won't judge Christianity, which is a tremendously beautiful thing, by some of those in the media who claim to be representing and teaching Christianity but who don't act in such a Christian way.

A reason that could be given for the above approach to religion (or for any imperfect approach to religion or philosophy) is that it has been said that people are only able to grow in small *gradient* increments. That is, they're just being introduced to God and can't quite yet let go of their sins (egotism, vanity, anger, self-righteousness, sexual sins, greed, insensitivity, etc.). Therefore they create religions that reach for God, yet simultaneously are non-judgmental towards their sins (2 Timothy 4:3-4 *"For the time will come when they will not endure sound doctrine; but wanting to have their ears tickled, they will accumulate for themselves teachers in accordance to their own desires; and will turn away from the truth, and will turn aside to myths"*). They probably do so because they are still centered *in their mind,* and not sensitive to the messages that come from God through *their spirit.* (And in the mind, anything can be justified). They are in transition from being mind controlled to being spirit controlled. Therefore, this is not to say that they won't someday come to the realization and inner conviction that some of their behaviors have been unholy. But while we should be patient with each other as we grow, we also should not enter into *agreement* with or raise up any less high of a standard than that which we know to be true (2 Timothy 4:2 *"..reprove, rebuke, exhort, with great patience and instruction"*).

Having their ears tickled with all positive, soothing words about God and about how great they are and how their dreams will come true is very pleasant (for some). But it is an avoidance of the real problem of this existence: sin. And if the problem is being avoided, a solution will never be sought...or found (God's solution will be spelled out in the upcoming chapters).

2 Timothy 4:5 says that we will have to do some work and endure some hardship along the way. But it will be worth it because a tremendously more positive existence

awaits us, now and in heaven, if we face this existence realistically. That is: it is much better to really clean a house, than to live in a dirty one pretending that it's clean.

By the way, I primarily used 'hyper preachers' here as an example of 'using emotionalism to present a philosophy'. But what was basically said here applies to anyone presenting any philosophy with emotionalism. In this sense, a lot of secular approaches can be found in the paragraph before this one as well.

How to search for the truth

The steps to finding truth are: experience a desire to know the truth; define the truth you are seeking to know; ask every pertinent question; actively seek answers (both inside and outside of yourself); and then listen to your mind, heart and spirit either verifying the answers you've found or asking more questions.

If a person accepts the wrong answer to a question, they may never ask that question again, and therefore might never learn its true answer. (But they will have to [consciously and subconsciously] fight off the intuitive part of them that tries to let them know that what they've considered to be an answer isn't really true. I call this intuitive part 'the truth meter').

It is frustrating (to someone who knows particular truths) when someone adamantly defends false answers as if they were true. It also does the damage of confusing a seeker of true knowledge (in the particular areas being presented and defended). But once again, a false preacher's fruit gives them away. If you really know the truth, you don't have to be overly adamant....and if you surrender to a Christian heart (the Holy Spirit), you will be patient, kind and gentle. However, this doesn't exclude 'righteous anger'. But it does exclude basing your whole 'act' (i.e. presentation style) on "righteous" anger. I mean, how often did Jesus get angry? Very rarely. The Bible tells us to be slow to anger. Why? Because we also once lived in error (and still do to some degree), and we appreciated it when someone was loving and patient enough with us to teach us the errors in our ways, rather than angrily scolding us.

How points are made with faulty logic

In conversations, we attempt to be attuned to the truth all the time. But if a person starts out to deliver a point that they have strong feelings about, and in mid-stream their attempt to persuade meets with a logically stronger than expected counter-argument that they don't have a defense for, their passion might cause them to sacrifice the pureness of their logic either for the sake of winning the argument or so that they won't have to abandon or modify their point. In philosophy these violations of logic are called 'fallacies'.

There are many different types of fallacies, each with their own name. For those who want to understand what constitutes a perfectly logical argument, and what violates logic, I encourage you to get a philosophy or logic book that lists and defines all of the fallacies. But for now, here are a few examples.

There's the 'argument ad hominem', where instead of addressing a person's point directly, an attempt is made to discredit their point by criticizing some other unrelated flaw of that person. For example, "You're wrong about that because I've caught you exaggerating before." This fact has nothing objectively to do with the point at hand, and certainly is not strong enough to discredit it on its own.

Then there's the 'fallacy of division', where an

attribute of a larger classification is passed on to something smaller that would fit in that classification. For example, "Pakistan is the world's largest per capita importer of candy. Therefore, you know all Pakistanis love candy."

The reverse of this would be the 'fallacy of composition': "You can't trust teenage drivers. I saw three accidents last week and they all involved teenagers." This fallacy would also support a point I made earlier stating: it is illogical to anthropomorphically project human limits onto the universe and God.

Here are some points of logic I've come up with that are relevant to the issue of whether or not God exists.

Flowers

The theory of evolution states that all living things have evolved: from plasma to atom to molecule to amoeba to plant to fish to reptile to mammal to human. And each change in the evolutionary process was (supposedly) made for the purpose of 'better survival'. So then, if everything has *evolved*, based on better *survival*: why the flower? It has no utilitarian purpose having to do with survival (ours or its own). It exists purely for aesthetic reasons (fragrance and visual beauty). This fact not only puts a dent in the theory of evolution, but it also suggests a designer/creator who is artistic, playful and loving in that He desired to create something just to share beauty and give us pleasure.

Also, on God's creative easel, as He painted this creation, why should we consider His palette of non-living (i.e. spiritless) paints to have been made up only of inanimate objects? Such a creative God would definitely give Himself *mechanical atomic volatility* to play with, as creative building blocks...with *genes* as their engines, and *genetic coding* as their computer drivers.

The present existence of the inferior model

Here is another flaw in the theory of evolution (a theory which secular society blindly and religiously accepts and teaches as true, on faith in what they've heard. And yet they use the *faith* argument to exclude the Bible).

If apes, through the process of *natural selection*, have slowly evolved into becoming human beings, for the sake of advancement and better survival, then why is the inferior model (the ape) still around? And if the initial model is still around, why aren't any of the more advanced in-between models still around? Or, if humans evolved through another line of apes (or a common ancestor that they share with the ape), why didn't all lines of apes in the same geographical area evolve in the same way (at least somewhat), being that they were presented with the same environmental conditions? These points of logic can conclude that it always has been nature's intention to have a number of distinct species that don't evolve. Further evidence of this is that 'missing links' have never been found.

Speaking of evolution (and other such "science" that is the basis for the secular world's philosophy of life), when modern science's theories and methods are closely scrutinized, many problems are found (especially in the 'dating methods' which are used to determine how old things are and how long ago things happened). Many would be surprised to find out how much of what is presented in schools, books and on television as 'science fact' is really 'science fiction'. Rather than include all of this information in this book, let me suggest a few other books:

The Collapse of Evolution   by Scott M. Huse
Scientific Creationism   by Dr. Henry Morris
The Fingerprint of God   by Dr. Hugh Ross

All were written by top scientists and are available

at Christian Bookstores. If you wish to have a complete argument that includes all of the specific scientific data available, I highly recommend reading these books.

This reading will also help break the *illusion* of a 'good world with trustworthy authorities' (which might then open up a space to discover a <u>truly</u> good and trustworthy God). This will especially ring true when you see how 'extremely weak data', 'slanted presentations' and even 'hoaxes' have been the norm in the formation and perpetuation of the theory of evolution (which has never been, and many top scientists now say never will be proven).

When a psychological and spiritual light is shed upon the 'religion of secular science' (and it is a religion because it is based on a set of unprovable <u>beliefs</u>), it can be seen that the base <u>motives</u> behind those who push such weak arguments as the theory of evolution and other secular science theories (and at the exclusion of what the Bible has to say) is either to take the glory away from God and give it to humans; or as a reaction to trauma perpetuated on them (falsely) in the name of religion; or as a desire to be alienated from the bad-fruit preachers in the media and anything they stand for (in this case: Christianity); or because they just don't want to confront their own sin.

Regarding 'faith': it is generally held as the doctrine of the school system, the government and most of the media, that the conclusion of the science community, that there is no God, is fact. Now it has been put upon religious people to prove that there is a God. But <u>assuming that there is no God is just as much an act of faith as assuming that there is one</u>. (And when you read my upcoming proof that 'atheism is impossible', you'll realize that there is no basis for this faith). And, being that most people aren't scientists, believing *the world's* scientists is also an <u>act of faith</u> (in them). I mean, *logically* looking at the question "Is there a God?"--on first inspection, "yes" and "no" both have a 50/50 chance of being correct. But when an effort is made to view all of the data (pro and con), the evidence is overwhelmingly in favor of the fact that there is a God. (And instead of presenting just the myths, why aren't schools presenting all of the data?)

The coordination of life forms in nature for the benefit of human beings and not for themselves

If the impetus of nature is for life forms to evolve (which is how they all supposedly got to their present evolved state, through evolution, originating with molecules spontaneously generating into amoebae, and so on), then how is it that some life forms appear to exist solely for the needs and pleasure of human beings (e.g. food-bearing plants, flowers, trees, etc.)? Wouldn't they have evolved for their own benefit? And how could they know the needs of humans (whom they seem to be alive for) without an intelligence (who does know) directing them?

And there are many intelligent interactions in the living world by non-thinking lifeforms which aren't just for their benefit (e.g. bees pollinating flowers, vultures eating dead carcasses, fungus decomposing rotten fruit, etc.).

Another example: trees shed their leaves in winter so people can have direct warmth from the sun, and then grow leaves in warm seasons so that people are protected from the sun. Where is the purpose in this activity for the trees and their evolution? And yet they don't die out as a species, feeling they're in a no-win environment of slavery.

Also, a friend of mine, who bought a farm, phoned me and said "Have you ever looked into the eyes of a cow? I just did for the first time, and now I know that their only purpose is to feed human beings." And cows don't appear to have a problem with this kind of existence. I mean, they don't try to run away, they don't make a fuss, and they just keep producing milk and more cows.

Humans have animal behaviors also. But even as socially organized as some animals and insects are, <u>only</u> humans are inspired to recognize deity (with religious cere-monies, churches, temples, etc.). This tends to show that only humans have a higher purpose than survival.

All of these realities that can be observed in the physical world are not consistent with evolution, but rather they support the Bible's explanation (Gen. 1:26-29), which says that God gave humanity dominion over all living things. Nature is a virtual orchestra of chain reactions, all leading to the apex of human beings (with God above them as the composer and orchestra leader). Although, many work to try to reverse this, e.g. making humans lose their logging jobs because of the spotted owl - which anyway, has been proven to migrate...not stay and die. They also need to recognize that trees are plants...for human con-sumption...like asparagus. And, environmentalists had bet-ter not be eating <u>any</u> fish, chicken or meat...or setting mousetraps. That would make them hypocrites. But their hypocrisy is also evident in that although they claim to be "sensitive", their actions show that they are extremely insensitive in that they support abortion (not to mention their support of other insensitivities to nature such as: fem-inism, atheism, pornography, sexual perversion, etc.).

Also supporting the Biblical position is the fact that human beings stand alone at the top of the food/predator chain, with no natural predators who crave their flesh. This fact is nature's testimony that human beings are separated at the top of this creation. If we were to assume otherwise and anthropomorphically project a spiritual essence onto animals, one viewing of a nature documentary would leave us traumatized as we watch (e.g.) a mountain lion hunt down, kill and rip the flesh off of a baby lamb (which we eat also).

Death

Another reality of life that can motivate us to deal with the question "Is there a God?" is the phenomenon of 'death'. But, preoccupation with the world (aided by the ease of turning on the television and getting *hypnotized* by its hyperness, sensationalism and melodrama) leads many to place 'death' in a *mental* box and put it out of their con-sciousness altogether (that is, until that time when it might come as quite an <u>experiential</u> shock). It is far better to dwell on the reality of death now, which might then leave a yearning in our heart to make sure that we're at peace with the One who invented and holds the power over our death and after-life. Thank God (literally), that power has made a way for us to be comforted about the reality of death (with the condition of that comfort being that we've made peace with that power <u>in a specific way</u>, which is <u>on its terms</u>, which I'll describe later). A good way that I recently heard the above concept put: "Death has not yet reached out to us. Let it rattle its chains at us (<u>now</u>), and stir us into action (<u>now</u>)" (my parenthetical adds).

<u>An analogy showing how God can be simultaneously com-prehensible and incomprehensible</u>

God is a being in the same way that infinity (∞) is a number. That is, ∞ isn't a *specific* number and therefore it is hard to *conceive* it as even being a number. Yet, it is often used in math and is very practical and necessary in the system of math and numbers. Therefore, it <u>is</u> a number. Yet, as a <u>concept</u> it has an <u>infinite aura</u> around it, and can't be visualized, like a number can be. This is very similar to the situation with God, who also has an infinite nature. He can be conceived and experienced as real and is very practical and necessary to our finite lives, yet His fullness can't be portrayed in a simple, visual picture. His infinite nature can be acknowledged, but not completely perceived or understood (although, parts of it can be).

<u>It is impossible for a human being to be an atheist</u>
There is so much going on in this universe that we can't see. Therefore, how can anyone say for certain that there is no God? And a chapter like this could never be written to support atheism because it is much easier to gather evidence that something exists than to put forth evidence that something doesn't exist. This is because, in order to prove that something doesn't exist, your evidence would have to be total and all-conclusive. Otherwise, the possibility would still be there that the something exists. Therefore, the most anti-God position a human being could logically take would be agnostic (that is: "I don't know").

<u>'What we experience' is also scientific data</u>
'Psychology' is defined as being: the scientific study of human behavior (both outer and inner).
The reason why psychology is probably given somewhat of a second class status by many in the sciences is because a great deal of its activity is in the 'hypothesis' phase of the scientific method. And the hypotheses that psychologists have come up with aren't doing a very good job (of helping people with their psychological problems and problems in 'how to approach life'). Like in the other

sciences, psychology observes (inner and outer human behavior). Then it tries to classify and categorize what it has observed so as to come up with conclusive definitions of *how* human beings uniformly behave, and *why* they do so in these specific ways. The problem here is, like with the questions about God, we are dealing with the invisible.

Nevertheless, the science of logic tells us that there exists only one description of the basic mechanics of the inner workings of a human being. But psychology is still in the dark ages in being able to give this description fully and accurately (whereas I have scientifically proven to myself that the Bible does accomplish this task).

Now because psychology, and no longer the Bible, is the guru of modern society, and because psychology is as undeveloped as it is, there is a great amount of suffering and dysfunction going on in this society, while it waits as psychology gropes for *the truth*. If this society was based on the Bible, it would be much more psychologically healthy. This is proven by statistics in this nation's past on divorce, crime, etc. when the Bible was the most revered thing in our society and the inspiration for its laws. It is also proven by the healthier emotions that were expressed in the media of these past generations (which is the general fruit of those living under its laws). Adding to this proof, there are many individual lives that have become healthier, happier and less problemated when they switched from psychology to the Bible (my life included).

So then, why does this society choose the psychology community as its guru (many of whose precepts have been proving to not work) over the Bible (whose precepts have proven to work much better)? (This question will be answered in later chapters. I'm just posing it now as an astonishing point.)

This next section contains the highlights from my 28 years of research in psychology that pertain to the question of God's existence.

What is 'absolute scientific proof'?

'Absolute scientific proof of something existing' could be defined as 'that which can be experienced by <u>our senses</u>'. But I've already shown in this chapter that there are many things that can be proven to exist (by scientific instruments) that our senses can't detect. Even very powerful things. In this way, 'scientific instruments' give human beings extra 'senses' to detect phenomena in the environment that we don't naturally have senses to detect. But we do have more scientifically viable senses than what has been generally acknowledged.

What makes sense?

The deepest definition of a 'sense' would be: a means by which a person (an observer/experiencer) can perceive an environment. Human beings have been said to have only 5 senses (taste, touch, smell, sight and hearing). But by the above definition, there are 3 more senses that are at least as real to our experience as are the basic 5. They are: heart, mind, and what I call 'the truth channel'. <u>Between us</u> (the observer/experiencer) <u>and the physical universe</u> are these 3 very real phenomena

The mind

We are not the mind, as psychology says, any more than we are the eyes, nose, tongue, etc. This is because the mind can be seen by the observer/experiencer (us) as being something <u>outside</u> of us.The mind can have words in it that were originated by us. But it can also have words in it that weren't originated by us. Therefore, we are not the mind. It is a phenomenon on its own. It can be seen to be like a two-way radio. That is: we can *talk* into it, but also: talk happens on it that we didn't initiate.

The mind also presents visions and thoughts <u>to</u> us, either for our evaluation, executive decision making, information, entertainment, or to try to motivate us to action. It gives us dreams, songs, and lines of thought. It is sometimes our inner television, and sometimes just a radio.

The truth channel communicates to us mainly in impressions. An impression is a feeling (but not an emotion), coupled with an intelligent content. And impressions happen instantaneously (whereas words happen slowly, one at a time, in linear thought).

Like with the other senses: (1)the mind is something that we only have limited control over, (2)its function can be impaired and yet *we** still exist (e.g. lobotomies, brain injuries, drugs), (3)the mind can even stop and yet we still exist (as in meditation), and (4)the mind can continue to function and yet *we** are not there (e.g. comas, deep sleep, dreams that we never become aware of). (*We are: a conscious, aware, observer/experiencer.)

So then, if we can observe thoughts, impressions, feelings, visions, and responses-to-stimuli happening spontaneously within us (and that aren't originated by us), and if we can observe them to happen in consistently specific ways, this can be considered to be real scientific data.

The reason why this data has been given less credibility in the science community, the media and the intelligentsia in this country is because, unlike an apple, it can't always be <u>simultaneously experienced in the same way</u> by all human beings. That is, when many people can visually <u>see</u> the same thing at once, they all will agree on what it is.

But people might <u>feel and think differently</u> about something that is not visible (e.g. religion).

For example, when presented with the question "Do you believe there is a God?", a person tends to quickly glance at the involuntary reactions of their heart, mind and truth channel, and then respond with what is there.

Now as to 'what is there' in many people's hearts is a secure feeling that there is a God. But they often can't explain it. I also feel this secure feeling. Now I'm using this book to explain why....and how this belief can peacefully coexist with a very logical, scrutinous, scientifically-trained mind. Why? In an attempt to bring this same sureness to others. Why? To share what I've found to be the greatest treasure that a person can have in this life.

<u>The heart</u>

The heart is just an emotional <u>re</u>actor to what comes from the subconscious and conscious minds, the truth channel, and life. 'What comes from life' is also heavily influenced (before it gets to the heart) by how the minds evaluate it. This is why some people are scared of dogs and others aren't. (Understanding this phenomenon of 'emotions-<u>re</u>acting-to-the-mind's-evaluations' is an extremely valuable piece of psychology information for those who want to gain control over negative emotions.)

Therefore, all the data in this book you agree with is reprogramming your subconscious mind, which will make you <u>feel</u> more secure and sure in your belief in God.

<u>The 'truth channel'</u>

The 'truth channel' is a fountain* of information, visions, feelings and impressions that manifest in us near the top of our stomach. It's been called: intuition, gut feeling, 6th sense, a place of knowing, soul, inspiration, God in our hearts, the higher self, conscience, the Holy Spirit, etc. Nevertheless, it is another *force* within us that is not originated by us, and that doesn't come from our mind(s).

I call it the truth channel because I've continually tested what it's given me, and (unlike with my heart, my mind, and what others have said) it's never been wrong.

(*This fountain that I physically observed, I later saw Jesus describe in John 4:11,13,14; *The woman said to Him, "Sir, You have nothing to draw with, and the well is deep. Where then do you get that living water? Jesus answered and said to her, "Whoever drinks of this water will thirst again, but whoever drinks of the water that I shall give will never thirst; the water I shall give will become in them a fountain.* This is just another proof to me that the Bible comes from the same God that designed and made me, because here it is describing an obscure, physical reality I've observed, with an accuracy I never see anywhere else. And I can testify that what this verse is saying is true in that once I accepted Jesus' offer, I never again felt the thirst of needing to search for something higher.)

How to observe the truth channel

The way to identify and observe the truth channel is to isolate it, amid all of the other inner voices. The best way to do that is to stop the other voices (mind, subconscious mind and heart). Being that the heart is a reactor, only the mind needs to be quieted. But we can't stand at the threshold of the mind and forcefully stop thoughts from coming in, because this also would be a mental action ("you can't fight fire with fire"). We need to let mental activity ebb away. And we can do this by focusing our attention on our breathing, right above the stomach. But while we are *just observing*, thoughts will be flying around us, trying to break in to our widening peaceful center. Don't fight them off. Just don't listen to them, or follow their train, or get in a conversation with them, or make plans to take action on what they're telling you to do.

After observing for awhile, you'll notice that there is a non-verbal stream inside that is trying to influence us and give us wisdom. You will also notice that the voice of this stream is not ours (i.e. we don't initiate it). And it can *say* things we've never heard before. And it shows us visions we've never seen before. And all of these things are very beautiful and inspiring. None of them take away our peace. Only fighting them takes away our peace.

Now when we *come back to life* (that is become fully outer-focused again), we'll see that this voice never leaves, and does try to continually influence us. I see this voice as the voice of God because (1)I don't initiate it, (2)it is in perfect agreement with the Bible, (3)it only expresses that which is positive, health-causing, and constructive, and (4)is in perfect peace with itself.

After spending a lot of time formally practicing the observing of this inner *voice*, I gradually became less inclined to let it slip out of my consciousness during my life when I was outer-focused. That is, through meditation, I was able to retrain myself to maintain a greater sensitivity to God for a greater amount of time in my life.

I have since observed that the more that my focus is both inner and outer simultaneously, the more peaceful I am. I believe that this is what St. Paul was talking about in the Bible when he said to "pray without ceasing". It would be impossible to literally verbally pray without ceasing while conducting our life. But we could non-verbally pray without ceasing in the way I described above. That is, always walk with (an awareness of and partial focus on) God (in our heart). And the longer we do this, the clearer we become about what the very specific philosophy and heart-nature of this inner voice is.

Before moving on though, let me clarify something about the truth channel. I'm not saying that any voice or impression that happens inside us is from God. There have been too many dangerous and harmful people in this world who've said that they've done what they've done because God told them to. It is critical that a person knows how to discern the source of the messages that happen within them. The truth channel's source is not the *subconscious mind* or *emotions*. One way to know if a message is or isn't from God is: does it agree with God's word - the Bible? This will become a more valid test for the reader after finishing the next chapter. Also the reader will learn how to know the Bible's complete message on a topic, so that they won't fall into the error of relying on a misinterpretation based on just one verse. And still, because self-deceit is a possibility, check your results with those who you are accountable to, trust and respect in the Church and in life.

Also, if you have a heart (not mind) inspiration to try meditation, my recommendation is to get initiated into it within a Christian organization that is devoted to it. You don't want to cast your fate to just any spiritual wind. These organizations can be found in some Christian book/cassette catalogues and retreats.

And when you meditate, do so by surrendering to and resting in the God of the Bible. A main purpose of meditation is to show us how to find strength and guidance in our one-on-One connection to God. And being that God is love, if meditating properly we should be immersed in peace...somewhere on a peace-to-bliss spectrum.

I would also like to point out that a church service intently followed is a meditation (which is one reason why we feel *high* after church). Deep prayer is also a form of meditation. And praying the rosary is even better than a mantra-style meditation when it is prayed as a series of heartfelt messages directed towards God. Spontaneous prayer is good too. The bottom-line reason to meditate is to transform to a more agape state, in communion with God.

Polls

In the *sense* of all that I just described, polls can now be seen as even more of a credible source of scientific data (that is, when they are expressions of people's intuitions, not minds). And in response to the question "Is there a God?", the numbers are very strong in support of "Yes".

The heart of America

Two 1992 polls support the hypothesis: human beings were designed with an experiential awareness of their designer built into their hearts. A poll in the Utne Reader says that 9 out of 10 Americans have never doubted God's existence. And, a USA Today poll said that 61% of Americans say that religion is very important in their lives; and 26% say that it is 'fairly important'. This means that the mainstream media is ignoring something that is dear to a minimum of 87% of Americans. This is an insult and a disservice to the great majority of people in America.

The heart of the media

In a poll of the mainstream media, in which religion is almost non-existent, only 14% of its main participants said that they were even somewhat religious. Obviously, the media does not represent the heart of America.

The spiritual feelings inherent in human beings

Another noteworthy poll result (which I mentioned in the beginning of this chapter) said that 96% of Americans believe in God. This is a very high percentage of individual hearts and minds to have come to this conclusion, having had years to ponder this question, while living in a society whose mainstream media rarely acknowledges God, and whose government often fights to have public mentions of Him removed. It shows the *feeling* that is *inherent* in our beings.

And, speaking of what is *inherent in human beings* (like I said earlier) out of all of the living creatures on earth, who inherently do most of the same things (eating, sleeping, playing, etc.), only humans worship God. And nearly all human cultures throughout history, even though many of them were (and some still are) isolated from each other and therefore incommunicado, have worshiped deity; had religious practices; and have had thoughts, feelings and discussions about deity. This heavily alludes to the probability that human beings were designed with an experiential awareness of their designer built into their hearts, by their designer, and for a purpose.

And, like I said before, only human beings were designed this way. That is, apes, ants, cats and dogs (and all other non-human life) who are instinctively highly organized as social creatures, have never had churches, temples or religious practices...only human beings have.

In this light, many people should question their political priorities. That is: the same people who are in an uproar over the treatment given to spotted owls, whales, etc. (creatures who aren't made in God's image or designed with a heart for God) are pushing for the liberalization of social policies (such as abortion, divorce, pornography, atheism, homosexuality, the de-feminization and divisive separation of women, alcohol, drugs, etc.) which are creating a lot of suffering for human beings (who <u>are</u> made in God's image and who are designed with a heart for God). These people are also cruel to God's most important creatures in that the policies they create and support are driving many people to homelessness, divorce, suicide, drugs, alcohol, dysfunctional lives, painful and deadly diseases, psychological disorders, crime, gangs, broken hearts, and the general suffering and emptiness that comes from having to deal with the aforementioned liberal social policies.

<u>How we've grown experientially distant from our intuitive knowledge of God</u>

Our relationship with God doesn't have to be as complicated as this chapter has presented it. But it's become so because humanity has separated itself from its Creator, and has become dulled and blinded by alcohol, drugs, and the drugs of: media, hyperness, idol worship, bad habits, etc. Most modern societies have egotistically chosen to glorify the (imperfect) creature rather than the (perfect) Creator.

Because of technological advancements, there are presently many smoke screens and diversions in this world. And all of them are aggressively fighting for our attention (and money). So if we want to sort out the basic truths of life amidst all of this, we must try to *eliminate* all of the empty focuses, and *illuminate* the most grounded and *real* focuses. Individually, our logical intellect and our innate sense of what is real can guide us and help us do this.

Also, much of modern humanity, through technology, has been increasingly able to insulate itself from experiencing the power in nature, and its dependence on nature.

(Although, notice how in recent years nature has increased its intensity, and still accomplishes the intended function of natural disasters, which is to remind us that we're not as omnipotent as we think, and to express the fact that God is not happy with how we're conducting ourselves). The issue of God was much simpler for people in past generations and past centuries. They held a high reverence for and focus on God because they moreso directly experienced Him in nature. I don't just mean in natural disasters, but also in the weather (due to a lack of air conditioning, heating and even electricity). And they knew that they got their much needed food every day from the ground, not from (human operated) buildings (supermarkets).

The validity of using 'circumstantial evidence' to scientifically prove the existence of God

Has anyone ever actually seen God? No.

Has anyone ever seen an atom, its nucleus, nuclear particles, or electrons? No. (Even if it were possible to see an atom, it would look like a fuzzball because the electrons are orbiting the nucleus so fast).

Yet, all of science is operating quite well based on the principles of atomic and nuclear *theories*, which have been determined to be true from circumstantial evidence.

Well the same holds true for God. My scientific analyses of the circumstantial evidence regarding God is as strong a proof for the existence and nature of God as science's proof for the existence and nature of the atom.

Further support for my hypotheses (besides logic) is that they've passed 'the experimental phase' of the 'scientific method' in that: a life submitted to the Bible's truths works well (just like scientific and industrial practices, which assume the atomic theories to be true work well).

Conclusion: my circumstantial proof of God is <u>as valid</u> and <u>admissible into the science community</u> as is the atomic theory.

Also, the Bible (which will be similarly proven in Chapter 2) is as <u>practical</u> to the 'science of living' (i.e. how we conduct our lives) as the atomic theory is to chemistry.

The following is an excerpt from a grade school chemistry book that simply illustrates and supports the two points I just made.

"In ancient times the atom was just a 'hunch'. Much later, scientists were able to show that atoms really did exist, and that with this <u>idea</u> many things could be explained. It turned out that atoms are even smaller than the ancients dreamed. They are far too tiny to be seen even with the strongest microscopes. Since <u>nobody has ever even seen an atom directly</u>, how do we know there are such things? The answer is that scientists have discovered many facts which can be explained only if we <u>take for granted</u> that there are such atoms. This is just as reliable as actually seeing the atoms. Do not doubt this kind of explanation, because we use it all the time in many familiar cases. For example, suppose you see a hunter raise a gun to his shoulder and aim at a squirrel. Then you hear a loud BANG and see the squirrel drop dead in his tracks. You would naturally take it for granted that a bullet killed the animal, although you did not actually see the bullet in flight. You would not even listen to any other explanation. That is how it is with our knowledge of atoms. It is an idea that works, and atoms are just as real to a scientist as marbles and baseballs are to you. Not only does he believe in atoms, but he is able to count them, to weigh them and to find out how big they are - all without ever having seen one."

Seeing is believing?

There've been many examples in this chapter of things that really do exist but that we can't see (magnetism, radio waves, etc.). And these things can have very dynamic effects (ultraviolet waves can give sunburn, microwaves cook food, radio waves cause radios to make music, etc).

Father Ken Roberts, on his show on EWTN, gave a great analogy regarding the unreality of only believing what we can see. An agnostic once said to him "You've never seen God, right?" He said "No, I've never seen him". Then the agnostic said "It would make more sense to me to worship something powerful that you can see." Father Roberts then said "Such as?" The agnostic said "Well I can see the sun. And I know that if the sun wasn't there, I couldn't live". Father Roberts said "Well then, you would have the same problem with a blind person that I'm having here with you. That is, how are you going to convince a blind person to believe in something they can't see, but that you know to be real? I mean, if you were blind, you could live without believing that the sun exists, couldn't you? But you couldn't live without it. Same with God. Just because a person is spiritually blind, it doesn't mean that they're not dependent on God" (slightly paraphrased). Father Roberts and many others actually do *see* God (with the inner *eye* I earlier described as the 'truth channel').

Also, Paul Stukey (of Peter, Paul and Mary), in a hit record he had as a solo artist, described a major benefit that happens when we accept the reality of God: when "you believe in something that you've never seen before....there is <u>love</u>." (The rest of the song makes it clear that it's God he's speaking of, e.g. "He is now to be among you", and "Whenever two or more of you are gathered in His name" Matthew 18:20).

I think this chapter has done a good job of logically proving that there has to be a power/intelligence/being other than humans[3]. In the next chapter the same scrutiny will be used to see if the Bible was authored by this power/intelligence/being.

([3] Perhaps you still don't agree. If not, write down any points that would argue against the existence of God that you think wouldn't be disputed by the contents of this chapter. Then go over the chapter again to <u>make sure</u> that these points weren't addressed. If there are no points that you can come up with that can't be handled, or if your points can't overtake the entire body of data, then realize that you have no *reason* to not accept a belief in God. Also, on the positive side, once you've accepted the existence of God and the realness of the Bible, the greatest of <u>all possible</u> worlds in this life will be available to you if you seek it: the Kingdom of God.)

An aside for believers

If you want to realize how fortunate and blessed your life is, imagine that the quote by Hume mentioned earlier in this chapter was true ("our world is [perhaps] a poor first attempt of an infant deity who afterwards <u>abandoned</u> it, ashamed of his lame performance"). Imagine that there was no Bible, no churches, no Jesus, no Holy Spirit. How empty, mundane and hopeless our life would be without this story of beauty amidst a world with so much ugliness.....without a Holy Spirit in our heart to guide, comfort, strengthen, inspire and just be with us. Actually, for many who don't know God, this is their reality (that is, unless they are on the *inspired* adventure of seeking and being reeled in by God). And were this also true for us, we'd probably find ourselves approaching life in ways that most of them do: trying to extract pleasure out of every moment with no consideration for the future, their bodies, or others; trying to find meaning in mundane things; worshiping imperfect systems and people in the world; etc.

Now...realize that this statement isn't true...you do have a Bible....a perfect God....a Jesus.....a Holy Spirit....a beautiful story....a beautiful meaning and purpose to your life (and life in general)....perfect guidance for every moment of your life and every possible situation....churches....holy fellowship, etc. Reflect on how fortunate you are. Every time this hits me, I gratefully thank God. But, unfortunately, only those who experience these great blessings know what I'm talking about. This is why, out of our love for God and compassion for others, we need to gently try to convince others of the great treasures that are available, and how much we value them.

A life that is centered around the Bible and the Holy Spirit is a very rich and fulfilling life. Whereas, a life that denies them (because it is atheistic, agnostic or distracted by 'the world', 'the mind' or 'habits'), is often empty, lost, confused, and highly prone to calamity (I unfortunately found this out by living the latter way first).

A key piece of wisdom: when you take these blessings for granted and/or complain about the life that God is giving you, He might (as a loving father who disciplines his children) allow you pain or loss in some form to remind you of your blessings, so that you can appreciate them when He gives them back to you. So, if you don't like pain or loss, don't whine or take your blessings for granted. The statement in Proverbs that says "Wisdom begins with the fear of the Lord" actually means 'the fear of what God can do to us (e.g. pain, from a disciplinary action)', not of God Himself (whom we should love, not fear).

In summary

The modern humanistic theory that says that 'conscious human awareness and intelligence is the pinnacle of existence' must be considered to be impossible. This is because: we do not embody the greatest intelligence in the universe. Even the bodies that we *find ourselves in* (which we didn't design) have a tremendously greater amount of intelligence than we have.

Humanity's advancements in technology have come from its attempts to imitate (whether consciously or intuitively) the designs that are in our bodies and in nature (e.g. electrical wiring=nervous system, computer=brain, plumbing=circulatory system, etc.).

Also, we do not embody the greatest power. There is so much power in the universe compared to us. We even only have very little power over *our own* bodies, which are teeming with life that is independent from us: red and white blood cells, digestive system, circulatory system, emotional system, reproductive system, conscience, computer-like brain, etc. Plus, not within our power is the ability to choose to keep *our* bodies alive forever.

And to think that we're just an isolated incident amidst all of this power and intelligence is also an extremely improbable thought. *The intelligence* shows that it is very meticulous by its extremely detailed work in the design of atomic structure. Therefore, it doesn't make sense that this intelligent power would abandon us, being that we are on a much larger scale than atoms, and are much more meticulous in design. But, psychology and the Bible (once proven) give us evidence that we weren't abandoned. Therefore, in the next chapter it will be shown how psychology and logic combined can be used to prove that the Bible and the truth channel had the same author.

Plus, a lot of other evidence that God inspired the Bible will be presented.

In the final analysis, the case for the existence of God, and that He authored the Bible, comes from a total body of evidence (logic, psychology, polls, archaeology, science and history). When viewed all at once, it is a very strong case....much stronger than the case against His existence...which is probably why 96% of Americans agree. (But, like St. Gregory said: "It is one thing to be persuaded of the existence of a thing, and quite another to know [it]").

Actually, the Bible says that all will be held accountable for believing or not believing in God because He has made the fact that He exists very obvious through this Creation. It's really that simple. Just walk outside some evening and look up into the sky. While looking out into this immense universe (keeping in mind how far away the things are that you are looking at) it will probably hit you as being absurd to think that human beings are the only intelligent life and that there isn't an immense power behind it all. And as this chapter has pointed out, nearly all people agree with this. (So being that atheists are such a small minority, isn't it tragic how they [by the energy generated from their psychological, spiritual, intellectual and emotional problems] have come to dominate America's national philosophy [in the media, government, psychology community, and education system]?)

The reason why some don't accept God's existence, and instead have mental walls built up against this obvious realization, is because they either have problems with submitting, peer pressure, or they don't want to give up their sins to a holy set of rules. But the Bible says that even these people will be held accountable and won't be able to use ignorance or non-belief as excuses. It says that this is so because the laws of God are "written on their hearts". It's unfortunate that they don't see the dysfunction and harm of what they're enslaved to, and the beauty of what they're missing out on.

A lot of these people just cruise along in a comfort zone (or semi-comfort or discomfort zone), and rarely, if ever, give death, God, or the meaning of their present existence a second thought. Also there are those whose lives are completely filled with the demands of goals and commitments...or just habits. But God deals with everyone in some way at some point. If this wasn't true, there would be no way for these people to enter into a higher existence in the afterlife. This will be more obvious as we move along in this book. But, like I've said, He is dealing with everyone now...via their conscience and Creation.

But regardless of a person's circumstances, a great reason to believe in God and live by the Bible is that doing so elevates our life. As we become proficient in applying the Bible's principles, it makes our life work <u>much</u> better, and it makes us feel better. Not that there won't be trials, but there will be silver linings to these trials, amidst a great sense of purpose, and a coming out on the other side much better off. My testimony is: life as an obedient Christian is the most sane, exciting, adventuresome, secure, beautiful, peaceful, intellectually stimulating, purposeful, joyful, motivating, challenging, love-filled, guiltless, fulfilling and inspiring way to approach life (and this testimony is even more credibile given that, as can be seen on the *About The Author* page, I've had many of what the world would consider to be top experiences in this life). Also, it makes us more enjoyable and helpful to others. And my testimony can be considered to be a piece of evidence in favor of the Bible. So now, on with proving the Bible.

Chapter 2

Was The Bible Authored By God?

I chose this point in the book to prove that God authored the Bible because I wanted to be able to use Biblical references and Biblical accounts of history from here on. But I still will be primarily explaining the logical 'whys' and 'meanings' behind what the Bible has to say.

In short, my proof of the Bible will include: (1)proving that it has 100% credibility in logic (no contradictions, and nothing that can be proven to be untrue); (2)proving that its principles, when applied, work as stated; (3)examining the credibility and motives of its human authors (e.g. why would such intelligent, articulate men allow themselves to be martyred in such horrible ways for something they knew wasn't true? And remember, most of these men testified as <u>eyewitnesses</u> to Jesus' miracles, teachings and resurrection); (4)archaeological evidence and historical accounts given both by credible Christian and non-Christian sources (including the most acknowledged Roman and Jewish historians of the first century); (5)examining the credibility of Jesus (e.g. why would a man, who was intelligent and wise enough to put forth wisdom and insights about life and living that haven't been topped in 2000 years, lie about His deity and knowledge of God's ways, especially since He spoke out so heavily against lying?); (6)comparing the Bible to my own scientific studies of the inner workings of human beings, which includes involvements in nearly all forms of psychology, and nearly all of the world's major philosophies and methods (and lots of minor and experimental ones too).

My studies spanned 14 years (nearly full-time) without Christianity, and then 14 years almost exclusively in Christianity. One of the findings of my studies is: having deeply and carefully observed the inner workings of a human being (through self-observation, meditation and being a counselor), and having carefully studied the most popular explanations given by others about these workings, I've found the Bible to be the only document that is 100% accurate in describing what goes on in a person.

The Bible has also proven to be a very credible revelatory tool in that 100% of the advice that is in it that I've tried (while not knowing if it was true or not) has turned out to be true (and very helpful). Many others also have given this same testimony.

But before getting into my detailed proofs, let me first make a couple of quick overviews regarding the Bible's place in human history.

The Bible is the best selling book of all time

The fact that the Bible is the most popular book of all time (by far) shows the natural attraction that the human heart, mind and spirit has for this book. It is not only the most read, but also the most revered, in that many large human institutions (churches) are based solely on it.

The Bible is the most scrutinized book in human history

The Bible is also the most scrutinized book in human history, by far. And although most of this scrutiny was done out of a loving attraction, it was also often done out of a hostile desire (especially by kings and rulers) to discredit and destroy it. But none succeeded for long. And the ones who resorted to censorship, suppression, torture and imprisonment, had their nations eventually witness a rebound enthusiasm for the Bible that surpassed their initial interest in it. For example: all of the ex-communist countries are experiencing great Christian revivals. One (Poland) has even produced a pope. And the once-mighty, pagan Roman Empire, which perpetrated many tortures upon Christians, eventually became the greatest preserver of Christianity for many centuries.

This book, that much of the modern world takes for granted, has often been regarded as gold by many who couldn't get it, or had a hard time getting it. In some places only a couple of pages were in a person's possession. And then a group of people would secretly get together to share each other's pages. And many have been tortured and killed merely for possessing the Bible or parts of the Bible.

Proving the Bible through our senses

To reiterate and expand on a point made in chapter 1, every radio station in the geographical area that we live in is playing in the air that we walk in all at once and continuously, emanating from very tall broadcast towers that serve as giant town criers that continually shout out sound (in electromagnetic form). Yet we don't hear any of it, and are not even aware of this tremendous amount of activity going on in our midst. Why? Because we have limited senses. That is, our ears can only pick up sound that is vibrating between 20 and 20,000 cycles per second, while *sounds* in the air from radio broadcasts are vibrating at between 10^4 and 3×10^{11} cycles per second.

And you can include in this mix of invisible, undetectable (by the human body) activity in the air: television broadcasts, cellular phone calls, and satellite emanations. But, we are able to detect some of the continuous occurrences in our midst because we have ears (to pick up a certain range of wave frequencies: 20-20,000 cycles per second) and eyes (to pick up another range of frequencies: appr. 10^{14} cycles per second). As for the other ranges of frequencies, we have nothing on this body to detect them with (X-rays, ultraviolet rays, etc.). But instruments have been developed to show us that they exist (radios, televisions, etc. - even a dog's ears). And, these undetectable-by-the-human-body waves can even be created by us (microwaves, media broadcasts, etc.). But, the invisible in the physical world can have a profound effect on us: sunburn, radiation poisoning, etc..

The spiritual analogy here is this: if so much potent activity can go on right next to us and inside of us that we can't sense with our bodies, but that instruments have been developed to show that it exists, how much more is there going on that we can't prove yet (e.g. a spirit world)?

It is also interesting to note that light is the <u>same physical thing</u> as radio waves: an electromagnetic wave. It's just that it is vibrating at different frequencies. Our body recognizes light but can't recognize radio waves. Yet they are in fact the same phenomenon. Even the different frequencies of light register within us as uniquely different: colors. And the different frequencies of radio waves register in a radio as completely different: radio stations. And the different frequencies of sound register within us as uniquely different: pitches.

This same-essence-but-different-manifestation property is also true of another phenomenon in the physical world. That is, most of the physical world (on earth) is made of the same physical thing: atoms. Yet, our body registers the differences in atom-groupings as very unique properties: solid, liquid, gas, hard, soft, etc. (Actually, the physical differences in this whole atomic soup that we find ourselves in can be seen as being merely (1)the difference in how tightly packed [through magnetism] different groupings of atoms are [that is, how hard or soft they are - with gas being the softest], and (2)the colors that their essence allows them to reflect.)

Therefore, this same-essence-but-different-manifestation property could also be true of the spirit world (which is made up of a completely different essence than the physical world). That is, it is made up of the same thing (spirit), but which, in slight variations, manifests as quite different entities: human spirits, different kinds of angels, satan, demons, God, the Holy Spirit, etc., each having different properties and a different range of powers.

(Also, reflecting back on a point in the last chapter, it is now even more clearly illogical to try to impose the properties and limitations* of one type of reality: physical, on a completely different type of reality: spiritual).
*[e.g. time and space]

Also, in the last chapter I showed how the spirit world is not totally undetectable. There is proof of the spirit world in that we do have scientific instruments to detect and verify its existence. We have a *sense* to experience it (our truth channel), and another *sense* to logically conclude its existence (our mind). Also, there's that box that they had in "Ghostbusters". (Just checking to see how well you're concentrating).

When all of the data is viewed at once, it can be seen that in our heart (not the physical one) is a place where the spirit world and the physical world intersect.

Our feelings

Everyone's first and foremost relationship is with their feelings. Therefore, if we want our feelings to be good and not bad, our primary interest should be with God, who is the designer of the rules that govern our feelings. After many years of very scrutinous observation of my feeling mechanism, I find that the Bible describes (with 100% accuracy) the cause and effect of what goes on there. That is, it describes the specifics of what causes me to feel good, and what causes me to feel bad....as well as why these need to happen in the specific ways that they do. No other body of thought in the world comes close to being as accurate or complete as the Bible.

This last fact is a solid piece of scientific *data* that can help support the *conclusion* that: God had a hand in the creation of the Bible. It couldn't be presented as proof in itself, but it is a strong cog in the many-cogged wheel that I'm presenting in this chapter.

The link in the scientific process that leads from *hypothesis* to *conclusion* is the creation and development of *data* through *experimentation*. The main place where this experimentation (observation and testing) is done is: within a person. I've done this almost continually for 28 years. If you want to come to the same unshakable conclusion that I've come to, you might also have to become a scientist (who specializes in feelings) and conduct your own experiments (i.e. objectively observing your own feelings at work, and then compare what you observe to what the Bible and other bodies of thought have to say). Some helpful ways to become aware of subconscious and conscious feelings are: journal keeping (where you write down the insights you have - [if you really get into this, you'll be fishing for receipts, grabbing for napkins - anything to write the very clear, important and inspiring things you'll be observing and realizing]), poem writing, songwriting, writing and meditation. These are also great ways to get the left lobe of your brain out of the way so that you can objectively watch God at work within you (i.e. the <u>involuntary</u> workings in, of and behind your feelings). And, an occasional drink of wine will often relax you enough to allow you to be able to see things about yourself that you weren't able to see when you were in a more tense state (of course, if you do this too often, it will lose its effect. As for me personally, I average about 1/2 glass every 4 months). Also, relaxed, spontaneous conversations with well-trusted friends will reveal to you deep truths that are within your being.

<u>Proving the Bible by objectively observing our heart</u>

Anyone who has extensively observed their heart (through continual, daily, thoughtful observation....and then in a deeper, more focused way, through meditation), and also has extensively studied the Bible, knows that the Bible accurately describes what goes on in the heart. And, the more extensive the observations and studies, the greater the Bible's credibility becomes.

I realize that due to economic pressures, the moral pressures of our time (and the media and peer pressures that promote and perpetuate them), and the continual blitz of media, most people are continually being pulled by <u>outer</u> focuses. But I have taken the time (and have tried to make it my continual life's purpose) to delve deeply into the <u>inner</u> realms. This pursuit was much easier (and more popular) in the '60s and '70s when financial pressures were much less and therefore people had more free time. But I was <u>so</u> inspired by the realness and rewards of this pursuit, I tried my best to continue and complete it (often at the expense of economic and physical well-being). Now I feel like an explorer who's come back to give his report.

After initially being fascinated and inspired by philosophy and psychology, and simultaneously recognizing a need for improvement both in my inner world and the outer world I lived in, I started carefully observing my heart, my mind, my ways, my life and life in general. I transferred my scientific scrutiny and sense of adventure from physical science to the sciences of living: psychology, philosophy, and sociology. I pursued a desire to absorb the best of all of the knowledge in these areas that existed on this planet. I would be attracted into a group or philosophy when *I* detected a ring of truth in what someone representing the group or philosophy said, or when I recognized a higher-than-normal state in their being. I spent many years doing a lot of meditation, doing a lot of mental investigation and studying, counseling, group therapies, classes, self-observation, and being a part of many groups of people who were inspired in the same way that I was. And when I would eventually realize that I hadn't found the highest truth, or that the philosophy or group that I was involved in was flawed, I would move on. I wanted to know perfection, or at least, the highest approach possible in this life.

The scientific side of me always kept a journal. It felt so much more <u>real</u> to write down what I *instinctively knew to be true* * and not true, than to be in total agreement with the people around me just for the sake of 'peace'. I realized early on that when I pursued peace with others, it often came at the expense of my own inner peace. Being that I deemed the latter to be the more important pursuit, and being that I realized that I had lost a lot of it in trying to keep peace with others, I would hold on to it and then try to not let it be intimidated by fears of rejection, disagreement, separation, criticism, argument or loneliness.

(*I was becoming aware that there was a voice within me that wasn't me, that had a settled feeling of *truth*, and that I had the ultimate respect for and a deep bond of love with. And my strongest desire had become to not want to go against this feeling anymore just for the sake of peace with the outer world, or to live out my own errant impulses, plans and confusions).

After 14 years of living like this, I moved to Los Angeles, where my cousin and his family were living. They had just gotten into Christianity, and were trying to enlighten me to it. But it didn't really take with me. I had so many negative feelings about it and its concepts, based on those in the media and on the street corners who *represented* it. Also, its precepts didn't completely go along with what I had been previously involved in. But my relatives said that I shouldn't judge Christianity so flippantly before I really read what it had to say in the Bible. This meant challenging all of my hippie 'peace, love and freedom' ways with the notion that there has to be a set of rules that accurately and exclusively describe how, by nature, our lives should be governed so as to run optimally. And these rules weren't ones that the editors of Rolling Stone or Playboy would agree with. I said 'fair enough'. So I began to study and grapple with the concepts in the Bible.

Proving the Bible with the truth channel

To make a long story short, what I found in the Bible was: perfect agreement with my rather voluminous collection of journals that I held sacred. Here the Bible was agreeing with things in my heart that I had not been able to find any person, group or philosophy to agree with. That was very exciting. It also greatly inspired me to <u>really</u> study this book. Could it be true? Did I finally find the apex of philosophy? (The fact that this has been the most revered book by much of the world for most of human history should have been a strong clue that it just might be).

<u>Proving the Bible with the mind</u>

To make another long story short (which I'll make long in another book), the Bible turned out to be a magic fountain of revelation (and has continued to be for the 14 years since). This magic has both been in my heart and my mind. The reason I had missed this great truth is that I had judged Christianity from observing the most visible and vocal Christians in the Christian media, and because I had joined in with the rebellious, "hip" counter-culture. These stances kept me from seeing how great a document the Bible is, and what Jesus <u>really</u> stands for. This cloud of bad PR still looms over Christianity today, which is why I had a lot to say about bad-fruit preachers in the last chapter. Mahatma Gandhi once said that if the world could see the Christ of Christianity...they would accept Him. But, because they see the Christians of Christ...they reject Him.

To make another even longer story short, my extensive observations and studies have yielded that the Bible has 100% credibility. That is: (1)I've found every statement in it (that I could test or observe) to be true, and (2)I've found nothing in it that I could prove to be untrue.

<u>Proving the Bible through 'experiential testing'</u>

And I have tried to find provable contradictions and fallacies in the Bible. My years of training in analysis didn't abandon me when I confronted philosophy and religion. It wouldn't let me endorse a philosophy or give myself to a religion without first scrutinizing and verifying them. This is why I've been through so many philosophies and religions (see page 301 as to which ones). But, having done so, I ended up greatly benefiting from trying out what I tried to disprove (in the process of trying to disprove it). And now, I point to 'knowing about and understanding the Bible, becoming a Christian, and having a close, continual access to God' as the greatest happening of my life. This is why I'm trying to share it here. Because I now know the great things it can do for an individual...and for a society.

Conclusion: The Bible has shown perfect accuracy in spelling out what I have observed in my heart. And what I have logically concluded about life in my mind, the Bible has turned out to be in perfect agreement with. Also, what it has pointed out that I didn't know, but which I've tested, has proven not only to be true, but also to be beauty-causing. The Bible has proven to be a resource of perfect advice in how to operate my mind, body and life.

Now, mine is just one testimony. But it is also one that has been repeated many times by others.

For many, these testimonies, plus their intuition, may not be enough to convince them (it wasn't for me). In which case I would suggest to do exactly what I've done. That is: carefully and objectively observe your heart, mind, complete inner workings, behavior, and life in general. Then read the Bible and see if indeed it is the most accurate and in depth in describing what you've observed. Also, test its other premises and advice to see if they in fact prove to be accurate and health-causing. And, like I said before, it is helpful to keep a journal or some other way of recording the results of your explorations (songs, poems, etc.). My experience has been that I absolutely have to write down or record higher-than-normal insights when I have them. Everything else stops at these moments.

You'll probably end up finding out that 'truth is greater than fiction', and much more inspiring and adventuresome than any fiction media you might read or watch.

Saying 'the Bible is perfectly true' is scientifically sound

If the Bible can be shown to have 100% credibility in making true statements (for the things in it that are provable/disprovable) then this would give a very high credibility for the things in it that aren't provable to also be true. Meaning: absolute proof of everything in the Bible may not be possible, but 'having faith in the fact that it's true' has good scientific credibility for being a sound position. Actually, this is a very common practice in science. That is: having *faith* in your hypothesis to the point of accepting it as being true (until it proves itself to not be true). A lot of what is assumed to be *science* is really just still in the hypothetical category of *premises of faith* (e.g. atoms, nuclear physics, the Big Bang, age of the universe, age of the earth, evolution, Neanderthals, etc.).

When we prove to ourselves that the Bible is the most practical guide for creating psychological, spiritual and emotional health (at least much more than anything else on the planet), this increases its scientific credibility even more. So then, an interesting question (which is a long topic for another book which I'm writing) is: how did it get replaced as the ultimate source of this society's wisdom and sanity, by an unwise and insane media?

Conducting the experiment of living under the hypothesis: the Bible is perfectly true

I continue to have an open and scrutinizing mind. But at one point, after much exhaustive study on all topics,

I realized that the Bible was almost assuredly going to continue to have perfect credibility. Therefore, I now just operate on the premise that all things in it are true (and enjoy the great feeling that happens when you accept this premise). I can't even imagine a better way to approach life (this is probably due to the fact that I tried nearly all of the other ways first).

I hope that my testimony here will inspire the reader to take the same course that I've taken, and thereby enjoy the same rewards I've found from taking this course. And then, to affect the whole of life in a positive way.

Also, as to when the spirit world interacts with the physical world: in the Bible God says that *"where two or more are gathered in My name, I will be there in their midst"* (Matt. 18:20). He's saying: here...in our midst. And like ultraviolet waves, He is a powerful invisible reality that has a tremendous effect on us. And, right now, (depending on how you're relating to what you're reading) you and I are gathered in His name.....which would account for the high experience you would be having while reading this book. That is: (1)God is love, (2)love is a very pleasurable experience, (3)the more that you allow God into your inner workings and life, the more you can feel His presence, which is love.

Examining the credibility of the writings of the human authors of the Bible...and of the human authors themselves

In the beginning of this chapter I said that one thing that I would use to prove the authenticity of the Bible is "(3)examining the credibility and motives of its human authors (e.g. why would such intelligent, articulate men allow themselves to be martyred in such horrible ways for something they knew wasn't true? Remember, most of these men are testifying as <u>eyewitnesses</u> to Jesus' miracles, teachings and resurrection)". Supreme Court Justice Antonin Scalia had a humorous way of pointing out how absurd it is to conclude that the apostles didn't really witness the resurrection like they said they did. He said "We must pray for the courage to endure the scorn of 'the sophisticated world'. The 'wise' do not believe in the resurrection of the dead. It is really quite absurd [to them]. The Ascension had to be made up by groveling enthusiasts as part of their plan to get themselves martyred". He's saying that the conclusion in this last sentence is what is really absurd here. Obviously, men who were intelligent enough to write the Bible wouldn't be so foolish as to make a plan to suffer being martyred for something that they knew wasn't true. Maybe an argument could be made for <u>one</u> mentally-deranged person doing this, but not <u>many</u> (and most of the apostles were martyred). Let's look at one these men...one of the main writers of the New Testament.

<u>Saul of Tarsus</u>

Here is an example of a conversion as drastic as Madonna (the pop singer, not Jesus' mother) becoming a nun. St. Paul, one of the main writers of the new testament and the main spreader of Christianity (after Jesus), wasn't always a lover of Christianity. In fact, he was one of the main persecutors of early Christians.

He was a Pharisee (an orthodox Jewish sect that strictly focused on the law) from Tarsus, born with the name Saul. He was obsessed with driving Christianity out of Jerusalem by having all of the Christians sought out and killed by being stoned to death (as you can imagine, a <u>very</u> painful way to die). Then he became obsessed with destroying Christianity altogether. He personally spread this crusade from town to town.

To make a long story short, he eventually became the leading evangelist of the early Christian church. He made many tours to different cities as a preacher in the town squares, for which he was stoned and beaten many times. How many of us would allow ourselves to be stoned for our beliefs? Therefore, he must have <u>really</u> believed in and loved Christianity. But why such a dramatic change of heart? To find this out, read about his conversion in Acts 9.

Also, read his other writings throughout the New Testament. Besides being a feast of wisdom, this reading will show you just how very intelligent and articulate he was. Now, would someone this intelligent and articulate allow themselves to endure so much suffering (and eventually, beheading) for something that they might have even an inkling that it wasn't true? Remember, Saul had very intimate contact with the apostles, who themselves had very intimate contact with Jesus and were eyewitnesses to His miracles, crucifixion and resurrection. By the way, Saul/Paul himself became empowered to perform miracles after his conversion.

Other martyrs

There have been <u>many</u> martyrs who have died <u>horrible</u> deaths (lions, upside-down crucifixions, stoning, amputations, being boiled in oil, etc.) rather than denounce their belief in Jesus. It's so easy to cast these bits of history aside, amidst so much history. But it would serve our purpose well here to stop and dwell on these facts of the martyrs for a moment.

Most of the apostles were martyred. Also, many entire families were martyred. They could <u>easily</u>* have been spared these horrible deaths by simply denouncing their belief in Christianity. Think about yourself being in this kind of predicament and how intensely sure you would have to be about Christianity (or any belief) to <u>allow</u> yourself to be horribly killed for it. Well, there are thousands of such testimonies from early Christianity (it is said that their blood is the seed of the Church), and also in modern ex-communist countries, and throughout history. Also, more priests and nuns have been martyred in the 20th century than in all of human history.

(*The punishment of execution was given in early Rome for the crime "the mere profession of Christianity". [This is what St. Paul was beheaded for]. But a Christian defendant could gain release <u>easily</u> by simply offering incense on a pagan alter).

Also, an interesting point to note here is that Peter, when challenged by the Roman guards who had come to get Jesus for crucifixion, denounced 3 times that he even knew Jesus. He obviously was more scared for his life than he was convinced of the importance of Jesus' work and teachings. Yet, later in his life, when he was told he was going to be crucified for his Christian views, he asked to be crucified upside down because he wasn't worthy to be crucified upright like his master, Jesus. Why this dramatic change of heart? A good scientist will point out the fact that where there is a dramatic change, something dramatic had to happen in between time A and time B. What was the cause of that dramatic change? The resurrection....which Peter personally experienced (the risen Jesus). Once again...dwell on this....people don't go from 'fear of being killed' to 'complete acceptance of a torturous death that they could have easily prevented' for no reason. This is a very strong proof that the resurrection really did occur.

Another strong testimony from a human being (in

this case, Peter) is that he said that he was an eyewitness to God manifesting Himself as a voice from heaven, giving testimony that Jesus was His Son. Peter did this in one of his writings in the Bible, 2 Peter 1:16-19:

"We did not follow cunningly devised fables when we made known to you the power and coming of our Lord Jesus Christ, but were eyewitnesses of His majesty. For He received honor and glory from God the Father when such a voice came to Him from the Excellent Glory: 'This is my beloved Son, in whom I am well pleased.' We heard this voice which came from heaven while we were with Him on the holy mountain."

Notice in the first sentence how he wanted to emphasize that 'witnessed truth' is what was being communicated here, not an orally transmitted, second hand, cleverly crafted myth (and there were many in those days).

But now you might say: "How do we even know that these accounts of history are true? I mean, it has been almost 2000 years." And the most common comment that I hear from non-Christians (and a pre-Christian argument that I used to use) is: "The Bible's been around for 2-4000 years. It must have been altered many times along the way. Therefore, how can we trust what the Bibles of today say?"

God knew that people would have this argument. So in His infinite wisdom, He inspired a monastic Jewish sect, the Essenes, to hide parchments of the entire Old Testament (minus the book of "Esther") in jars in caves in Qumran. Then He inspired a Bedouin goat herder to *stumble across* them in 1947. When checked, there was found to be no difference between the nearly 2000 year old scriptures and today's scriptures. Finding the Dead Sea scrolls has been called "the archaeological find of all time".

As for the New Testament, it is the most well-preserved of all ancient documents. We have more than 3,000 manuscripts today dating from the 2nd century.

Being that there are so many different explanations in the world as to what the Bible is saying, how do you know which ones are really true?

Now for some fun (if you're interested in improving your life, knowing the truth, and fascinated by discovering wisdom....and also, if you like philosophic adventure, and resolving religious controversy).

If you hear someone present something that is in the Bible, but it doesn't ring in your heart (actually, truth channel) as being true, chances are what they're saying isn't an accurate representation of what's in the Bible (and there's a whole lot of this kind of misrepresentation going around). Well, thank God, there is a way for you to know exactly what the truth is. Actually, there are 3 ways: (1)Bible study, (2)revelation in your heart by the Holy Spirit, and (3)logical scrutiny. And yes, there are plenty of misrepresenters who claim to have done all 3 of these, but when you get in and do your own study, you'll find that they really haven't. But in your heart of hearts (what I referred to in the last chapter as the 'truth channel') you really know if someone is speaking truth or not. Usually when people don't look to the truth channel it's because they are attached to 'things being a certain way'.

So, given all of this, the really inquisitive among us, who can't just base their basic life beliefs on 'accepting what someone else says', are just going to have to get in and do some Bible studies. But, when I do a Bible study, I become extremely focused and experience a great sense of purpose, peace, fullness, highness, love and (sometimes) excitement, like I'm about to uncover some buried treasures. And I guess that I feel this way because of my past experiences of actually uncovering treasures in this process. They are treasures because of how greatly they've helped my life, improved my feelings, changed courses in my thoughts and actions that would have brought me and others suffering, given me understandings that eliminated my backlog of 'questions about life', and resolved these mysteries in a way that has resonated true throughout my entire being. They also are treasures because amidst today's religious controversies, they confirm that what my heart-of-hearts is saying...is also what the Bible says.

The reason I keep saying heart-of-hearts instead of heart is because the heart can have flippant emotional reactions triggered by bad programming in the subconscious mind, not based on truth. Whereas, what comes through the truth channel is always true.

<u>How to do a Bible study</u>

First you start with a question that you want to get answered, e.g. how does God feel about divorce? Next you look in a *concordance* to show you every place in the Bible where your key word (divorce) is mentioned. Then you read all of these verses (and surrounding verses), and formulate a hypothesis that wouldn't be in disagreement with any of them, e.g. 'God hates divorce, but will allow it if there's been infidelity, or if an unbelieving spouse leaves'.

Now, pick some key words that relate to this topic, e.g. marriage. Look in the *concordance* to find every place in the Bible where your relative words are mentioned. Read all of them. But, while doing so, keep in mind your hypothesis, checking to see if any disagreements come up that might cause you to have to alter it.

After doing this, you should have a pretty solid idea

of what the Bible has to say about the question you've posed. But, if there is still some confusion or controversy, there are many other tools that can help you.

There are *topical* books, in which the Bible's contents are categorized by topic; there are commentaries by scholars and organizations who you trust; there's your *truth channel* (whereby wisdom can be accessed in focused states of prayer); there's your *mind*'s ability to logically analyze and discern; there's your ability to *observe* what's truly occurring in life; there are Bibles with footnotes by organizations and people you trust; you can read the verses around the verses you are studying; you can study and understand the full books that contain the verses you are studying (e.g who wrote them, to whom, and why, in what setting, under what circumstances, etc.); and last but not least, you can study the texts of the Bible in the original languages they were written in.

The original writings of the Bible were in Hebrew, Aramaic, and Greek. Therefore, any serious student of the Bible, or any person who is dubious about accepting what the Bible says by hearing it from another person, needs to go directly to the older Hebrew and Greek manuscripts. These are also available as computer software.

There are two ways to do this kind of a study: *surface* and *in-depth*. A surface study only requires a Greek or Hebrew Interlinear Bible, and a dictionary of the language you're studying. But an in-depth study requires that you master the grammar of the language, as well as know the idioms of the language of the times that the texts were written. Also, you'd have to know the customs of the day to fully grasp the meaning behind the idioms.

But, how much of all of this is really necessary? Just until you get to the point where you're sure that your hypothesis finds no contradiction from any of the above tests (and to the depths of your heart-of-hearts you know that you're not fooling yourself).

Archaeological support

Archaeology is the scientific study of ancient times. There are many books on Bible archaeology if you're interested. But to make a long story short, there has not been one archaeological finding that would dispute anything that's said in the Bible. On the contrary, there have been many findings that prove that the Bible's accounts of history are factual. Here are the major ones.

The history of Israel, as described in the Bible, is believed to be true because Egyptian and Assyrian historical records from the time of King Solomon on describe the same Kings and the same battles.

Israeli archaeologist Gabriel Barkay found two tiny silver scrolls inside a Jerusalem tomb in 1979. They were dated around 600 B.C. There was a benediction from the *Book of Numbers* etched onto them. The discovery made it clear that parts of the Old Testament were being copied long before some skeptics believed they were even written.

Archaeologists revealed in 1986 that several lumps of figured clay called bullae, bought from Arab dealers in 1975, had once been used to seal documents. Nahman Avigad of the Hebrew University of Jerusalem identified the impressions stamped into one piece of clay as coming from the seal of Baruch, son of Neriah, a scribe who recorded the doomsday proclamations of the prophet Jeremiah. Another bore the seal of Yerahme'el, son of King Jehoiakim's son, who the *Book of Jeremiah* says was sent on an unsuccessful mission to arrest both prophet and scribe - again confirming the existence of Bible characters.

In 1990 Frank Yurco, an Egyptologist at the Field Museum of Natural History in Chicago, used hieroglyphic clues from a monolith known as the Merneptah Stele to identify figures in a Luxor wall relief as ancient Israelites. The Stele itself, dated to 1207 B.C., celebrates a military victory by the Pharaoh Merneptah. "Israel is laid waste," it reads, suggesting that Israelites really existed more than 3,000 years ago, and not just because the Bible tells us so.

Avraham Biran of Union College - Jewish Institute of Religion and Joseph Naveh of the Hebrew University announced In 1993 that they had found an inscription carved into a chunk of basalt at an ancient mound called Tel Dan, in the north of Israel, bearing the phrases "House of David" and the "King of Israel". It is the first time the Jewish monarch's name has been found outside of the Bible. The writing, dated to the 9th century B.C., only a century after David's reign, described a victory of a neighboring king over the Israelites. The skeptics' claim that King David never existed is now hard to defend.

French scholar Andre Lemaire reported a related "House of David" discovery in *Biblical Archaeology Review* in 1994. His subject was the Meshe Stele (also known as the Moabite Stone), the most extensive inscription ever recovered from the state of Palestine. Found in 1868 at the ruins of the Biblical Dibon, the basalt stone wound up in the Louvre, where Lemaire spent seven years studying it. His conclusion: the phrase "House of David" appears there as well. As with the Tel Dan fragment, this inscription comes from an enemy of Israel boasting of a victory - King Mesha of Moab, who figured in the Bible.

In 1995, Egyptologist Kenneth Kitchen of the University of Liverpool offered what was called an "extraordinary demonstration" in *Biblical Archaeology Review* that the stories about Abraham are plausible. Drawing on non-Biblical records, Kitchen argued that everything from the quoted price of slaves to the style of warfare to the laws of inheritance in Abraham's day is amazingly consistent with the Bible accounts.

In 1990, diggers in the Jewish Quarter of Jerusalem's Old City uncovered an ossuary (repository for bones) with the inscription "Joseph son of Caiaphas". This marked the first archaeological evidence that the high priest Caiaphas, who according to the Gospels presided at the Sanhedrin's trial of Jesus, was a real person. So, indisputably was Pilate. In 1961, diggers in Caesarea found the fragment of a plaque indicating that a building had been dedicated by "Pontius Pilatus, Prefect of Judea".

And, of course, there is the "archaeological find of all time" that I mentioned earlier: the Dead Sea Scrolls. Before the Dead Sea Scrolls were discovered (in 1947), the earliest copy of the Old Testament that we had was written in 895 A.D. This fact left the door open for the criticism that I mentioned earlier: "The Bible's been around for 2-4000 years. It must have been altered many times along the way. Therefore, how can you even trust what the Bibles of today say?" And in the case of the Old Testament, if 895 A.D. is the oldest copy available, that allows this text some 1500-2500 years to have been altered. But paleographic and archaeological evidence indicates that most of the Dead Sea Scrolls were written between 200 B.C and 68 A.D., and no differences were found in them from the text we have today (which are an additional 1100 years removed from the original writings). So, combined with some of the even more recent archaeological findings I mentioned earlier, we can be assured that what we have today is an accurate text of the Old Testament.

One argument that anti-Bible archaeologists give is: if you can't prove the whole Bible archaeologically, then the Bible should be discounted. But this is a fallacy in logic (as I talked about in chapter 1). Also, not being able to prove a Biblical account doesn't prove that it didn't happen. This fact is concurred with by a truism in archaeology that says: the absence of evidence is not evidence of absence.

Two pieces of archaeological evidence that I didn't include here are the Shroud of Turin and Noah's Ark. Although there is some very convincing evidence for them, the science community at large has yet to give their findings its stamp of approval. But there are some very stirring and convincing TV shows and video tapes out about them. I would highly recommend watching them. *The Silent Witness* is good. For a recent update see USA Today (5/23/96) article "Turin shroud dated closer to Jesus' time".

There may not be physical evidence for every occurrence in the Bible (e.g. Adam and Eve). But as long as there isn't any evidence that disproves what the Bible says, then the Bible still has 100% credibility. And I point to this fact as a solid piece of logic data. This also allows the archaeological evidence which supports what the Bible says to be joined with all of the other evidence from other fields that I've been presenting (logic, psychology, physics, testimonies of practical effectiveness, history, etc.) to form a very strong pro-Bible argument.

Historians

Although the Bible writings had always been recorded on papyrus and leather, passing down scriptures by oral tradition was also very common. But sometimes the writings of the oral traditions wouldn't happen until years after they started. Now most of us have probably seen or participated in the demonstration where you get a line of people who whisper a phrase to the person next to them, which is then passed successively down a line, until it is revealed that the person at the end of the line has a completely different version of what was originally said. So now, if this could happen while being passed in such a short period of time, wouldn't there be an even greater breakdown of the original stories when passed over many years? Once again, God had this covered by having the very important gospel stories written by 4 different men, thus the 4 gospels: Matthew, Mark, Luke and John, all of which are in harmony. And two of these books (Matthew and John) weren't written by hearers of stories passed down by oral tradition. They were written by men who were eyewitnesses to the original events, experiencing them first hand. (The gospel of Mark was basically co-authored by Peter, his close companion and another eyewitness to the original events; and the gospel of Luke was basically co-authored by Paul, whom He spent a great amount of time with on his missionary journeys.)

I used to look for proofs of the Bible's authenticity outside of the Bible, until one day I realized 'Hey wait a minute. The writings of the Bible themselves are also proofs. This isn't just a book written by one person, but rather it was written by many people...all of whom can be considered to be just as credible of historians as any other writers of the day. In fact, they were so moved by what they had witnessed that they devoted their whole lives to it, and even allowed themselves to be martyred for it. I'd say that these are pretty dedicated historians. Therefore, why should their accounts of history be looked at with any less credibility?'

Once again, we have an entire New Testament filled with writings by a number of men, which are all in agreement, and most of these men came to torturous deaths only because of what they were writing. These facts give high credibility to the authenticity of the history that they were writing about.

Josephus Flavius

But, we don't need to just rely on the New Testament writers' accounts of history because the top non-Christian historians of the day also verify that what they've said is true, including the crucifixion and resurrection.

One such historian was Josephus Flavius, who was a first century Jewish historian born in Jerusalem. His family had both a royal and a priestly history. His original name was Joseph Ben Matthias. He was an educated man with public involvement, in that he was a member of the Pharisees, before the Jewish revolt against Rome (66), who had friends at the court of Emperor Nero.

In 67 A.D. he prepared Galilee for a coming onslaught (that he had inside information on) by the Romans, who were out to repel a rebellion by the Jews that had started in 66. The Jews were able to repulse the advance of Vespasian, the Roman general who was soon to become emperor, defending the fortress of Jotapata for 47 days before surrendering. Josephus would have been sent as a prisoner to Nero had he not had the wit to prophesy that his captor, Vespasian, would himself one day be emperor. This prophecy concurred with Vespasian's ambitions, and so the general kept Josephus with him, thus saving his life. While Vespasian's prisoner, Josephus saw the subjugation of Galilee and Judea. Subsequently freed, he adopted Vespasian's family name, Flavius. Accompanying another future emperor, Vespasian's son Titus, he witnessed Titus's siege of Jerusalem in 70. Thereafter, enjoying imperial patronage under Titus and his brother's successor, Domitian, Josephus lived until his death in Rome and devoted himself to his writing.

His works include *The Jewish War* (in 7 books), which he wrote to dissuade his people and other nations from courting annihilation by further revolt against an all-powerful Rome; *Jewish Antiquities* (in 20 books), a history of the Jews from the creation to 66 A.D. that eloquently demonstrates how his people had flourished under the law of God; an autobiography, *Life*; and *Against Apion*, a refutation of charges against the Jews made by the anti-Semitic Greek grammarian Apion (1st century) and other likeminded writers. This last book is invaluable, because Josephus recapitulates writings on Jewish history that are no longer available.

In *Jewish Antiquities*, this is what Josephus wrote about Jesus: "Now, there was about this time, Jesus, a wise man, if it be lawful to call him a man, for he was a doer of wonderful works - a teacher of such men as receive the truth with pleasure. He drew over to him both many of the Jews and many of the gentiles. He was [the] Christ. And when Pilate, at the suggestion of the principle men among us, had condemned him to the cross, those that loved him at first did not forsake him, for he appeared to them alive again the third day, as the divine prophets had foretold these and 10,000 other wonderful things concerning him. And the tribe of Christians, so named from him, are not extinct at this day."

This writing alone is in perfect agreement with what is written about Jesus in the New Testament. It also, in one paragraph, supports the most important historical

claims made about Jesus in the Bible: His miracles, crucifixion, fulfilling of Old Testament Jewish prophesies, and
resurrection. And many other details in Josephus' works
verify what's said in the Bible.

The credibility of Jesus

Proof of the existence of Jesus includes: the historical record of the New Testament writings, the writings of
Josephus and a number of other Jewish and Roman historians of His day, and the fact that Jesus was listed in a
Roman census.

Also, let me reiterate what I said at the beginning of
this chapter: "Why would a man, who was intelligent and
wise enough to put forth wisdom and insights about life
and living that haven't been topped in 2000 years, lie about
His deity and knowledge of God's ways, especially when
He spoke out so heavily against lying?" And like most of
the New Testament writers, Jesus also was put to a torturous death because of what He was saying. Such an intelligent and articulate man could have easily spared Himself
from such excrutiation. But obviously He, like most of the
apostles and many of the early Christians, felt that what
they were standing for was so important that even death by
torture wasn't enough to make them conceal it.

Miracles

One easy way that God could prove His existence
is to merely step in and do something supernatural (that is,
something that can't be explained by the normal laws of
nature). But He doesn't often do this because He wants our
love and willing submission to be based just on the goodness and rightness of His laws and love. But, some people
aren't that easily enlightened or convinced. And many oth-

ers are so distracted by the dominant media, their families and their work, that they never pay attention to God. One very potent tool that God invented to get people's attention is: pain (emotional and physical). But as awful as pain is, it often still isn't enough to get people's attention in the right direction. And even when it does, the attention usually drifts away as soon as the pain drifts away. But besides being a punishment for wrong-doing (for our guidance and for the protection of others), pain is mostly just used by God as a polishing tool. Therefore, He still must do something extraordinary to prove that there is a supernatural.

The Bible is filled with accounts of supernatural occurrences. Even the secular historian Josephus attests to the miracles that Jesus performed. And the early church fathers were given powers to perform extraordinary signs that showed that they truly represented God.

Also, there still are many miracles occurring today, both publicly (e.g. the miracles of the saints*) and in personal lives. They are there for those who need 'signs' (which is probably most of us at some point) that the God of the Bible and Jesus are who they say they are (of course the Bible does say that creation itself is a miraculous sign. Some question the miracle of the 'virgin birth'. But what about the miracle of birth itself? And what about the supernatural miracle of a seemingly endless universe?). (*Read about Padre Pio for some stunning modern-day miracles).

El Lazari

An historian said that you look for indirect evidence when you're investigating something that you can't prove directly. "El Lazari" is a strong piece of evidence both of Jesus' existence and the fact that He performed miracles. I'm sure most have heard about the fact that

Jesus raised Lazarus from the dead. Well right after it happened, the city where it happened (which was even mostly populated by Arabs) changed its name to "El Lazari". Now cities don't easily change their name. Therefore, it is extremely reasonable to assume that something spectacular happened there...and that that something involved Lazarus.

<u>Personal Signs</u>

I don't know what the percentage would be, but I'm sure if you started questioning Christians, you would hear many stories of divine intervention on the physical level in their lives. I'll give two examples from my own life.

In the late '50s and early '60s I was a '50s-kind-of-guy (I still am a 50s kind-of-guy, but not the 1950s...the 50s). I mopped my hair, loved '50s music, wore black suede boots, smoked, drank beer, loved to dance, etc. I started college in 1965 in San Francisco. And because I came in 2nd in an all-city math contest and scored in the 99th percentile on the SAT, I had dreams (and encouragement by teachers) to become an aerospace engineer.

But something exciting started brewing in San Francisco in late 1966: the hippie movement. Despite all of the negative repercussions that have happened as a result of the hippie movement, there was also a very sincere groundswell of 'love of realness and goodness', as well as a denouncement of 'phoniness and dysfunction'.

There were two kinds of hippies: the hedonistic hippie...and the organic hippie. The organic hippies, like with every new late-teen/early-adult generation, made an attempt to forge a better way of living, as well as repudiate what they perceived as the last generation's errors. But this generation's attempt was one of the most radical-ever departures from the previous generation.

And like all other new-generation-rebellions, this generation's attempt was two fold. On the one hand, there was anger, decadence, and a reaching for freedom. I imagine this mostly came from kids who had had their individuality and true connection to God unkindly suppressed.

On the other hand, there was a much higher motive. I was greatly inspired and excited by this motive (although, like most, I was also, unfortunately, influenced by the other side of the movement. I'm sure that relying on the music industry for my living didn't help in this regard).

The fact that the higher spiritual motive was going on en masse, especially in the San Francisco Bay Area, made it even more exciting. There were many people, stores, and events where this high feeling was shared.

But first you had to be inspired by a yearning for 'something better'. And before you could do that, you had to <u>know</u> that something better even existed.

For some, the "good vibes" (peace, love, laid-back approach, realness, and spirituality), repudiation of vanity, and the recognition of the importance of healthy food and healthy thoughts (wisdom) was enough. Most felt they needed to "turn on" (with drugs) before they could "tune in" (to the high). While others could get *there* via a "contact high" (i.e. being in contact with others who are high).

It took me a couple of years to feel this inspiration. It finally took hold rather dramatically while I was riding in a car and a very obscure (it never even made it to one of their albums) Rolling Stones song came on the radio called "We Love You".

As I listened to the song, whose lyrics consisted of a variety of pronouns sandwiched on both sides of the word 'love' (e.g. We love you...we love they...they love I...I love you, etc.), a <u>very clear realization completely</u>

overtook me that: we are living in a *sea* of love, and that we are only separated by consciously and subconsciously enforced walls (of protection, training, habits, fear, anger and reactive-ignorance). But nobody really wants to be this way. And when our walls are allowed to come down and we are immersed in this sea, it is the most pleasurable and beautiful of all experiences (hippies used marijuana, hash and LSD to try to get this experience [and later: meditation], but the same experience can be approached with deep, sincere 'prayer', Bible study, church, etc.). And I just intuitively *knew* that this sea was God (later confirmed by the Bible which says that God is love). I was so moved by the beauty of this experience, that I changed my life and made 'wanting to merge with love, God and beauty' my highest priority. The search and journey of trying to accomplish this was not an easy one though (although it had a happy ending, which is what I'm trying to inspire in other lives with this book).

I began my journey by trusting, hoping and reverently looking to the *accepted* source of wisdom of the day: psychology. I spent many hours in the offices of top psychologists and psychiatrists pouring out my heart and mind with the sincere expectation that I would get great answers that would change my life. I probably should've realized that the accepted system of the "plastic" world that I was trying to escape was not going to have the answers I was searching for. But I didn't know where else to turn.

To make a long story short (and get to the point of why this story is in this chapter), I got a few things out of psychology, but definitely not the cure-all. I had to go through many philosophies, religions and practices, picking up bits and pieces along the way. The problem here though is that while I was searching for the solution, my life was still manifesting in many unholy ways, for which I sometimes had to pay heavy emotional prices, the worst of which came in early 1980. My sins resulted in me experiencing such an intense, unbearable physical pain in my stomach, I couldn't take my mind off of it. It was so intensely painful, I concluded that I couldn't go on living with it. So I decided to end my life. Not that I wanted to...it's just that I couldn't bear the pain.

There's a 1960s song lyric in which the main person in the song said that they had a habit of just getting up and going to the corner when they felt the pain come on. One of the rituals that I used to do to try to accomplish this during this particularly bad time was to go to Tower Records (I was in too much pain to do my usual: eating).

When I'd go to Tower I would do a number of things. One is, I had some records out then, and I would look to see how they were selling. But on this particular night I was in too much pain to do the others. I somehow found my way over to the Oldies bin of 45 RPM records. It was about a 20 foot wide and 2 feet deep bin with dividers, in which all of the records were leaning against the wall at about a 30 degree angle. And that's the way I found them on this night. Except for in one spot, where the records were parted. I went over to see what this single record was that was exposed. It was "We Love You".

Seeing this <u>very</u> obscure record like this, I knew in my heart that it was a message from God to not end my life, but rather to just get through this pain, and then continue my search. This, to me, was a very direct-in-the-physical-world proof of the existence of God and angels. He mercifully stepped in right when it was necessary.

One other time that it was necessary was when I was riding in the second row of seats in a station wagon, going to a concert that I was going to perform at. I had laid my sax right behind the seat that I was sitting in. This section started the back half of the station wagon.

We had just finished doing another concert about 100 miles away so I was kind of exhausted. I decided that I was going to go and lay down back there where my sax was, just to rest. All of a sudden, as soon as I made that decision, a very heavy sleepiness came over me. Not only was I sleepy, but I was physically paralyzed and couldn't move. I was so perplexed by this, and I just remember saying in my mind "I've got to go back there and sleep....I've got to go back there and sleep". But it was no use. It was the same feeling as getting put out with ether before an operation. So I fell asleep.

The next thing I knew, my eyes opened, and the station wagon was stopped on the freeway. There was just enough time for my eyes *to be directed* to the rear view mirror in the front of the car to see the giant grill of a big truck crash into us. It was going about 50 miles per hour and didn't even put on its brakes. *Luckily* I hadn't fully awoken, so I experienced a peace throughout the whole incident. Plus I wasn't injured. But the guy next to me had his arm broken. And when I looked in back of me, the entire back end of the station wagon was crushed right up to the back of my seat and part way in on the seat next to me. When I looked at my sax, it was crushed almost completely flat. Then I got the chills when I realized that that's where I had tried so hard to lay. I would have been crushed had I laid there. Then I really got the chills when I realized how God had stepped in and saved my life. There is no other possible explanation as to why the ether-like experience came on and took me over. It's never happened at any other point in my life. Plus, the timing of when I fell asleep and the exact moment that I came to, and the fact that my eyes were directed to the rear view mirror, was too perfect.

And if in fact there was divine intervention in this incident, this is proof that the divine does possess at least some ability to read the future, because I was put to sleep with *someone* having a foreknowledge that the accident would happen. This leads to the next topic.

Fulfilled Prophesies

A form of a miracle is a 'prophesy'. To be able to accurately predict the future is truly a supernatural, extra-ordinary act. Therefore, proof of the divine authorship of the Bible should also include the many prophesies that are made in it that have been fulfilled. Also included should be the fact that there haven't been any Bible prophesies that have been proven to be false.

Just as Jesus used miracles to prove that He was not just a mere mortal, there are many prophets in the Bible who have shown their ties to God by the accuracy of their prophesies. And they not only were believed by Jews and Christians, but they were also believed by many great non-Jewish/non-Christian pharaohs and kings, even to the point where these pharaohs and kings made the prophets very close to them as confidants (e.g. Pharaoh and Joseph, and Nebuchadnezzar and Daniel).

Also, if God wanted to make a direct communication to people en masse, He would have to do it through a human being (aka prophet). That is, unless He wanted to pop into the sky. But He already did that and it didn't work, so now He operates on a more personal level, through people's hearts, via the Holy Spirit.

Regarding prophesies: why people look to tabloids, astrology, and psychic hotlines for prophesy (all of which have a near zero accuracy rate) when they have the Bible and the Holy Spirit (which have a 100% accuracy rate) is amazing. But they obviously do so because they don't <u>really</u> know what they have in the Bible and the Holy Spirit (which is a big reason why I'm writing this book).

The Bible has a lot of warnings about <u>false</u> prophets. Some of their modern day forms were just mentioned: the tabloids, astrologers, psychic hotlines (which hire and train almost anybody to do their dirty work), and even some religious people (including some "Christians").

Here's what Jesus had to say about them in Matthew 7: *"Beware of the false prophets, who come to you in sheep's clothing, but inwardly they are ravenous wolves. You will know them by their fruits. Do men gather grapes from thorn bushes or figs from thistles? Even so, every good tree bears good fruit, but a bad tree bears bad fruit."* He's saying to <u>beware</u>. And that the false prophets will come on innocently like sheep. But inwardly they are <u>ravenous</u> wolves, only out to get your money, praise and devotion. So how can we tell who they are? By their fruits. And in the case of prophets, one way that the goodness of their fruits can be determined is: how many of their prophesies actually come true. And Jesus is saying that those who produce untrue prophesies are 'bad trees'. And *"Every tree that does not bear good fruit is cut down and thrown into the fire"*, meaning: hell. If I was one of these celebrities who encouraged people to turn to psychics, I would be worried. Why? Because they're diverting people from the only true source they need to go to for advice in life: the Bible. And here's how God feels about the type of activities they promote: *There shall not be found among you one who practices witchcraft, or a sorcerer, fortune-teller, soothsayer, charmer, diviner, or caster of spells, nor one who consults ghosts and spirits or one who calls up the dead. Anyone who does such things is an abomination to the LORD* (Deut. 18:10-12). This would also include: tarot cards, astrology, and (black and white) witchcraft.

In Matthew 7, Jesus went on to say: *"Not everyone who says to Me, 'Lord, Lord' shall enter the kingdom of heaven, but those who do the will of My Father who is in heaven."* Here, the 'fruit' idea is expanded to include how holy and sinless a person is. Jesus is saying that calling Him Lord and calling yourself a Christian is no more a guarantee of getting into heaven than the false prophet has who is prophesying falsely (even) in His name. He goes on to clarify this in the following verse: *"Many will say to Me in that day, 'Lord, Lord, have we not prophesied in Your name, cast out demons in Your name, and in Your name perform many miracles?' And then I will declare to them 'I never knew you; depart from Me, you who practice law-lessness!"* The overwhelming point that is made here (which is further expounded on in 1 Corinthians 13) is that God is not interested in a religious *act*, He is primarily interested in our ability to obey His laws. These are the kind of people that He wants close to Him in heaven. This is the only way that heaven could work. This also is over-whelming what the theme of this book will be.

The following is a quick overview of 'prophesies in the Bible':
- •In the Bible there are 737 different prophesies (1,817 total, including 8,352 verses, making up 27% of the total Bible).
- •1,239 of them are in the Old Testament (6,641 verses, 28.5% of the Old Testament).
- •578 of them are in the New Testament (1,711 verses, 21.5% of the New Testament).

•Of the 1,239 Old Testament prophesies, 113 of them were about Jesus, describing in detail all of the major events that would happen in His life, as well as their meaning. All of them came true.

So, of the 737 different prophesies in the Bible, 610 of them have already been fulfilled (6,924 verses). This means that 127 are yet to be fulfilled (1,556 verses).

These facts yield two very important realizations: (1) <u>The Bible has proven to have 100% credibility in its ability to make prophesies</u> (based on the fact that all prophesies that should have happened by now have come true; and not one has proven to be false).

(2) This also means that <u>there is a 100% probability that the remaining prophesies in it will come true</u>.

In the book "Science Speaks", Peter Stoner said that if you were to make 11 prophesies, the Law of Compound Probabilities says that the chance of them coming true is 1 in 8,000,............000 (imagine 64 zeros in there). Well this did happen in the Bible. But not with just 11, but with 610 (6,924 verses). Imagine the astronomical probability number that this many would produce.

A point I made earlier: if the Bible can be proven to have 100% credibility in a given *area* (That is, many things that it says in this *area* can be proven to be true, whereas nothing that it says can be proven to be untrue), then all of the things in that *area* that can't be proven one way or the other also have a 100% probability of being true (based on the Bible's 100% credibility rating).

So now, let's summarize all of the *areas* in which the Bible has proven to have a 100% credibility rating.

As I said before, I've proven to myself (through direct experimentation) that the Bible has a 100% credibility rating in psychology and how-to-live. Because of this, it has become for me an 'owner and operator's manual' for the human experience. Can you imagine someone trying to overhaul a car without ever having had a manual? Well a lot of people live their lives this way, which is why they have so many troubles. Although....we all do have an inner 'owner and operator's manual' (for the experienced computer users: an 'onscreen help guide'). But this one doesn't just wait for us to turn to it for advice, it pushes its guidance onto our psyche. But many people, due to forceful people outside of themselves - especially in childhood - have come to where they rarely or barely hear that still, small voice inside of them, and have callously become accustomed to overriding it. But the Bible does say that, in spite of this, it is right that we all will be held accountable on judgment day because (1)God has proven that He exists, just from the unduplicatable miracle of the physical world that we see around us, and (2)because the rules He requires us to follow are written in our hearts, with our conscience bearing witness. None of us will be able to use the excuse that we didn't know.

The Bible has been proven to also have a 100% credibility rating in 'history'. What this means is: many of the historical accounts in the Bible have been proven to be true (through archaeology and historians), and not one of the Bible's historical accounts can be proven to be untrue. Therefore, there is a 100% probability that all of the Bible's historical accounts are true. Therefore, many *believe* that they are true. But what has been delegated to the realms of *belief* and *faith,* to me, is really science (albeit the sciences of *logic* and *probabilities*). I mean, even though the atom has never been absolutely proven to be true, we don't call atomic scientists *believers* do we?

No, we call them scientists. Well what I'm putting forth here in philosophy, religion, physical science and psychology is just as, if not more, scientific.

And, as stated before, the Bible has a 100% credibility rating in the area of 'prophesy'. That is, all future predictions that were made in it have already come true or are yet to come true. And there have been no false predictions. This means that there is a 100% probability that all of the rest of the Bible's prophesies will come true.

There is a science that is dedicated to the study of all of the yet-to-be fulfilled prophesies in the Bible called eschatology (which is just a fancy name for 'very curious about what the Bible says is going to happen in the future'). There is a lot of fun and excitement in eschatology, similar to the fun and adventure of a good mystery movie or novel. The difference here (and cause for extra fun and excitement) is: this is reality. And it is especially chilling and exciting to watch the Bible's prophesies come true in the news of our day.

I suggest that you do the Bible studies on the remaining unfulfilled prophesies yourself. You become Perry Mason and enjoy uncovering the mysteries. But, to get you started there are a lot of enthusiastic eschatologists out there who would love to help.

Eschatology comes in two forms: scholarly investigations and novels/movies that spell out potential scenarios. Some of the movies are: "The Late Great Planet Earth" (based on the New York times best-selling novel of the same name by Hal Lindsay), "A Thief In The Night", "A Distant Thunder", and the 1980's Hollywood release starring Demi Moore "The Seventh Sign". Some novels are "The End Of The Age" by Pat Robertson, and Hal Lindsay has many other books out as well. (All of these have some

Biblical inaccuracies, but they're still very informative and a lot of fun.) Three popular investigative eschatologists are Dr. John MacArthur Jr., David Breese and Jack Van Impe, who has a weekly TV show on several different channels. Then there are many books, video and audio cassettes. And you can always get good information in liner notes and writings in Bibles, as well as "The Catholic Catechism".

But, eschatology abounds with speculations and disagreements, so do plan on forming your own eschatological opinions based on your own studies. You'll find it to be a very big challenge to sort through all of the theories out there until you land on your own. But it is an adventure well worth undertaking because it gets you thinking and you end up knowing the Bible much better in the process.

I'll deal with the specifics of eschatology in the upcoming chapter on end times. But as this book develops, you'll understand <u>why</u> the end-time prophesies have to be fulfilled, and what the perfect logic is behind them. Also, it is very comforting and satisfying to know that God didn't just become disgusted and destroy the dysfunctional mess that the free-will beings here on earth created (although He once did, but left the rainbow as a sign that He would never do it again - more on this later).

<u>Did God author the Bible?</u>

So now, back to the question that the title of this chapter posed: Was the Bible authored by God? It was obviously written down by human beings, so then how can it be claimed that God authored it? Well first we had to establish that the Bible has 100% credibility - which we did. Now, based on this, we can go into the Bible and use what it has to say to support our arguments. And, in regard to the question of who authored the Bible, here is what the

Bible has to say: (2Timothy 3:16) *"All scripture is inspired by God"*. It says here that all scripture is inspired by God. And if you break down the word 'inspired' to its Latin derivatives, it reads: *in - spired*, with *spire*'s root word meaning "breathed". Therefore, in-spired means 'breathed in'. And the understanding in the Bible and throughout history is that God is the One doing the breathing.

This shows how the creators and early users of the English language viewed all inspiration as coming from God within us - unlike today, where human beings like to take the credit for themselves.

Many people recognize the supernatural inspiration in inspired works and erroneously worship the human beings that they come through. But we know that God isn't pleased with this because His very first commandment is that we not worship false idols. Unfortunately, the idols of today are nearly all humans. And these human idols are too greedy and egotistic to push away the worship, fame and fortune they receive to give God His due credit.

The verse in 2Timothy 3:16 goes on to say that all scripture *"is useful for teaching, for refutation, for correction, and for training in righteousness"*.

The fact that inspiration comes through the 'truth channel' within us is confirmed in Romans 8:16:*"The Spirit Himself bears witness with our spirit"*.

And to further clarify some things said in chapter 1, we now can credibly add the Bible's description of the subdivisions of our inner workings: *"You shall love the Lord, your God, with all your heart, with all your soul, and with all your mind"* (Matthew 22:37). "You" is your 'spirit', the observer/experiencer, which then has the following things to work "with": your heart (center of feeling, including feelings that are triggered by what comes through the truth channel), your mind (including the computer-like subconscious mind), and your soul (your free will).

Conclusion

Now that you've seen all of the proof that there is regarding the authenticity of the Bible, were you surprised by how much there is and by how overwhelmingly convincing it is?[1] To some, certain points are more important than others. As for me, the fact that the Bible has proven to be an incomparable handbook for how to fix and elevate my life, my mind and my feelings, is enough (plus the fact that I've found no contradictions or untruths). All else that Christianity has given me (and there's been a lot) have been beautiful bonuses.

The Bible shows how to elevate your state of being. If you've been *there* (that is, in a high state of being), you know* that nothing else on earth can compare...no other mindset, philosophy, viewpoint or approach-to-living. Getting involved with the Bible and following what it says *magically transforms* us to a clear, knowing, peaceful state...even ecstacy. This inner transformation can also be counted as data that the Bible is true because it in reality affects our being in such a positive way.

*A simplistic analogy of this would be comparing a northern California beach to a Hawaii beach. If you've been to both, you know the difference. The California beach water is shockingly cold, the air is cold, the sand is very coarse, and the water is murky. Whereas, at the beach in Hawaii, the water temperature is very comfortable, it's also very clear and beautiful, the air is warm, and the sand is very fine and comfortable. All of this yields a very relaxing and pleasurable experience. The reason that some people will put up with the shocks and harshnesses of a north-

ern California beach is because they <u>desire</u> a beach experience and don't <u>know</u> how good the experience in Hawaii
is. And just like a vacationer in Hawaii would enthusiasti-
cally urge someone to 'come to Hawaii'...I'm enthusiasti-
cally writing this book to say 'come to God'.

[1]So then why is the media, intelligencia, government and education community so *hell*-bent on keeping the
Bible out of the public forums? (You'll understand the
answer to this question more as you move on in this book.)
Let me give you just one of <u>many</u> examples of how this
occurs, which will hit you as even more unbelievable,
given what you've been reading in this book.

In The Oregonian in 1994, there was an article enti-
tled: *Scientist stifled from teaching life's origins*, subtitled:
*Academic freedom stomped on by hidebound secular
administrators.*

This article trails a professor of biology at San
Francisco State, Dean Kenyon, who was stopped from
teaching introductory biology because he not only taught
evolution, but he also discussed the problems with it and
stated that some biologists see evidence of *intelligent
design*. He has a Ph.D. in biophysics from Stanford and co-
authored "Biochemical Predestination" in 1969, a book
that supported humanistic evolutionary thought by articu-
lating what was arguably the most plausible evolutionary
account of how a living cell might have organized itself
from chemicals in the "primordial soup". Quoting from the
article: "Kenyon's subsequent work resulted in numerous
scientific publications on the origin-of-life problem. By the
late 1970s, however, Kenyon began to question some of his
own earlier ideas. Experiments (some performed by
Kenyon himself) increasingly contradict the dominant view
in his field. Laboratory work suggested that simple chemi-

cals do not arrange themselves into complex information-bearing molecules such as DNA - without, that is, "guidance" from human experimenters.

To Kenyon and others, such results raised important questions about how "naturalistic" the origin of life really was. If undirected chemical processes cannot produce the coded strands of information found in even the simplest cells, could perhaps a directing intelligence have played a role? By the 1980s, Kenyon had become sympathetic to the second idea. That a man of Kenyon's stature should now be forced to lobby for the right to teach introductory biology, whatever his current view of origins, is absurdly comic. Kenyon knows perhaps as much as anyone in the world about a problem that has stymied an entire generation of research scientists. Yet he now finds that he may not report the negative results of research or give students his candid assessment of it." (The article later says):

"Such intellectual strictures reflect the very essence of political correctness: the suppression of critical discourse by enforced rules of thought." The article ends by calling Kenyon a world-class scientist who is yet another casualty of <u>America's peculiar academic fundamentalism</u>.

But even this example pales compared to the many examples of children who have been harshly reprimanded and threatened with expulsion *just for bringing a Bible to school.* (The ACLJ - the American Center for Law and Justice - has <u>many</u> such cases that they're defending against the ACLU. And by the way, they've been winning all of them). I mean, shouldn't the number one and most influential book of all time be included in what students are exposed to? This is not a 'separation of church and state' problem..it's a 'history-and-philosophy-censorship' problem. It's ironic that the liberals who used to parade the book "1984" with a paranoia of a coming 'big brother' have now become the 'politically correct big brother' themselves. What are these powers-that-be so afraid of? And what motivates them? (You'll have very clear answers to these questions by time you finish this book.)

An editorial aside: given the huge decline in our society since the advent of secular humanism and the expulsion of God from the mainstream, I think that we very badly need to become a religious society again. The person who started this religious oppression, Madeleine Murray O'Hare, did so to protect her son from having to pray in school. Isn't it ironic that her son now spends a great deal of his time praying, being that he's a Christian preacher. This also shows how effective and persuasive her philosophy was....she couldn't even convince her own son.

Talk show host Dennis Prager had a great comment about all of this. He said that if it meant the moral downfall of this society (which it has) he doesn't care if a few (and that's all there are) atheists are offended by prayer in school, religious study in school, nativity scenes, God in the media, etc. And, Dennis Prager is a religious Jew, who is not only not offended by Christianity, but he sees great value in it, even for Jews. I'm sure that he'd agree with me that the greatest reason to be offended today is by how this society has been tricked into being non-religious.

A note to anti-Bible critics

If you don't test the Bible's precepts for yourself, you have no right to criticize it. When formulating your *hypotheses*, the *experimental testing* phase can't just be foregone. Otherwise, your *conclusions* are not credible. Also, you can't judge the Bible based on your judgments of people who claim to be into it. If you want your opinions to be considered valid, you have to study, test and judge the Bible itself. A friend once said to someone who was criticizing the Bible: "Have you read the whole Bible?" The other person said "No". Then he said "How can you criticize a book you haven't read?" (Another thing that he said, which is a good guideline in a discussion: "It's not a matter of 'who's right', but 'what's right'").

<u>Why I believe that the Bible is the only document on the planet (that serves as a basis for a religious system) that can claim complete authorship by God</u>

I put this section in this chapter not to judge or alienate <u>anybody</u>. These are the last things that I want to do. My mission is to enlighten. (Later in the book I'll show how God judges people, and how people can be saved with or without being Christian). Nevertheless, I've been making the statement that the Bible is the <u>only</u> perfect religious document on the planet. Therefore, I feel I need to explain why I ruled the others out. It's basically because I find logical and scientific *flaws* and *lackings* in all of the other documents. I also find *contradictions* with and *inaccurate descriptions* of what I have observed to be true nature. Whereas, I don't find any of these problems with the Bible.

Let me be more specific. I found <u>eastern religion</u>, and the <u>new age</u> movement in general, to have the same limitation as the hippie movement. That is, they are able to chime in on the mindset of spirituality (agape/love), but they don't understand the critical importance of having a strict set of rules for the nuts and bolts of living (holiness).

The problem here is: while people are 'turning on' to the high of God, they still suffer from dysfunctional lives. This is because they don't know how to properly operate a marriage (which is a very fragile hotbed of potential emotional turmoil), they don't know how to operate a society or its economy, they don't understand nature's guidelines for and meaning of sex and romance, they're confused about who they are (as human beings, as men and women, as citizens, as workers, etc.), and they don't know how to properly operate their inner workings (thoughts, feelings, decisions about living, etc.).

Yes, meditation is a great means to stop the mind long enough to see and fall in love with God by experiencing the very pleasurable feeling of His Spirit. But the practice of it is just a temporary solution. The reason being: the mind can't be continually and forcefully held back forever. It is an invention by God, and therefore is important to our natural functioning. 'Operating it as it was designed to function' is the challenge, not 'eliminating it'. Problems happen in its operations because its subconscious was mis-programmed (due to trauma and unwise influences). Therefore, in order to have it not push dysfunction on our psyche, it must be *reprogrammed* (changed in a computer-programming-like fashion): Rom. 12:2 *"Do not be conformed to this world, but be transformed by the <u>renewing</u> of your mind"*. But reprogrammed with what?

(This also is where <u>psychology</u> fails...which usually just amounts to many fishing expeditions in many expensive therapy sessions, but where no consistent standards are imparted - as well as explanations as to why they should be <u>the</u> standards for living).

For the mind to be *naturally* at peace, it must be (re)programmed with <u>true knowledge</u> of how our insides and lives were <u>designed</u> to be operated:*be transformed by the renewing of your mind.* It must be focused on truth...and it must verify that we are <u>in</u> the truth. Otherwise, it will keep pushing on our psyche with error messages, which are meant to trigger emotions and energy to try to prompt us to solve our out-of-tuneness with true nature (kind of like an automatic self-cleaning mode).

So, in my studies, and also in my restless desire to continue searching until I could feel throughout my whole being that I had found the complete truth, I've found that the Bible is the only book that both understands the high of agape as well as the nuts and bolts of our *design*. This is yet another strong testimony that the Bible comes from the *designer*. (Of course, here I am trying to convince others that the Bible is the ultimate approach to life. But a most solid piece of evidence for me is that when I became a Christian, the 'searching antsyness' that semi-tormented me for many years was completely gone. For me, this piece of evidence is very, very major. Nothing else could bring me that specific relief - and as you know, I sincerely and diligently tried most of what is in the world. It was like being healed of a disease...or chronic back-pain. It's this simple: when I got into the Bible...the antsyness and the emptiness just turned off. Kind of like finally taking the right wonder drug and the disease goes away. "The proof is in the putting". My wish is that others will benefit from this experience that happened within me. Hopefully my enthusiastic testimony will have some persuasive impact).

Another point against eastern religion is: 'reincarnation' is in contradiction with the Bible: *"It is appointed that human beings die once, and after this the judgment"* (Heb. 9:27). Therefore, we can't believe in both the Bible and a philosophy or religion that believes in reincarnation.

Regarding Judaism: the Old Testament is perfect, but not complete. Why? Because the sacrificial system didn't work. Even today's Judaism is a testimony to this fact, being that it no longer practices the sacrificial system.

Plus, it doesn't include the sacrifice that does work, Jesus. This last fact is even attested to by the prophesies in the Jewish Bible. The story of Judaism is so important though, that rather than try to deal with it all now, it is given an entire chapter later in this book.

Regarding the Koran: although I greatly admire the strict importance placed on holiness by Muslims, and the amount of time and devotion they give to religious practices, I do find the following flaws. (By the way, I'm not holding up many of the ways that Christianity is practiced in the world today as being all-superior to other religions. There are definitely things that I've observed and experienced in other religions and practices that I miss in Christianity, and that are advised in the Bible. For example, more time devoted to religion - both on a personal level and on a group level; a greater intolerance and disgust for the dysfunctions of the world - e.g. most of the entertainment industry, vanity, greed, etc.; more holiness and less taking liberties; more reverence; more submission and less obsession with personal freedom; etc. There is some truth in 'the great Satan' label put on the U.S. And even the Bible agrees with this label, as you'll see in Chapter 11. By the way, I'm also not making a judgment here as to what the exact nature of the relationship is that God has with other religions and the many varied individuals in them. [There is also great in-fighting even within *Christianity*.] This is a long subject for another book. I'm just saying that my heart and my mind were not completely satisfied that I had found complete perfection until I got to the Bible).

If 'miraculous signs' are a proof that a prophet is representing God, Mohammed never exhibited any. There is a myth that says he passed the moon up one arm sleeve and out the other. But this supposedly happened so fast that nobody saw it. So then what good is this sign? Plus, this myth wasn't started until long after Mohammed's time.

Christianity has <u>many</u> miraculous signs, witnessed and recorded in history (as has been pointed out). No other religion can exhibit direct physical proof like this. Non-Bible religions' claims to the supernatural are based on 'visions', and only by one person.

The Koran is based on just such a vision by Mohammed. But even Mohammed was skeptical about the supernatural source of his vision, thinking it to be demonic. He was even inclined to question his own sanity, until he was convinced otherwise by his wife.

And, once again, we can't believe in the Bible <u>and</u> the Koran because the Bible says: "*Add nothing to His words, lest He reprove you, and you be exposed as a deceiver*" (Prov. 30:6). And in Deut. 4:2 "*In your observance of the commandments of the LORD, your God, which I enjoin upon you, you shall not add to what I command you nor subtract from it.*" These verses have been violated many times, even by (so-called) Christians.

And Mohammed, who wasn't even born until the late 6th century A.D., didn't need to add anything to an already perfect book (which he knew well, having traveled to Palestine and Syria). He just needed to bring Christianity as is to his native land. But that wasn't well-received, which is probably why he came up with a hybrid bible.

Here are some interesting facts about Mohammed.

Mohammed was an orphan at the age of six. His guardians were zealous for the special religious superstitions of Mecca. As a young man Mohammed was troubled by the evil features of Arabian religion as it existed at that time, especially its quarreling, idolatry, immorality and intemperance. A specially revolting custom was the burying alive of unwanted infant daughters. Mohammed was outraged, too, by the needless, endless bloodshed in wars between different Arabian tribes.

From the age of 12 Mohammed went on caravan trips to Palestine and Syria. Thus he came in contact with Jewish and Christian beliefs. These experiences led him to question many Arabian beliefs and practices. Mohammed began preaching in his home city, Mecca, but met with bitter opposition. This continued for 10 years. You can now see why I made my 'hybrid bible' conclusion.

Another reason that I wasn't attracted to Mohammedism is because there's always been an air of hostility and violence surrounding it (Gihad, suicide bombings, kidnappings, terrorism, wars, etc.). This is further exemplified by the fact that Mohammedism was mostly spread throughout the Arab world and some of the surrounding countries by means of military victories, not by the attraction of love or by intellectual persuasion.

By the way, it is interesting to note that the 3 major religions all believe in God and Moses, and the Koran also includes Jesus. And, most other religions and philosophies acknowledge Jesus (if not His deity, at least His teachings).

It is also interesting to note that Ishmael, who with his sons started the Arab world, was the natural son of Abraham, who started the Jewish world. He didn't leave the Jewish land until he was an adult. And he returned to the Jewish land to help bury his father when he died.

I must also point out here that my evaluations of Islam and the other religions that follow are intellectual and spiritual evaluations, but not first hand inside-evaluations. I've never been a Muslim, etc. My inside, in-depth, first hand experiences are limited to what is listed in the Preface, including: Christianity (3 forms), psychology (many forms), new age (many forms), secular humanism (the current unstated religion of the American society), and the basic religious approach in India. Therefore, I don't want to present myself as a first hand expert in any other religion or philosophy. I'm just making evaluations from the outside based on the literature that I've read.

But I can say this: Christianity is complete in my mind and my heart and my spirit (although I do wish the Christian communities were, well, more Christian...more reverent, more sacred, more peaceful, more agape-high, more holy, more focused on God, etc.). The void-in-my-heart search that drove me for 14 years has been over for 14 years. Plus, no other religion or body of thought has the intellectual completeness as a total plan for a human being and for humanity that Christianity has (which will have been totally spelled out by the completion of this book).

Also, there's a very important observation that I must acknowledge: despite all of my many spiritual experiences, and very extensive personal growth studies, and my many evaluations...the bottom-line is......I still had the <u>feeling</u> of being blind.....until I became a Christian.

I can now make this retrospective observation of 'blindness' only because I don't have it anymore. When I was blind, I felt like something was missing, but at the time I didn't know exactly what it was....although I was both driven and inspired to search for a solution to the 'being blind' feeling. But I can still become *partially* blind if I let myself get hyped-up or hypnotized or thrown-off by the 'fruits of the god of this age': secular-humanistic activities and media..or even by the thoughts that happen in my mind, or another person's unconnected words and vibe. But never: blind-to-the-point-of-being-lost anymore.

Another analogy that partially illustrates this blind-

ness is: seeing the Kingdom of God is like one of the currently popular 'Magic 3-D' pictures. That is: if you don't
maintain your focus, you lose the beautiful vision (and the
feeling that goes along with it). Instead, the plain vision
comes back, and you lose an entire dimension.

Regarding Buddhism: I don't have to have tried
Buddhism to know that it is not in sync with truth. Its basic
principle is that a person's troubles come from *desire*. And
that if you eliminate desire, you will eliminate your troubles and have peace. Well this is partially true, but it is
somewhat like saying that you can eliminate getting the flu
by eliminating being around people. Yes, you would probably eliminate the possibility of getting the flu, but you
would create the problem of loneliness. Therefore, you
would be without the trouble, but you still wouldn't have
peace. The thinking here is similar to that of Hinduism
(both of these religions were born in India). That is,
Hinduism says that if you eliminate the mind you will find
peace. Buddhism says that if you eliminate desire you will
find peace. But, based on my experience, this is like saying
that you can experience a dry land if you keep your thumb
in the hole in the dam. This is fine until you get tired and
bored with standing at the dam all of the time.

Christianity spares us the pains of an over-acetic
lifestyle by giving us holy standards. That is, the problem
is not that we have desires, it's that we don't live them out
in the way that our designer planned for us to.

This one flaw discredits Buddhism as being able to
be looked at as a complete philosophy. Not that there aren't
benefits from living an acetic life....but just for a season (or
seasons, if necessary). The inspiration for an acetic life is:
the world is so off (and our mind also - from how it's been
affected by the world), it is a nice vacation to completely

detach from it. And hopefully during the vacation many insights are gotten, so that the world, when re-entered, can be viewed with a fresh, clearer perspective, making it easier to live in it in a more positive and healthy way. But God built us with desires for involvement with others. And He wants us to try to satisfy these desires. Why? So we can discover that when we do it our way, or the world's way, we have troubles...but when we do it His way, it goes much better. Life is not something to run from, rather it is a good gift from God. Also, Jesus said *"I came so that they might have life, and that they might have it more abundantly"* (John 10:10). I do feel though that acetic retreats should be much more popular in the Christian community.

People's innate desire for there to be a God-in-the-flesh

I won't even get into a discussion of the massive idolatry of sports and entertainment stars that goes on ad nauseum, other than to say that it is pure sublimation and a substitution of the ungodly for God (which He's extremely angry about, as is expressed in the first commandment and throughout Bible history).

But this also goes on in religion. When I was involved in Divine Light Mission, many of the "premies" said that Guru Maharaj Ji was God in a body. There was even a secret paper going around to attest to this. But when Guru Maharaj Ji was on "The Tomorrow Show", Tom Snyder asked him: "Now I'm not trying to be disrespectful, but I've got to ask you this question. Many of your followers say that you are God. What do you have to say about this?" Guru Maharaj Ji replied: "No, I'm not God. I am only a humble servant of God." I was very happy to hear this and have what I knew wasn't true cleared up.

I guess this desire for God-incarnate is mostly an

expression of a person's desire to have a 'physical sign' as proof of deity. But, in the current frenzy of human-idol-worship: 'touchdowns', 'vocal performances', 'looks', and 'acting' are setting one's sights pretty low when looking for 'signs'. This is also the main reason that this nation is having so many problems. Its gods are just entertainers, who are imperfect and also have many problems. When its role models once again become the spiritually mature (who point us to God, His Bible, and the godly), then this nation will be on the right path to health, sanity and happiness.

Speaking of physical, supernatural signs, besides the recorded history of Jesus' signs, there have been many appearances by His mother Mary in the last century. And they have been verified by scientists and have produced many photographs. Don't be quick to push this off (as many do) or take it lightly until you've seen one of the documentaries on it. EWTN often runs "Marian Apparitions Of The Twentieth Century". For those who have a problem with the Catholic emphasis on Mary, let me offer this introductory, logical thought: Jesus' ministry lasted only 3 years. This means that He spent nearly 10 times as many years with His mother. Don't you think that He would have given her a special place and ministry in heaven?

The universe is God's physical body

(Indulge me for a moment while a make a specula-tion.) Is it possible that the universe is God's physical body just like our human body is the physical body that cloaks our spirit? That is: we have a thought...which then sets our body, or some part of it, in motion. Similarly, God has a thought...which then sets the universe, or some part of it, in motion. This idea would actually find support in the Bible when it says that God is omnipresent. My idea would just propose that God (the spirit) has the same attachment to the physical universe that we have to our physical body. Our bodies could even be seen as part of His body. It's just that He gives us limited control over them for a limited time.

Another speculation could be that God's physical body is similar to our physical body, it's just that ours is on a much smaller scale (*"Then God said: 'Let Us make man in Our image, after Our likeness.'"* Genesis 1:26). That is, our body is made up of atoms. And an atom is a nucleus with electrons continually and smoothly orbiting around it. Well, isn't this the same model as the solar system? It's just that it's on a much smaller scale. Also (while we're still speculating), the universe might not be infinite, but just a much, much, much bigger version of our body, with even a calculable size based on the proportional scale: 'the size of our solar system' to 'the size of a 9 electron (ala: 9 planets) atom: Fluorine'. Some Bible support for this is that the Bible always mentions heaven as being "up". Well, being that we're on a sphere (earth), if "up" applies to all points on the sphere, then the only visual picture that would satisfy this description is: the universe also is a sphere, which is enveloped by 'heaven'. Recent science has also been alluding to the universe as a sphere.

Hubbell telescope photos point to a very young universe

A recent study of super nova expansion, coupled with the data being brought back by the Hubbell telescope (in particular the very low number of red dwarf stars) points to a young universe, not an old one. How young? The super nova expansion study says 6,900 years old. The Hubbell telescope data says less than 10,000 years old.

Because of these findings, many astronomers and

astrophysicists now say they are going to have a hard time holding on to the idea that the universe is old. They expected the Hubbell telescope to finally support their old-universe theory, but in fact just the opposite has happened. Astronomer Todd Lowe said: "Listen. We knew this was a shocking result. That's why we spent over a year trying to debunk it ourselves before we went public." So what is the shocking result that he's talking about? When presenting the Hubbell photos to the national press in November 1994, Dr. Parice of John Hopkins University said this: "We expected the image to be covered wall to wall by faint red stars. There were just a handful there. This was a disaster for the whole way that astronomers are developing the idea of an old universe." These findings support the Bible's explanation of history, not the science community's.

For more information on this write to: This Week In Bible Prophecy, PO Box 583, Niagara Falls, NY 14302.

Introduction to Chapter 3

Now that a scientifically solid foundation has been laid for accepting the Bible as truth, let's see how what the Bible says can help us to uncover the logical and scientific truths about (1)the Creator's motives for making this life specifically as it is, (2)His plan for carrying out those motives, (3)the past, present and future of the carrying out of this plan, and (4)the ramifications that this plan has on us individually and on the societies of this world. This will all be done in the upcoming chapters. But of course, 'using Bible proofs' will only be one piece of our puzzle. We will also continue to use the other sciences we've been using: logic, psychology, history, archaeology, etc.

Chapter 3

God's Motive For Making Us

Why......would a being who is powerful enough to make this universe......who is so intricately creative as to be able to design and make this earth and all that is on it...whose heart essence is pure and sensitive love....want to create human beings - especially given how imperfect and grief-causing they've turned out to be?

Well, the bottom-line is: He did decide to make us. Therefore, there has to be a good reason. No, it would have to be a great reason, because a being who is so creative and intelligent in every other way must have been equally creative and intelligent in His plan to make human beings. And actually, the Bible says that human beings are God's greatest creation on earth...in His own image and likeness...having dominion over every living thing.

So, let's examine what God's good reason for making us might be.

There are many possible ways to *speculate* as to what God's motive was for making us. One such speculation would be Hume's assumption (stated in Chapter 1) that we are an experiment that's gone awry and will eventually be branded as a 'failure'. Another speculation says that there are many such experiments throughout the universe, including extra-terrestrials.

Another scenario would be: if in fact God is the

greatest phenomenon in all of existence, perhaps He is trying to expand the universe to include more beings similar
to Him. This speculation has some Biblical support in that
it says that God *breathed* a bit of His essence into each one
of us, and that we're made in His *image* and *likeness*. This
speculation could take an unbiblical offshoot by saying that
we are the second in a line of building experiments that
lead up to an end, with the animals being the first. (Getting
back to Biblical) the next in this line of experiments would
be: human beings. The third would be: human beings who
would successfully graduate from this planet, and be given
more functional and powerful *bodies* in a heaven.

We could go on and on with speculative possibilities. And actually, isn't this one of the main functions of
science fiction That is: to speculate on possible explanations to the mysteries of life, in hopes that one of them will
strike a harmonious chord in us that says that we might
have stumbled onto the truth, or at least a part of it? In fact,
as has already been pointed out, a good deal of our *science*
is often just the best scenarios that have been proposed in
science fiction. But eventually we forget this and *act as if*
these science fiction premises are true. Some examples:
atomic theories, evolution, dinosaurs, cavemen, the history
and age of the earth, the origin and nature of the universe,
panicky environmental theories such as 'global warming',
and 'species extinction'. A big problem in this country is
that the sensationalistic, ratings-and-sales-starved media
and the psychodramatically-inclined liberal element of our
society are addicted to creating emotional fervors. The
most positive thing I could say about some of the people
given to liberal philosophies is that they have good intentions, but they also have impulsive hearts and lack a
knowledge of the truth. That is, in their hearts they quite

rightly *feel* that 'something is wrong'. But they have a weakness for buying into whatever trendy complaints are being amplified in the media. I'm sure they do this mostly to release the frustration, anger, pain, fear and indignation they feel about *something* being wrong in the world. But the state of 'something wrong' is also usually in their own lives (primarily from their past, their current circumstances, not really knowing God). Therefore, this book is also written for them (as is the Bible). Hopefully what's written here can show them what's <u>really</u> wrong and what's <u>really</u> right, which would then liberate them from liberalism (which, actually, is a big contributor to what's wrong). This can then make their efforts be not so much 'shots in the dark', but rather: on target.

This book is only interested in science, not science fiction. And being that each simple (not compound) question in life can have only one true answer, we want to see how many of these <u>one true</u> answers we can uncover regarding life's basic questions. This is why 'proving that the Bible was authored by God' was so important. It can now be seen as a great *deductive reasoning* source of data that can give us hypotheses, which we can then test and scrutinize for contradictions and untruths. So then what does the Bible say about God's motives for making us?

<u>What the Bible says about God's motive for making us</u>

The Bible says that God made us for fellowship and pleasure for Himself. More specifically: the pleasure of 'making something nice for someone and then seeing them enjoy it' (i.e. the pleasure of giving pleasure); the pleasure of sharing (experiences, pleasurable settings, responsibilities contributing toward common good goals); the pleasure of being creative; the pleasure of agreement; pleasurable emotions; the pleasure of company; the pleasure of giving and receiving love, gifts, attention and appreciation; the pleasure of others recognizing and devoting themselves to your good ideals, etc. *For we are His workmanship, created in Christ Jesus for the good works which God prepared beforehand, that we should walk in them* (Eph. 2:10).

Here are some Bible verses that say that God finds pleasure in us. (Luke 12:32) *"Do not fear little flock, for it is your Father's good pleasure to give you the kingdom."*; (Col. 3:20) *"Children, obey your parents in all things, for this is well pleasing to the Lord."*; (1John 3:22) *"keep His commandments and do the things that are pleasing in His sight."*; (Ps. 149:4) *"For the Lord takes pleasure in His people"*; (Num. 24:1) *"it pleased the Lord to bless Israel"*; (1Kgs. 3:10) *"And the speech pleased the Lord that Solomon had asked this thing."*; (Isa. 42:21) *"it pleased the LORD in His justice to make His law great and glorious"*; (Matt. 3:17) *"And suddenly a voice came from heaven saying, 'This is my beloved Son, in whom I am well pleased'."*; (Matt. 12:18) *"Behold, My Servant whom I have chosen, My Beloved in whom My soul is well pleased"*; (Gal. 1:15,16) *"God, was pleased to reveal His Son to me"*; (Hebr. 11:5) *"By faith Enoch was taken up so that he should not see death, and 'he was found no more because God had taken him'. Before he was taken up, he was attested to have pleased God."*; (Hebr. 13:16) *"Do not forget to do good and to share, for with such sacrifices God is well pleased."*; (Eccl. 7:26) *"More bitter than death I find the woman who is a hunter's trap, whose heart is a snare and whose hands are prison bonds. He who is pleasing to God will escape her, but the sinner will be entrapped by her."*; (Ps. 69:31)*"My song will please the Lord"*; (1Ths. 4:1) *"conduct yourselves to please God"*; (Prov.

16:7) *"When a man's ways please the Lord, He makes even his enemies be at peace with him"*; and Eph. 1:5 says that it is God's pleasure that we become His children. And, there are many, many verses that say that God loves us.

God has a heart

In order for God to experience pleasure, He has to have a means by which to experience this feeling. Genesis 6:6 says that He has the same means that we have: a heart (which makes sense if we were made in His likeness). And His heart (or at least part of it) is very similar to ours. The Bible is full of examples of God experiencing all of the same experiences that we experience.....joy, anger, love, grief, compassion, jealousy, etc.

You Bless God

When I first saw the phrase "bless God" (e.g. Ps. 68:26), I thought to myself 'Wait a minute. God is God. How can we bless Him? We don't have that power. He blesses us. God is all-powerful, and therefore we can't have any effect on Him. Or can we? Well, as we just saw, God has a heart, and we definitely do have an effect on Him. And, as we will now see, we would be much less pleasurable to Him if we didn't.

Free will

Consider this analogy: how enjoyable of a marriage would it be if your mate said they loved you only because they were intimidated to do so, or their motive was money? Another analogy: a musician creates a song, and then plays it for a group of robots that he or she has programmed to say things like "Great!" and "The best I've ever heard!". These situations would not yield an experience of pleasure.

Thus, it was necessary for God to give us free will (the next chapter deals with the issue of 'free will' in depth). But, 'free will' not only gives us the potential to create pleasure (for God and for each other), but it also gives us the potential to create harm and pain. And history, the news, and perhaps our own lives, bear out that this very much has been what has happened, and is still happening.

So, God made us for His (and our) pleasure. But is pleasure what He has found? Yes...and no. I've already spelled out some of the yesses, now here are some of the nos: *And the Lord was <u>sorry</u> that He had made man on the earth, and He was <u>grieved</u> in His heart* (Gen.6:6); *How often they provoked Him in the wilderness, and <u>grieved</u> Him in the desert* (Ps. 78:40); *God is a just judge, and God is <u>angry</u> with the wicked <u>every day</u>* (Ps. 7:11); *Now the people complained....and when He heard it His <u>wrath</u> flared up* (Num. 11:1); *You shall not worship any other god, for the LORD is a <u>jealous</u> God* (Exod. 34:14). And He's been made to have the unpleasant experience of jealousy (and all of the other above-mentioned negative experiences) <u>many</u> times. (If you are pondering whether to judge God for being jealous, realize that this is a modern judgment...which is incorrect and unhealthy. God invented jealousy for a good reason. It is a warning signal that the glue that keeps marriages and families and important relationships together is being threatened. And it is especially needed in these days, in which many of people's and society's ills can be traced back to 'broken families' and 'not having a good relationship with God').

So, because of people's generally poor performance in bringing God pleasure, and because <u>total love</u> (which God is) <u>requires total holiness</u> (perfect function) <u>in order to be totally and intensely pleasurable</u> , God has had to devise a <u>plan</u> by which 'many free will beings can operate in sync, so as to create pleasure - for Him and each other - and not pain'. (Chapter 4 describes the essence of this plan, and Chapters 5 through 11 describe how this plan has been, is being, and will continue to be carried out in history). But first, let's take a closer look at how pleasure is gotten from a relationship.

Pleasure is an *experience*. And the most pleasurable of all experiences is *love* (I'm speaking about agape love, not the act of commitment). And the Bible says that God <u>is</u> love: *He who does not love does not know God, for God is love* (1John 4:8); *And we have known and believed the love that God has for us. God is love, and he who abides in love abides in God and God in him* (1John 4:16). But the part of our being that allows us to experience love, also has the same potential to experience pain, (which is just as unpleasurable as love is pleasurable). And there is a complete spectrum of 'pleasurableness of feeling' that runs from 'very intensely unpleasurable pain' at one end to 'very intensely pleasurable love' at the other end.

So then, why did God invent this spectrum of pleasure and pain? Why not just pleasure only? Very simply, He needed to have a way to experientially show and guide us towards right, and away from wrong. This fact alone shows us how important it is to God that we live by absolute standards of right and wrong (shortly I'll explain *why* it is so important). And He demonstrated just how important it is by allowing HImself to be tied to this spectrum (which means He was going to have to suffer too).

So, God has given us a way to *experientially* know right from wrong (our heart and conscience), and a way to *mentally* know right from wrong (the Bible and logic).

A way to visualize our heart is to see it as having,

like a camera has over its lens, an aperture, which dilates, depending on how safe and loving or hostile the environment is deemed to be. The bigger the dilation, the greater the flow of feeling allowed, and therefore the more intense the experience (good or bad).

And although there are fluctuations in the widening and narrowing of this port, each person will generally set it at a fixed position, depending on how much trauma and love they've experienced in their life. But little do most people know of the tremendous potential this port has for positive and negative intensity. I know that most people don't know the high degrees of potential on the positive side that I've experienced (most of which happened due to spiritual disciplines), because I rarely see them being expressed anywhere...especially in the public forums (which is one reason why I'm writing this book). Human manifestation and experience, as is currently being expressed in this life, fall <u>far</u> below the potential that God designed for them (which should give us a great expectation for a great heaven). I know this not only intellectually as a scientist, but also experientially.

This is the main reason why people use drugs and alcohol. If a person has their aperture clenched to a certain degree of closure (which we all do to some degree), they instinctively crave to have it open more. But the reason why they don't open it more is because they are afraid of experiencing the same degrees of pain that they have in past traumas that they were unable to prevent and defend themselves against. So now they (subconsciously) try to prevent this pain by fearfully avoiding anything that resembles what caused the pain in the first place. Kind of like: you're not going to drown if you don't go in water. But, on the other hand, you're also not going to enjoy the fun of swimming and playing in water. But, when a person *happens* into an experience of using drugs or alcohol, and finds their *guard* anesthetized and therefore their aperture somewhat forced open wider, and they experience the pleasure that comes from this, it has a lasting effect on them. They realize that they like the heart ramifications of this experience and value it above the normal humdrum. It also lets them know that higher states do exist. But, drugs and alcohol are not *the* way to get to these higher states. I wrote a book to describe why ("Sweeping It Under The Drug"). In essence, I said that drugs and alcohol usually end up creating just as much pain as they do pleasure. They are an artificial way to get to the higher states. Kind of like eating saccharin when you are hungry for something sweet. Also, God won't allow us to artificially get to the higher states without Him for too long because it defeats His purpose of wanting fellowship with us, and gets in the way of Him teaching us the lessons of love and holiness. Therefore He's designed into drugs and alcohol a potential for unpleasant physical and emotional experiences to guide us away from depending on drugs and alcohol for being in higher states (and, as some know, 'unpleasant' is a <u>very</u> mild word for the intense pain that can come upon us as when using drugs or alcohol).

On the positive side, some people use drugs and alcohol to allow themselves to be reminded of the great potential for beauty this life has (which their aperture setting has stopped allowing them to see and feel). But, like I've said, I'm not advocating drugs here because even though I've had some 'awakening experiences' with drugs, I've also had such intensely painful experiences that they were even life threatening. No, there are other ways to be 'awakened': prayer, meditation, Bible study, church, good conversations, serving, music, etc. Although, an occasional glass of wine can prove to be beneficial and not harmful. And the Bible does allow for this. The benefit of wine is that by being *instantly* taken to a more relaxed state, we get inspired to do the work that will allow us to more and more experience this state naturally. Analogously, once a person has experienced having money, they are more likely to do the work necessary to make sure that they never have to experience being poor.

Why absolute standards of right and wrong are important
(1) Informative. Simply, they allow the Designer to describe to us what specifically would cause harm to others' feelings, physical well-being, possessions, property, works, in-progress-developments, and stations-in-life. And 'others' also includes the Designer.
(2) Protection. Obedience to these standards keeps the environment safe, so that our apertures can stay wide open. A safe environment also prevents the shocks and traumas that would cause our heart-aperture to protectively narrow.
(3) Pleasure. Love is the highest emotional pleasure (and because of the ways of the world and its priorities, I don't think many really know how intensely pleasurable love can be). Love is an unefforted, natural state. The Bible says that God (who is love) is omnipresent. Therefore, letting God (and therefore love) into our hearts is no more an effort than letting fresh air into a room. The window needs merely to be opened, and the fresh air will gently come in.
(4) Performance. An automobile is a pile of materials (metal, rubber, plastic, wood, gasoline, etc.). But when that pile is arranged as an automobile with an engine, it does far greater wonders than just a pile of materials could do.
(5) Beauty. If certain correct notes are played together on a

guitar or piano or harp, an experience of beauty is created (harmony). If one of these instruments is out of tune, or *wrong* notes are played, an unpleasant experience is created (disharmony). And the rules as to what these notes can or cannot be is <u>fixed</u>. A very important piece of wisdom then is: the rules describing which human behaviors would cause harmony or disharmony is also fixed. This is one giant reason why the Bible is so valuable. It tells us what these rules are more accurately and thoroughly than any other religion, philosophy or branch of psychology.

So, the overriding rule that governs where our experience will be on the pleasure/pain spectrum is: how harmonious (or unharmonious) with God's perfect design are our (external and internal) actions. The more harmonious, the more pleasurable. The more discordant, the more unpleasurable. (Of course, our experience is also affected by the actions of others).

Therefore, the reason God tied this invention of pleasure and pain indelibly to our experience is: there needs to be a built-in feedback system that will guide all of our actions and intentions into being in harmony with perfect nature, others and God. And this emotional guidance is there even when we are not conscious of whether what we're doing is right or wrong.

Given all of this, it is easy to understand the (unfortunate) necessity of the pleasure/pain spectrum. And it is very loving of God to allow Himself to be tied to us and this spectrum (because it means He'll have to also go through unpleasant experiences). This shows just how important this spectrum is, for Him to not do without it.

Like with the strings on a guitar, when we operate in harmony, beauty is created (which is pleasurable).

And this invention itself is actually beautiful.

The God-void
> *Thou has made us for Thyself,*
> *and our heart is restless until it rests in Thee.*
>   St. Augustine

If psychology and sociology are the studies of human behavior, an important observation seems to be consistently overlooked, or at least, underplayed by them. And that observation is: all peoples in all societies (now and throughout history) <u>inherently</u> <u>desire(d)</u> to have a relationship with God, as is expressed in the many examples given in Chapter 1. Aldous Huxley, in *The Perennial Philosophy*, said that all groupings of people throughout all of the ages have had 3 things in common (as was expressed in their artifacts [totem poles, cave drawings, etc.] and by their group spokespersons/philosophers [witch doctors, priests, etc]. And these groups include cavemen, Africans, Asians, Europeans, New Guinea tribes, etc., etc., many of whom never had physical contact with any other group): (1)They all believed in an invisible intelligence and world beyond the physical one, (2)They believed that this invisible intelligence is a part of every human being, and (3)The purpose of life is to discover God.

And when this last desire is pursued and developed, fulfillment is achieved: inner fellowship and dialogue (praying and listening), security, inner strength, clarity, confidence, purpose, knowing, verbal guidance (the Bible, people being used by the Holy Spirit), in*spir*ation, religious feelings (reverence, awe, worship, agape), knowing perfection, hope for a higher afterlife, sense of belonging (to God and to a holy community: the church), etc. All of these are ways that God <u>gives us</u> pleasure.

I, and many others, can personally testify to the experience of: having a specific desire that <u>only</u> found fulfillment with God. But I first tried many other things to try to satisfy this very specific longing. The scientific report that I would give on my search would yield these conclusions: God and the Bible not only satisfied this desire, but did so in an even greater way than I had hoped for. Nothing else that I tried could satisfy it (and my efforts did include most of the popular 'worldly' approaches). But I was always left with a spiritual hunger and emptiness, which drove me to keep on searching.

A song that greatly describes this kind of searching is "Take It To The Limit" by The Eagles. Every word in it is great. "So put me on a highway, and show me a sign, and (I'll) take it to the limit, one more time." But it becomes frustrating, disheartening, and sometimes even survival-testing when you keep not finding the satisfaction that you had hoped for at those limit points. But thank God that I can finally say that I did find that satisfaction...in God.

This is why this longing has been appropriately called the 'God-void', because: only God can fill this particular void. He designed us with this void because <u>He</u> desires to have a relationship with us. This is a fact that we all should be very happy about, instead of increasingly kicking Him out of the public forums, which is what has been happening for the last 30 years.

And because of these efforts to erase God from public visibility, when people experience the hunger in their God-void, they often "look for love in all the wrong places". They choose to look up to: the media, television (the secular church), movie stars, music stars, politicians, mates, other people, sports teams, sports stars, social groups, gangs, lifestyles, clubs, organizations, food, habits, etc. But none of these can fill the God-void. Therefore, their experience of life will be less than glorious.

All of this heavily points to the fact that the God in the sky...the God in our hearts...the author of the Bible, <u>desires</u> to have a relationship with us. Otherwise, He wouldn't have designed us with this yearning God-void, which can only be satisfied when we turn to Him (in spirit and in word).

Reiterating a point made earlier: to think that an intelligence as great as the one that designed this universe, planet earth and the life on it, would do so for no <u>reason,</u> is a highly improbable thought. It also wouldn't be a very intelligent thing for a high-level intelligence to do. I mean, wouldn't an intelligence who put <u>such</u> meticulous design into the physical part of the universe and planet earth, put just as meticulous and purposeful a design into the spiritual/experiential side of this life?

So, In this chapter we've been examining what this intelligence's (God's) design and motives might be. For answers, we've looked to the Bible...and we've looked to psychology (the God-void).

By the way, our observations in psychology are just as strong of evidence as those that are in the hard, physical sciences. It's just that we are dealing with the invisible. But why should the observations made by one of our senses (vision) be considered to be any more scientific than three of our other senses (mind, heart and truth channel)? It seems that only those who are strongly attached to an outer focus on the physical world, and who've done little observing of the mind, heart and truth channel, would discredit them as being able to produce real, scientific data. And the secular world is very backward in its approach to the 'mind, heart and truth channel'.

It seems like most people in the world are like goats following carrots, with little understanding of the carrot, or the goat. This is why they're not recognizing that the reason for their unhappiness is that *someone* has been working hard to replace their *natural* carrot with an *artificial* one (that is, replace God and the Bible with secular humanism).

But this dangerous new carrot is not just artificial. It is also poisonous. And we can see (by observing television, the music industry, movies, the news, etc.) that the *heart* of this society is exhibiting a condition of ' poisoned' (i.e. negative emotions). And being that the heart is a reactor to the mind, this is definite proof that there is something wrong with the mind of this society...which is secular-humanism without God.

Now if the heart of this society were to be the Holy Spirit, and the mind of this society were to be the Bible, and the head of this society were to be God and Jesus, health would start returning.

Now I'm not sure exactly how many people in this society are lost, but I do know that *the world's* shepherds are poisoning *their sheep* (that is, people whose religion is this world, not the kingdom of God). But, nevertheless, this all is leading toward a happy ending because, even though God has given us free will, our reins can only stretch so far, and He will allow this problem to go on for only so long. The rest of this book describes how God has and will triumph over the problem of free will, and how we can be a part of this triumph.

Conclusion about God's motive for making us

We must be very important God, being that He's had to break His comfort zone and suffer through the headache and heartache that the human race has been.

A simple summary of Chapters 1, 2 and 3

(1) One look out into the universe let's us know that there is *something* going on out there that is more powerful than us.

(2) The many possible explanations as to what that *something* could be are all boiled down to just one explanation when we look within ourselves and see:

    (A)There are things going on within us that are more powerful than us (e.g. sleep, death, romance, various hungers, etc.).

    (B)The Bible is the only body of knowledge on earth that accurately, and without flaw, describes what we can observe going on within us.

    (C)The Bible has 100% credibility in what it says (from a number of perspectives: psychology, history, prophesy, etc.), therefore the probability stands that the Bible is 100% true.

(3) The greater power outside and inside of us made us for an ultimate good reason....for an intensely great pleasure, both for itself and for us.

(4) Planet earth is a place where certain developments take place to properly prepare the individuals who will become eligible for a place of greater pleasure in the afterlife. (The rest of this book deals with this last point.)

Chapter 4
God's Solution To The Problem Of Free Will

Being that the Creator needs to give free will in order to receive the 'pleasure of shared experience with intelligent/feeling beings', the basic problem in His creation then becomes: what if the free willed beings <u>decide</u> to not cooperate with His plan, or even pay any attention to Him at all?

However, like in any engineering problem, this is not to be initially seen as a roadblock, but rather only as an obstacle to which a solution must be found.

In making an existence with a number of free will beings, the Creator of it inherits the basic problem of government and sociology: how to organize many free will beings so that they will peacefully coexist. Of course, any being who is intelligent enough to make this creation (which is much greater than anything that humans have made), is also going to have a solution to the basic problem of sociology that far outshines any system humans have invented (e.g. kingdoms, communism, capitalism, tribes, dictatorships, naziism, anarchy, secular humanism, etc.).

God's solution to the basic problem of government and sociology is this:

<u>The only way that free will beings can peacefully coexist is for ALL of them to submit to doing ONLY what is best for the whole (as opposed to: doing anything that would cause physical or emotional harm to others or themselves; or abandoning their God-given responsibilities).</u>

'What is best for the whole' is defined by a set of (holy) rules....a specific set of inner and outer behaviors that each person (and society as a whole) must adhere to, which: (1)are perfectly in sync with the basic design of how the beings were made to optimally operate, (2)reflect a collective fairness to all, and (3)prevent beings from causing pain in other beings.

The Creator's challenge now becomes: how to create a place where <u>all</u> the free-will beings will adhere to this solution. Simply stated, His solution to this dilemma is: first prove that free will beings can't (won't) accomplish this by themselves; then set up a system where those free will beings who choose submission to holiness, instead of selfishness, are eligible to be closer to Him, now and in heaven; and those who don't choose allegiance to holiness can't go to heaven (otherwise it wouldn't be a heaven).

But, the Bible tells us that no one in history (except Jesus) has been able to completely and continually choose holiness: "<u>All</u> have sinned" (Romans 3:23). Because of this fact, God had to create a solution to the problem of free will that would need to go through a number of phases and span thousands of years. (Part 2 of this book describes each of these phases, and the necessary reasons for each one.)

It might be said: "Why doesn't a loving God just pop into the sky and tell us to wake up and follow His ways?" He doesn't do so (anymore - although He once did and it didn't work, which I'll describe in this and upcoming chapters) because this would go against one of the main things He's accomplishing here, which is to prove that: <u>When He gives free will to many beings, they make a horrible mess of things. And therefore, if we want to live in dangerless peace, we need only Him (and His perfect standards) to be sovereign, and the rest of us to be submissive.</u>

It took 6,000 years of human history to make this point indelibly (that is, to those who would get the point).

Once this concept is understood, and a person realizes that they don't need to play god or follow false gods (and that it's actually harmful to do either of these), they now have the <u>freedom</u> to relax (into just submitting to perfect function). And the more that a person understands and adheres to this concept, the more they become <u>liberated</u> (from the pain and damage that often results from 'trial and error attempts to learn how to correctly live this life'). The underlined statement on the last page answers the question 'why are we here - collectively?' But we as individuals have little control over the collective. Therefore, what's more important to us is: why are we here - individually? This question will be answered in this chapter.

Three of my reasons to write this book were (1)to show how to become liberated from suffering, confusion and lostness (as Christianity once liberated me from these), (2)to show how to be in beauty and perfection (not dysfunction), and (3)to set the record straight in Christianity's debate against "the world" by showing that <u>there indeed are absolutes in this life</u>: God, His plan, His specific design of the human being, and His holy standards in the Bible for a human's behavior. Science recognizes a lot of absolutes in this life. Now it is time for science to also include these.

As I showed earlier, the Bible is equivalent to an auto mechanic's repair manual, which describes the <u>only</u>, absolute ways that a specific car and its many parts were <u>designed</u> to operate. Similarly, we were designed to operate in only very specific ways (that is if we want to experience happiness, fulfillment and peace). A line from a song puts this nicely: "Wonderful is what you'll feel in you, when you do the things you're made to do".

Do we, in fact, even have free will?

I've been to Bible studies where it was said that we don't. In fact, this is a popular position in parts of the Protestant community. They say that God *predestined* only specific people to become Christians and be saved, and had *foreknowledge* that these specific people would do so....and these things prove that we have no free will.

While trying this philosophy on for size, I used to say "Yes, this is possible, because God could show us what He wants to show us in this life simply by *taking us on a ride* in which we'd have the *illusion of free will,* just enough for Him to prove that free will doesn't work."

I ended up rejecting this notion though because: (1)I could observe within my being that, although there were forces acting within me trying to prompt me to do certain things, I still did retain some executive power to choose to do or not to do these things. (2)I couldn't conclude that God is completely holy <u>and</u> observe myself doing unholy things <u>and</u> conclude that God was totally moving me. This would mean that God also authored unholiness. (3)2Pet. 3:9 says that God doesn't **want** <u>any</u> to perish, and **wants** <u>all</u> to come to repentance. Therefore, if predestination were true, this is how he would have made it (otherwise He's not omnipotent). So being that many will perish (Matt. 7:13-14), predestination cannot be true. It is the free will of others that denies God what He wants. (4)I would regularly run across Bible verses that said that we did have free will. Just to name a few: Pr. 1:24, Jos. 24:15, De. 7:12, 30:19, 1Ki. 18:21, Gen. 2:16,7, Ex. 19:5, Lev. 26:3, Rev. 22:17, 2Pet. 2:10, Acts 57:51, 2Ch. 36:15,6, Heb. 3:8,14, 4:7, Ps. 78:8, 95:8.

Now whether or not you accept the Apochrypha as part of the Bible, these writings have always been highly revered, and are accepted as part of the Bible by the largest church in the world: the Roman Catholic Church. Also, they are starting to be included in some Protestant Bibles. Given all of this, there are some great verses in the book of Sirach regarding free will. *"Unseemly is praise on a sinner's lips, for it is not accorded to him by God. Say not: 'It was God's doing that I fell away'; for what He hates He does not do. Say not: 'It was He who set me astray'; for He has no need of wicked man. When God, in the beginning, created man, He made him subject to his own free choice. If you choose you can keep the commandments; it is loyalty to do His will. There are set before you fire and water; to whichever you choose, stretch forth your hand. Before man are life and death, whichever he chooses shall be given him. No man does He command to sin, to none does He give strength for lies."* (Sirach 15:9,11,12,14-17,20)

The *predestined* and *foreknowledge* verses can be explained by the fact that God did predestine a plan to save a part of humanity for heaven. But to say that we don't have free will to choose whether or not to be a part of that plan would negate the very reason He made us in the first place, as was pointed out in the last chapter. Otherwise, He wouldn't *"stand at the door"* of our heart *"and knock"* (Rev. 3:20), waiting for a response. He'd just come in. But then once we answer the door, He can respond in great ways, such as boosting our faith.

Also, in not one of the verses that mention *predestined*, *foreknowledge* and *elect,* is there an inference that 'individuals' are being referred to. If you were to reread these verses with the meaning: us - collectively, instead of us - individually, this would eliminate the notion that we individually were predestined. These verses would then simply mean that God had predestined to bring out of all humanity an elect group of people who loved Him and desired to submit totally to Him being their only ruler. The possibility of this 'collective' idea is verified in Romans 11, where the word 'foreknew' is used in reference to 'a group of people': *"God has not cast away His people whom He foreknew"* (Rom. 11:2). The previous verses show that it is the Jewish people <u>as a whole</u> that is being referred to.

The above is an examination of the 'English' text. But when we look at the Greek (original) text, the plural theory is even more confirmed. The Greek word for "us" in Ephesians 1:5 is: ημας (hemas). The Greek dictionary defines this as: "the accusative <u>plural</u> of us". In Romans 8:28-30, "those" in the English can be read to mean either "those (individuals)" or "those (the collection of individuals)". The Greek word is: τουτοις (toutois), which is the dative <u>plural</u> and means: "these (persons or things)". On its own, this could be inconclusive. But in light of Romans 11:2, which shows God foreknowing people as a group, and in light of the fact that God does change His mind (which I will shortly prove), and also the fact that we have free will, I think that it's evident that God predestined that He would have a group of people for Himself, but that the individuals that formed that group were given the freedom to choose to be in it or not. Also, if God wanted to communicate '*individual* predestination' He would have used singular words. I think that it's illogical to think that a God who is omnipotent, loves His church, and whose Spirit dwells within many of its members, would wait 1500 years to communicate such an important fact as individual predestination (via John Calvin).

Another point is: if we don't <u>freely</u> choose our actions, then we're not responsible. And if we're not responsible, then there wasn't any need for God to have rebuked people...or for Jesus to have died on the cross.

It has been rationalized that the way that 'predestination, foreknowledge and free will' can coexist is to visualize human history as being like a movie. The movie will play out frame by frame, in sequence, but the entire film itself can be held up and every frame can be viewed all at once (with only God having this option). (But then the rationalizer went on to say that this is all still a *mystery*).

The reason that I would refute this visualization is because there are instances in the Bible where God has changed His course in midstream. For example:*"the Lord regretted that He had made man on the earth, and He was grieved in His heart"*. (Gen. 6:6). Webster's Dictionary says that 'regret' means: "To feel remorseful over one's own acts", with 'remorse' being defined as: "A deep, torturing sense of guilt over a wrong that one has done". Therefore, why would He be remorseful if He knew that bad things were going to happen which He could have prevented? He simply would not have allowed the circumstances that would cause them in the first place, knowing He'd be sorry about the outcome. An analogy here would be: why would we open our heart and fall in love with someone, if we <u>knew</u> that it was going to end up disastrously?

Other examples of God changing His mind: (Exod. *32:7-14)...the LORD said to Moses, "Go, get down! For your people, whom you brought out of the land of Egypt have corrupted themselves. They have turned aside quickly out of the way which I commanded them. They have made themselves a molded calf, and worshipped it and sacrificed to it and said 'This is your God, O Israel, that brought you out of the land of Egypt!'" And the LORD said to Moses,*

"I have seen this people, and indeed it is a stiff-necked people! Now, therefore, let Me alone, that My wrath may burn hot against them and I many consume them. And I will make of you a great nation." Then Moses pleaded with the LORD his God, and said: "LORD, why does Your wrath burn hot against Your people, whom You have brought out of the land of Egypt with great power and with a mighty hand? Why should the Egyptians speak and say, 'With evil intent He brought them out to harm them, to kill them in the mountains, and to consume them from the face of the earth'? Turn from Your fierce wrath, and relent from this harm to Your people. Remember Abraham, Isaac, and Israel, Your servants, to whom You swore by Your own self, and said to them, 'I will multiply your descendants as the stars of heaven; and all this land that I have spoken of, I give to your descendants, and they shall inherit it forever.'" So the LORD relented from the harm which He said He would do to His people.

Also, God <u>changed His mind</u> about destroying the Ninevites; Jonah 3:10*"Then God saw their works, that they turned from their evil way; and God relented from the disaster that He said He would bring upon them, and He did not do it."*

In Exodus 4:24 *"the Lord came upon Moses and sought to kill him."* But then God <u>changed His mind</u>, and Exodus 4:26 says that *"God let Moses go"*.

You see, what's at stake here is the resolution of two conflicting concepts: (1)that God could have handed us the Bible, complete with the history that's in it, before the beginning of time, and (2)that He had an initial desire to have fellowship with free will beings, and a basic plan, and then jumped right into it with them and tried to make it work. If God had been able to <u>totally</u> predict what the free will beings were going to do, this would not only mean that they didn't really have free will, but for God this would be a much less adventuresome, exciting, interesting, fun and challenging endeavor.

But I'd like to make the point here that it wouldn't <u>really</u> matter which of these is true because, whichever one it is, we are still just left with: do we love God and His Bible, support them in life, and conduct our lives in obedience to His holy laws? A problem here is that some people enter into this debate with such fervor that they end up committing sins in doing so. But the Bible warns against this by saying in Rom. 1:21, 22:*"they became vain in their reasoning, and their senseless minds were darkened. While claiming to be wise, they became fools"*. 2Tim. 2:23-3:2: *"Avoid foolish and ignorant debates, for you know that they breed quarrels. A slave of the Lord should not quarrel, but should be gentle with everyone, able to teach, tolerant, correcting opponents with kindness. It may be that God will grant them repentance that leads to knowledge of the truth, and that they may return to their senses out of the devil's snare, where they are entrapped by him, for his will. But understand this: there will be terrifying times in the last days. People will be self-centered and lovers of money, boastful, arrogant, abusive"* (Another Bible uses the word *"speculations"* instead of *"debates"*. This is a good slant because it implies: why enter into ungodliness [quarrels] over a speculation, which is something that you don't know for absolute sure is true?). 1Cor. 13:2 *"And if I have...all knowledge;...but do not have love, I am nothing"*.

Therefore it boils down to: are we being loving and submitting our lives to obedience to God's laws? In the final analysis, sincere Christian life is this simple. And <u>anything</u> that pulls us away from these things is evil..even if it is a (heated) religious debate: *Whoever teaches some-thing different and does not agree with the sound words of our Lord Jesus Christ and the religious teaching is conceit-ed, understanding nothing, and has a <u>morbid disposition for arguments and verbal disputes</u>. From these come envy, rivalry, insults, evil suspicions, and mutual friction among people with corrupted minds, who are deprived of the truth, supposing religion to be a means of gain. Indeed, religion with contentment is a great gain."* (1Tim. 6:3-6).

Catholics don't show an inclination for *"arguing"* or *"verbal disputes"* (although many Protestants do); they don't *"envy"*, acknowledge a *"rivalry"* with Protestants (like many Protestants do), they don't have ready, manu-factured *"insults"* for Protestants (although many Protestants do against them), and many Protestants are *"deprived of the truth"* that peace and love should never be sacrificed to defend speculative theological positions that are penny wise and pound foolish compared to what's real-ly important: our daily duties of love, growth and holiness.

One last note on discussing/debating/arguing: In our heart of hearts we all agree, because there is only one truth. It then just becomes a matter of taming our ego, let-ting go of our attachments to and defenses of untruths, giv-ing priority to the Holy Spirit when it tries to convict us, and then working out our semantic differences.....without becoming disagreeable, arrogant, addicted-to-having-to-be-right, defensive, mean, insulting, belittling, pushing lies, closed-minded, etc.

The Circle of Submission

It's very common nowadays for people to reject 'submission' in favor of the more popular, modern pursuits of: 'personal freedom', 'self-autonomy', and 'shirking of responsibilities'. It seems like the phrase "It's better to give than receive" has been changed to "It's better to receive (or do nothing) than to give".

It's often hard for a woman today, who's been inundated with messages in the media saying she's supposed to compete with men in the workplace, to hear that the Bible says that she is to submit to her husband as being her authority: *"But I want you to know that Christ is the head of every man, and a husband the head of his wife, and God the head of Christ"* (1Cor. 11:3). But this wouldn't be a bitter pill to swallow if she would look at the fact that there is a circle of submission, in which we all must submit.

Yes, a wife must submit to her husband (which just means that she must consider her duties to him and her family as being more important than her personal whims...plus she must treat him with respect and love). But, the husband is also in the same position. That is, he also must consider his duties to his wife and family as more important than his personal whims. Plus, besides preserving God's law in his family, he must treat his family with gentleness and love. A husband's submission also includes: submitting to his employer and his responsibility to provide for the physical needs of his family.

When speaking about submission, I'm not saying: 'total submission'. The first and foremost submission for all of us is: to God and His holy laws. Therefore, if a submittor was to ask a submitter to do something that was unbiblical, the submitter could <u>respectfully</u> refuse. This is exemplified when Jesus was asked whether it was right to pay taxes to the Roman government. He replied: *"Render unto Caesar what is Caesar's, and render unto God what is God's."* The point being: Caesar was due only their taxes (because of the services and public utilities that the Roman government provided). But a godly person did not owe him the right for him to expect them to do unbiblical things.

But I also want to heavily emphasize: <u>respectfully</u>. As this book has pointed out, all of the problems in the history of free will beings has as their root: beings wanting to do things their own way....sometimes even to the point of rejecting God and His Bible as authorities. This is how new religions and denominations have been started....and often by disagreeing over just one theological issue. Then these offshoots have spawned even more offshoots, which then spawned even more offshoots, etc., etc...and usually with each new offshoot taking greater liberties and becoming even more bizarre and unholy than its predecessor.

But this all would never have happened if the disagreements would have been presented respectfully, patiently and in submission (once again, submission just means 'respecting authority', not blindly agreeing with everything it says). I mean, how could anyone go to the extent of thinking they have the right to splinter God's people.....or the arrogance and energy to reinvent His church? I mean, the Church is referred to in the Bible as "Christ's bride". Have the denominationalists then presumed that Jesus is a polygamist? The Bible says that when those who have created these *"dissensions"* and *"factions"* (Gal. 5:20) have to face God, it will be very harsh for them (*"Let every soul be subject to the governing authorities. For there is no authority except from God, and the authorities that exist are appointed by God. Therefore whoever resists authority resists the ordinance of God, and those who resist will bring judgment on themselves"* Romans 13:1, 2).

I'm not *"rebuking"* and *"exhorting"* all members and pastors in offshoot religions and denominations, many of whom I know love God very much, being that I was one of them. I'm just trying to point out the sinful roots in how these religions and denominations got their start. Think how much stronger Christianity would be in the world and in our unlawful societies if God's Church hadn't been splintered (Satan's M.O.: divide and conquer).

In regards to my going from the Protestant church to the Catholic Church: When I was a Protestant, I had a ready barrage of knee-jerk anti-Catholic remarks...all of which I was just parroting other Protestants. But I found that when I examined Catholicism first-hand, and was open-minded and didn't engage the knee-jerk remarks, I found a reverent Church with a history of beauty, a beautiful feeling, a history of saints and of preserving Christianity since the first century, more agape-like music, etc. I was drawn into the Catholic Church because these agape-like characteristics were very pleasurable and felt much more godly, as opposed to the bad feelings I always had for the basic sins of many people in the Protestant church - vanity, drawing-attention-to-self, argumentativeness, money-mania, bombastic entertainment and music, unpeaceful preachers, syrupyness, a general air of worldliness and trying-too-hard, etc. I feel much closer to God in peace and beauty. And eventually I found that logic and scripture was actually on the Catholic's side, not the Protestants. Now instead of knee-jerk condemnations, I have true explanations...maintained in peace, not *"rivalry"*.

For those who thought the Church was erring in some way, the proper thing to do would have been for them to respectfully communicate the errors they (thought they) saw (to as many people as it took before they felt that they'd been heard) and then just <u>leave it in God's hands,</u> not take matters into their own hands...especially not to the point of starting a new church. If there's more communicating and work you need to do, the Holy Spirit will let you know and energize you. (Remember, in Romans 13 we are told to submit to authorities. And this was even a pagan government that people were being told to submit to [at the time of that writing]..let alone God's Church.) 'Taking matters into our own hands' is the basic sin and error of this life (us playing God). But out of this also comes the basic lesson of this life: only 'total submission to God and His holy laws' works. And that we learn this basic lesson (which makes us eligible for Heaven) is the answer to the question posed by this book: Why Are We Here?.

Let's look at the basic structures of some of this life's *circles of submission*.

<u>The Family</u>: The children submit to the parents; the wife submits to her husband and her homemaking duties; the husband submits to his employment duties; the parents submit to their duties and responsibilities to raise their children correctly....and they all submit to God and his holy laws on how a family should be run, and how people should interact. And when this is all done correctly, God blesses them with the very pleasurable feeling of love.

But if one cog in this wheel stands in rebellion, it hurts the whole wheel and hurts God's plan....which God will then judge with very unpleasant feelings.

<u>A Business</u>: The employees submit to their manager; the managers submit to the boss; the boss submits to the owner; the owner submits to the customers; the customers submit to the employees (by surrendering their money to them)....and they all submit to God and His holy laws on how a business should be run and how people should interact.

Of course, there are many possible variations in this structure (board of directors, stockholders, etc.). But the basic concept is always the same. And to the degree that this is carried out correctly, God will bless this business with success.

The Church: The church members submit to the pastor; the pastor submits to the elders; the elders submit to the needs of the flock.....and they all submit to God and His laws on how a church should be run.

Creator/creations: The creations submit to their Creator, who in turn submits to going the extra mile for developing them (which is very fair of Him, and under-standable why He accepts this responsibility: because He put us into this situation in the first place - ultimately for our gain and for His). Examples of His submission to us are: (1)He's had to suffer through a lot of sinning human history, (2)Jesus washing the disciples feet, and (3)Jesus dying on the cross.

The Joy Of Submission

I'm very, very, very glad that there's a God, a Jesus, a Holy Spirit, a Bible.....all of whom I'm supposed to look up to and submit to. This makes life so much simpler. I don't want to have to take the responsibility of deciding what is right and what is wrong....or to have to take the new age position that says that "I am a part of the God authority" and that "all things are possible". When I used to live life that way, a lot of traumatic possibilities also happened. It's so much easier to know that there's a perfect God and a perfect Bible, and that I really have only one basic responsibility: to obey what's in the Bible.

Of course, this wouldn't be possible if I didn't feel that the Bible is perfect and that God is truly worthy of my respect and love. I mean, we can't submit to just anything or anyone. But this is what many people do, which is why they develop a bitter taste for submission. But there is so much freedom and joy and weightlessness in submission. This is the basic paradox of this life. This is also why I spent a large part of this book proving that God is real and that His Bible is perfect.......to uncover the key to the life of freedom, joy, meaning and love.

In any other philosophy we'd be submitting to something that is less than perfect (and possibly evil and damaging)....or, if we were to choose ourself to be sovereign, we'd be forced to take on the burden of reinventing the wheel (and suffering from many stumbles along the way).

As for those who have a problem with submission... they're denying themselves a very pleasurable deep inner peace and satisfaction. This satisfaction comes from 'doing the right thing', and the peace is the absence of guilt and upset from doing wrong things.

Some might say to me "Well it's easy for you to say that a wife must submit being that you're a man." My response is: As I've spelled out, I've also had to submit to a lifetime of hard work (and most of the time, work that I would have preferred to not have had to do). I've suffered a lot to do the right thing. But that's because I consider it to be a greater suffering (in my spirit) to do the wrong thing, or to not do the right thing.

And it doesn't matter what position of submission God put me in, I would do it, because the main thing in this life is that we learn to submit. And all those who we submit to (except God) will have some degree of imperfection. If God were to say that husbands were to submit to their wives, that's what I'd do. And I would have no problem with it. Or even if He were to say to submit to trees, or flowers, or gravel, I would do it. Why? Because I trust Him (and I'm sure His Bible would have a good explanation as to why - which, of course, I would investigate)....and because I know that submission is the only way that life can work. Therefore, those who don't submit, no matter who or what their *natural* (God-invented) place in life requires them to submit to, are without excuse before God.

We are all the same

A lot of people see themselves as different from others: male, female, black, white, a certain nationality, a certain age, a certain lifestyle, etc. But at the core, we are all the same: spirits in the image of God in a human body, with the choice of submitting to God's holy standards...or to not submit (and/or to submit to imperfection). What kind of body we're in, and what kinds of talents it has, will determine how our submission will manifest. But the basic challenge, dilemma and test of this life is the same for us all. To submit or not to submit....that is the question.

The bottom-line answer to the question: why are we here?

In order to create a peaceful, loving, joyful, danger-less heaven filled with free-will beings, God needs all of its inhabitants to have their free will tamed (away from unholy tendencies....and to holiness), and to unquestion-ably know that this is the only way that a heaven as described above could be accomplished. While on earth, the ways in which a free-will being would exhibit that this taming is taking place is by having the following as their fruit and basic approach to life:

(mind:) willing submission to holiness;

(heart:) in a spirit of positiveness and love;

and when need be, to accept sacrifice and suffering

(for the sake of God's holy standards).

Chapter 5

Phase 1

Powerful Beings
(Satan And The Angels)

Seven phases were necessary in God's plan for resolving the problem of free will. Each phase had a definite purpose and had to occur in order for God to make a complete argument in proving that: it is not possible for a large group of free will beings on their own to submit to holiness, no matter what degree of power and freedom they have, or what form or setting they're in.

We start with the first phase: Satan and the angels. This phase of God's experiment yields the theorem: a high degree of power, freedom, knowledge and closeness to God does not necessarily yield submission.

I use a scene from a movie to illustrate this point. The scene starts with a man who is drowning in the ocean and pleading with God for help. He promises God that he will devote his life to Him if He helps him get to the shore. To make a long story short, as God helps him move closer to the shore, he gradually lessens his pledges of what he'll do for God with his life and money. When he's finally at the shore, he says to God "Well, you're omnipotent and own everything, so you really don't need my help." This illustrates how a person's response to increased power and freedom often is: increased selfishness. This also shows why God had to invent pain and knock us down occasionally: so that we can get centered, focused on Him, rightly fearful and humble, and back on track to accomplishing the real purpose of our lives (which is not continual, impulsive self-gratification). (Looking at our own lives: when we are given more power, love, money, health and free time, [after taking care of our own and our family's needs] do we spend it on God and others, or on frivolous impulses? Later I'll show how we'll be rewarded or punished based on these kinds of decisions that we make in our lifetime.) The opposite lesson that we can see from this story is that when God puts us into a trial, we usually turn to Him, but as He lessens the peril, we lessen our attention on Him, His holiness, and His purpose for our lives. Because of this unfortunate fact (and the overall understanding of why this life even exists), there is really no basis for complaining about the trials in our lives.

Ezekial 28:12 says that Satan's original form had *"the seal of perfection, full of wisdom and perfect in beauty."* He was even *"blameless in his ways."* The name Lucifer means: light-bearer, shining one. In Isaiah 14:12 he is addressed as: *"O morning star, son of the dawn"*.

But then he developed pride over his elevated stature and wanted to be God:*"You said in your heart:...I will exalt my throne above the stars of God;...I will ascend above the heights of the clouds; I will be like the Most High!"* (Is. 14:13,14). This is what caused Satan's downfall (that is if God was going to be able to maintain a perfect, orderly, no-fear-of-turmoil heaven). Like with Adam and Eve, just one sin by Satan has lead to the great amount of demonic activity that we are now in. It all started with just one sin. (Why can't beings just be happy with what they've got...especially when they have so much?)

And 'not even tolerating one sin' is important because: one sin leads to another...which then leads to another, etc., etc. One sin might not seem so bad, but it would never end there. For instance: a marriage doesn't go from 'the beauty, gentleness and sweetness of romance', to 'the ugliness, irresponsibility, harshness, and insensitivity of divorce' in one move. There usually is a long series of small, gradual breakdowns in kindness, civility, submissiveness and positive outlook...but with all of this starting with one small breakdown. This proves the necessity of beings to have to be perfectly sinless in order for there to be a holy environment.

Names for Satan in the Bible show some of his activities on earth: Satan (adversary), devil (slanderer), the prince of the power of the air, the god of this age, the prince of this world (these last 3 show who's really behind the current media, entertainment industry, etc. This will be further expounded on near the end of chapter 10 under: 'the Kingdom of God' vs. 'the kingdom of *the world*'), the ruler of darkness, Leviathan (one who dwells in the sea of humanity), the king of death, the dragon, the deceiver, Apollyon (destroyer), Beelzebub (prince of demons), Belial (vileness, ruthlessness), the wicked one, the tempter, the accuser of the brethren, an angel of light, a liar, a murderer, the enemy, and a roaring lion. *Be sober; be vigilant. because your adversary the devil walks about like a roaring lion, seeking whom he may devour* (1Pet. 5:8).

Satan also: instigates false doctrine (1Tim. 4:1-3); perverts the word of God (Gen.3:1-4); hinders the works of God's servants (1Thes.2:18); blinds people from seeing that the Bible is the truth (*The god of this age has blinded the minds of the unbelievers, so that they may not see the light of the gospel of the glory of Christ, who is the image of God*. 2Cor. 4:4); prevents some of those who have heard the gospel from understanding it (*When anyone hears the word of the kingdom, and does not understanding it, then the wicked ones comes and snatches away what was sown in his heart*. Matt. 13:19); lays snares for people (2Tim. 2:26); tempts (Matt. 4:1, Eph. 6:11); imprisons people (Luke 13:16); afflicts suffering (Job 2:7); oppresses (Acts 10:38); deceives the whole world (but not all the people in it) (Rev. 12:9); tries to destroy marriages (1Cor: 7:3-5). His end-times fate (when he no longer will "accuse the brethren" before God) can be read in Rev. 12:7-12. Also, his destruction can be read in Rev. 20:10.

Another very common attribute of Satan is that, being that he wants to be god, he tries to imitate what God does (this is also common among evil people in the world, i.e. they often try to imitate those who are ahead of them and then try to claim the creative credit for themselves. But their imitations often reek from the foul odors of falseness and evil slants). Some examples: he has a trinity (Rev. 13:2,11), synagogues (Rev.2:9), doctrines (1Tim4:1), mysteries (2Thes.2:7, Rev.2:24), a throne (Rev.2:13; 13:2), a kingdom (Luke4:6), worshippers (Rev.13:4), angels (Rev.12:7), ministers (2Cor.11:5), miracles (2Thes.2:9, Matt.7:21-23), sacrifices (1Cor.10:20), fellowship (1Cor.10:20) and armies (Rev.16:14).

The Bible says that Satan brought down with him many of the angels of heaven. Yes, there is another high level of free will beings that we need to be aware of: angels. They are <u>powerful beings</u> (*Bless the LORD, you His angels, who excel in strength, who do His word* Ps. 103:20; also: 2Thess.1:7, 2Pet.2:11) who either <u>minister for God</u> (*Bless the LORD, all you hosts, ministers who do God's will.* Ps. 103:21; *Are they not all ministering spirits*

sent forth to minister for those who will inherit salvation?
Hebr. 1:14; *When the poor man died, he was carried away*
by angels Luke 16:22; also: Acts 12:7-11; Acts 27:23,24;
Heb.1:7; Gen.19:1-27; 1Kgs. 19:5), or <u>minister for Satan</u>
(*For such are false apostles, deceitful workers, who mas-*
querade as apostles of Christ. And no wonder, for even
Satan masquerades as an angel of light. So it is not strange
that his ministers also masquerade as ministers of right-
eousness". 2Cor. 11:13-15; *Now the Spirit explicitly says*
that in the last times some will turn away from the faith by
paying attention to deceitful spirits and demonic instruc-
tions through the hypocrisy of liars with branded con-
sciences. They <u>forbid marriage</u> and <u>require abstinence</u>
<u>from foods that God created to be received with thanksgiv-</u>
<u>ing</u> by those who believe and know the truth. 1Tim. 4:1-3).
(Two things that are very prominent in the new age movement and the secular societies of today are prophesied
here: living-together/live-in-partners/non-traditional-fami-
lies and vegetarianism. Could we then be living in "the last
times"? Stay tuned for Chapter 11.)

The followers of God receive <u>protection</u> by angels
from Satan and his demons (the fallen angels that followed
Satan), (*You have the LORD for your refuge; No evil shall*
befall you. For God commands the angels to guard you in
all your ways. With their hands they shall support you.
Whoever clings to me I will deliver; whoever knows my
name I will set on high. All who call upon me I will
answer; I will be with them in distress; Ps. 91:9,10,12,15;
Behold, I send an angel before you, to keep you in the way
and to bring you into the place which I have prepared.
Exod. 23:20; *The angel of the LORD, encamps all around*
those who fear Him, and delivers them. Ps. 34:7; *My God*
has sent his angel and shut the lions' mouths so that they

have not hurt me Dan. 6:22; *And Jesus called a little child to Him, set him in the midst of them, and said "Take heed that you do not despise one of these little ones, for I say to you that in heaven their angels always see the face of My Father."* Matt. 18:2,3,10 ("one" says that we each have a Guardian Angel). And Satan and his demons can't harm God's children (unless God gives them permission to do so, for a good purpose: as in Job 1:12, 2:6).

Also, in terms of the theme of this book, there is a great thing to be realized from the world of angels. Angels are <u>free will beings</u> (Is. 14:12-15, Jude 6) who now live close to God, with the problem of free will having been resolved in them: *whereas angels, who are greater in power and might, do not bring a reviling accusation against them before the Lord* (2Pet. 2:11). This means that it is possible to resolve the problem of free will.

<u>Conclusion from Phase 1:</u> Although it would be more pleasurable for God to have company with beings who are closer to Him in level of power, wisdom and intelligence, He is not able to just rely on these kinds of beings because of the problem of 'pride', which leads to 'desire for sovereignty' which leads to 'competition' which leads to 'anarchy, strife and pain'. And on such a large scale, the problems and the pain are also much greater. Therefore, in phase 2, God continues the free-will experiment....but on a much smaller level. (But, like we'll see with humans, Phase 1 was still successful because He is able to enjoy fellowship with many angels, along with the fellowship that He already has within the Trinity).

Chapter 6

Phase 2
Less Powerful Beings
(Adam & Eve: Human Prototypes)

How's this for a smaller level: put the free will beings on a relatively tiny ball, suspended in space, in the middle of a seemingly infinite universe, with no chance of any of the beings on it escaping (and who says that God doesn't have a sense of humor?). Then, put them in physical bodies that are infinitesimally small compared to the size of the ball. Still, Adam and Eve, who even had direct fellowship with God and had to follow only one rule, failed.

Phase 2 of God's experiment with 'free will beings' started with the postulate: Can the new free will beings (humans) maintain holiness (i.e. do what's right, and not do what's wrong) <u>simply</u> by <u>trusting</u> and obeying what God said to do, and to not do?

You see, God always wants life to be <u>as good as possible</u>, both for the free-will beings He creates, and for Himself. So it was very gracious of Him to try to keep the free-will challenge in check with <u>just one rule</u>. He even withheld from them an <u>awareness</u> that anything bad could even happen by making them unaware of 'good and evil'. Now wouldn't this be nice....just one rule, and complete peace (because you're not even aware that something bad could happen.)

But at that point, He was not dealing with a clean slate. The picture was muddied by the fact that there were fallen angels, and there was a Satan, who would like to be sovereign and see God's plans fail (but God will use this <u>bad</u> energy, then and in the future, for <u>good</u> purposes: to test humans and aid them in their growth). So, God didn't allow Satan total power over Adam and Eve. That would defeat <u>His</u> purpose. If Phase 2 was going to fail, it would be because of Adam and Eve's own doing.

I'm sure we all know the story about how it went (if not, read Genesis 3:1-7). Only one tree, the tree of the knowledge of good and evil, stood as a gateway to a lower existence. But like the story in the last chapter from the movie, and as is exemplified in the phrase "curiosity killed the cat", the new free will beings couldn't handle even this one simple restraint.

God even trusted Adam and Eve to the point where He didn't feel like He had to constantly watch over them (at least He would have liked to have lived this way, so He tried it), as can be seen in Gen. 3:9: *"The LORD God then called to the man and asked him, 'Where are you?'"*.

<u>Conclusion from Phase 2:</u> The free will beings need to be given even less power, less freedom, and more rules.

(By the way, there is a misinterpretation among some in the Christian community that says that "We are condemned because of Adam's sin." No, we are condemned by our own sin. Adam and Eve merely showed what could be prototypically expected from human beings: sin.)

Chapter 7

Phase 3

Less Freedom, More Rules (Adam & Eve's Offspring)

So, given that Adam and Eve failed, this is how things were changed: *To the woman He said: I will greatly multiply your sorrow and conception; in pain shall you bring forth children. Your desire shall be for your husband, and he shall rule over you." Then to Adam He said: "Because you have heeded the voice of your wife, and have eaten from the tree of which I commanded you saying 'You shall not eat of it': Cursed is the ground...In toil shall you eat of it all the days of your life. Both thorns and thistles it shall bring forth to you. In the sweat of your face shall you eat bread, till you return to the ground. For out of it you were taken; For dust you are, and to dust you shall return." Then the LORD God said: "Behold, The man has become like one of Us, to know good and evil. And now, lest he put out his hand and take also of the tree of life, and eat and live forever -" therefore the LORD God sent him out of the garden of Eden.* (Gen. 3:16-19, 22,3).

So how did Adam and Eve's Offspring perform, now knowing that there is penalty for disobedience? Would this be enough to achieve God's purpose of having a relationship with human beings without holiness being sacrificed? *And it came to pass, when they were in the field, that Cain rose up against Abel his brother and killed him. Then*

*the LORD said to Cain, "Where is Abel your brother?"
And he said, "I do not know. Am I my brother's keep-
er?"(Gen. 4:8,9); Lamech said to his wives: Adah and
Zillah, hear my voice; O wives of Lamech, listen to my
speech! For I have killed a man for wounding me, Even a
young man for hurting me (Gen. 4:23); the LORD saw that
the wickedness of man was great in the earth, and that
every intent of the thoughts of his heart was only evil continually (Gen. 6:5).*

So then how did God <u>feel</u> about how poorly the
human beings that He loved were performing? He was
*sorry that He had made man on the earth, and He was
grieved in His heart. (Gen. 6:6).*

Sympathy for God

A situation in life that can help us understand and
relate to God's predicament in dealing with free will beings
is: being a parent. (Being that there can be great variations
from parent to parent and from child to child, I'll just relate
what I want to say by using my relationship with one of my
children - Timmy - as an example).

When Timmy was born I was very excited. And
even then I had no idea what a loving being he would soon
become. My relationship with him was what we'd like all
of our relationships in life to be: one that I could pour into
it as much love as I had, and where I got the same back in
return. And he frequently, every day, initiated very pleasurable, loving interactions. Timmy and I definitely were
attached to each other....and greatly enjoying it.

And I didn't want to lose the great quality that this
relationship had. This often meant that whatever Timmy
wanted I would try to give to him. Not because I was afraid
that if I didn't I would lose his love and affection, but

because I loved him so much, I enjoyed giving to him and seeing how happy it made him; (similarly with God, *"It's the Father's good pleasure to give the kingdom to His children."* Luke 12:32). And because I loved him I didn't like to see him be disappointed.

This went on for years. He was one of the best things that ever happened to me in my life...partly because he <u>also</u> enjoyed our relationship so much and was very attached to me.

Everywhere I went he also wanted to go (and it's still pretty much like this). And I always tried to accommodate him. But in those times when I just couldn't take him with me, he'd always stand at the side window waving kisses at me as I got in the car. And I'd do the same back. Then he'd run to the front window and we'd wave more kisses at each other as I drove away. And we'd continue doing this until we were absolutely out of sight from each other. His brother Tony said that he'd continue doing this even after I was out of sight (which he'd also do when he was riding in the car and I was at the window).

And every day there were many instances of great interactions between him and me. In his artwork, he would come up with some of the happiest and most loving viewpoints I'd ever seen. And they would fill my heart with love and joy. They were especially a blessing in a world where most people have become (at least somewhat) calloused, and therefore incapable of this high degree of love. Therefore, I didn't want to see this ability tarnished in him in any way. To a parent who is capable of a high degree of love, with each new child comes a fresh hope for them to be able to maintain a higher state of love (which is the <u>natural</u> state of everyone) than what the world has come to accept as the norm.

Well, in my enjoyment of this relationship, I was unable to foresee the potential problems that might arise out of a person who has pretty much had what they wanted, and also consistently could rely on a very forgiving person to lean on, who would sometimes overlook their faults and faulty reactions for the sake of *peace*. The problem becomes: they'll have a hard time handling the times when they don't get their way. And when they don't, they express emotions that are taxing and toxic to those around them, e.g. disgust, temper, whining, etc. (This also violates the 'what's best for the whole' aspect of God's solution).

But I could never bring myself to be harsh with Timmy (let alone even fathom the thought of spanking him). But then there would be times when I would <u>gently</u> try to explain to him how some of his ways were upsetting people and/or making them angry and not liking him. Well, he'd get upset, angry and cry, thinking that I was mad at him. But I wasn't. I was being very deliberately gentle. Well, his emotional explosions would break the sensitive, loving peace and shock those emotions out of me. These situations would make me sad, mad, emotionally upset, etc. Alas, was our relationship starting to come down a notch or two?

I knew that I didn't want to experience this any-more. And I started noticing that him having this problem was not only starting to hurt his relationship with me, but it was also hurting his relationships with other people (kids and grown-ups). It was not going to be good for him to carry this baggage of bad-habits-in-relating-to-others through life. And it was my responsibility as a parent to see that he (and myself and others) wouldn't have to suffer this burden....even if it meant suffering short periods of distance between him and me to accomplish this.

So I looked to God for guidance in what I should do. Well, there are many examples of this kind of relationship (and its inherent free-will problems) throughout the Bible because: God is our father...and we are His children. And there are two main parallels between my relationship with Timmy and God's relationship with us: (1)the desire to have as loving a relationship as possible ; and (2)the problems of free-will: sometimes wanting its way instead of God's way, sometimes wanting more than it needs, and insensitivity to the fact that these might unfairly come at the expense of others.

What God inspired me to do in my dealings with Timmy is: first try to gently and lovingly explain to him the important lessons I wanted him to learn and understand. But because free will doesn't always want to pay attention, I might sometimes have to withhold something that is dear to him (e.g. part of his allowance, or my willingness to play a game with him at a time when I'd rather do something else, etc.) in order to get his attention and communicate how really important this is.

'Reward and loss' is a great invention by God. He really had to set life up this way if the parts of His solution that say 'fair to all' and 'cause no harm' were going to be fulfilled. Therefore, we all need to be aware that there are things that we will lose (emotionally, physically, and in the quality of our relationships) when we do wrong things. As well, we need to remember that there are things that are gained (emotionally, physically, and in the quality of our relationships) when we do right things...not the least of which is our own inner peace.

Unfortunately, God has had to go to great lengths many times in dealing with people (individually and collectively). And sometimes to very harsh degrees, as is evidenced in God's relationship with the Jewish people in Deuteronomy 28 and 29, where He holds a terrible curse over their head as a threat <u>if</u> they are disobedient. We will look at this very revealing passage in detail in the chapter on the Jewish people. His dealings with people have slipped many more notches down than what I've experience with Timmy (but who knows what the future will bring...he's only 8 years old as of this writing. But, I'm very optimistic because he's very sharp, understands the concepts of God, and although energetic and impulsive, he sides with God and wants to see himself as 'good').

Regarding the popular Bible paraphrase "Spare the rod and spoil the child", the rod being talked about is a <u>guiding</u> rod, not a hitting rod. My assumption that "the rod" can be something other than a hitting rod, or even a physical rod at all, is supported by the following verses: *Who will apply the lash to my thoughts, <u>to my mind the rod of discipline</u>, That my failings may not be spared, nor the sins of my heart overlooked* (Sir. 23:2); *He shall strike the earth with the <u>rod of his mouth</u>* (Isa. 11:4); *I am a man who has seen affliction by the <u>rod of his wrath</u>* (Lam. 3:1); *Foolishness is bound up in the heart of a child, but the <u>rod of correction</u> will drive it far from him.* (Prov. 22:15).

Yes I realize that the Bible does allow for hitting, but only in extreme situations (and heaven knows that God has done some major hitting in His day, as will be evidenced in the next chapter).

When there is a grey area in the Bible, such as: when to hit or when not to hit, the answer must then be revealed to us through our truth channel by the Holy Spirit. If you can't go into deep prayer and feel a peace about a position you've taken, then the wise thing to do is to concentrate on the unpeaceful part of the voice that's coming through you until its message is amplified to where you know what it's trying to say to you. Then look for Biblical support for what it's saying, and modify your position accordingly. Then, if need be, repeat this process until you can go into deep prayer and have a pure peace. (When I say deep prayer, I mean: where we don't manipulate the dialogue...we just listen).

An example of how rods were used in Bible times is 'a shepherd's rod'. When a sheep would go astray, the shepherd would <u>gently</u> guide it back into the fold. He would <u>only</u> increase the force behind his rod <u>as was necessary</u>. And if he were a loving and compassionate shepherd, he would always lean towards being as gentle as possible, and deeply regret ever having to be harsh. Out of all of this, a statement can be made about what a rod is: a fence that keeps behavior within holy guidelines, which exerts its containing force only as much as is necessary.

I hope that Timmy will always value our relationship so much that he'll be willing to submit to my and the Church's Biblical guidance, instead of submitting to his desire for <u>all</u> of his free will impulses (including emotional outbursts that have no consideration for others) to find fulfillment. This is how many of God's children feel towards Him (present company included). And the Bible says that this pleases God: *"Do not forget to do good and to share, for with such sacrifices God is well pleased"* (Heb. 13:16).

But, as we'll see in the upcoming phases, God still has had a tough time of it with people. With Timmy, I'm only dealing with one person (and God has had many successes on the individual level). But God has had to deal with a great number of people...including very stubborn, selfish, self-centered, evildoing and insensitive people, who care nothing about Him.

So now, as you read about the phases that God has gone through with free will beings, keep in mind the inherent problems in the parent/child relationship....especially if you've experienced being a parent. This should give you a new sympathy for God and His predicament, and an understanding of why He's done (He does) what He's done (He does). Also, it will give you a new appreciation for just how much He loves us. Because, as you'll see, we've really been a problem child.

In light of what I just wrote here about the parent/child relationship, what I wrote in chapter 3 under "You bless God" can now be seen much clearer. That is: can your child bless you? Or, to rephrase this, can your child be a blessing to you? Yes, of course. If they are nice and polite, doesn't this make you happy?

Well, when we live in this existence (that God made) the way He would like to see us live in it, don't you think it makes Him happy? Reread the verses in Chapter 3 (the second paragraph under "<u>What the Bible says about God's motive for making us</u>") telling how God finds pleasure in us and you'll see that it obviously does. One of the great shortcomings of modern society is that people don't realize how much of an interactive relationship we have with God. We're not just detached beings floating in space.

So, "glorifying God" doesn't just mean 'holding <u>Him</u> up above everything', it also means 'holding His <u>lifestyle</u> above all lifestyles'. And this doesn't just mean preaching it...it also means: living it.

(Back to our Bible story). Because the descendants of Adam and Eve weren't following the rules, God was grieved (because He is spiritually heart-bonded to them).

So now what was God going to do? How was He going to respond? Was He going to abandon the human experiment altogether...or did He feel like it was worth pressing on? *So the LORD said, "I will destroy man whom I have created from the face of the earth, both man and beast, creeping things and birds of the air, for I am sorry that I have made them."* (Gen. 6:7).

Remember whose experiment this life is

One thing that many (who criticize God, ignore God, follow false gods, or forge their own path) fail to realize is: we are in God's experiment...He's not (supposed to be) in ours. Oh He's allowing us to (semi-)carry on like it's ours....but only for 1 lifetime.

Many new-age philosophies take the position that it's a joint experiment between us and God, where we are a part of God, and have infinite possibilities. But I've seen many of these cosmic fishing expeditions end in disappointment.

The end result of this life is simple: either the spark plug learns to spark when the key is turned....or it is cast into the garbage pile of bad spark plugs.

If this seems harsh to you, once you understand the concept behind this book you'll realize that it isn't. God made holy standards (and built-in punishments if they're not kept) for the protection of others. Spiritual anarchy is good only for those who are on top. It can be hell for those on the bottom. Therefore, realize that the only reasonable bottom-line is: God cannot lower His standards.

Natural disasters

An atheist once said that people believe in God only because they're reaching for comfort from natural disasters and other natural problems (e.g. floods, diseases, death, etc.). But this is not the position of the Bible. The

Bible says that we are sinners. And from the perspective of a perfect God, sinners don't merit comfort, they merit extermination (because they destroy the harmony in a perfect creation that He's trying to maintain). It is an act of mercy for God to spare sinners the death that they deserve (which He didn't do for the flood victims in Noah's time).

The reason why He doesn't spare us from natural disasters is so we won't get too comfortable, and so that our attention will draw to Him, so that we can then see the solution that He's made to save us from our sin tendencies, allowing Him to maintain a sinless existence (which is what we'd all really like). With natural disasters and other discomforts, He is only rebounding the discomfort that our sin is causing Him. In this life, we can try to carve out a comfortable little niche and then live it out or hide away in it. But no one can hide from death. And if we didn't achieve our basic purpose in this life (which I've been explaining) we could end up with a disastrous afterlife. Therefore God, being the loving father that He is, will attempt to work with us throughout our lives in order to try to get us prepared for the judgment after our death of the decisions we made throughout our life. Unfortunately (due to our stubbornness, laziness, and the distractions of this world) He is probably going to have to on occasion rattle our comfort. But the truly wise learn how to flow with this, as well as see the good purposes and lessons in these trials.

God also accomplishes the above through unnatural disasters (man-made and self-made). An example of Him doing this in a man-made disaster is nicely expressed in the phrase: "there are no atheists in a foxhole".

Conclusion from Phase 3: Eliminate all people with a flood and start all over again...but do so with only the holiest people (Noah and his family).

Chapter 8

Phase 4

Start Over With The Holiest (Noah's Offspring)

Noah found grace in the eyes of the LORD. When God saw how corrupt the earth had become, since all mortals led depraved lives on earth, He said to Noah: "I have decided to put an end to all mortals on earth; the earth is full of lawlessness because of them. So I will destroy them and all life on earth. Make yourself an ark of gopherwood. I Myself am bringing the flood of waters on the earth, and everything that is on earth shall die. But I will establish My covenant with you (Gen. 6:8, 12-14, 17, 18).

God sadly had to finally accept the fact that the free-will humans were not capable of holiness, and therefore it was no use in wiping them out again. But He still wanted to work with them.

The LORD said to himself: "Never again will I doom the earth because of man, since the desires of man's heart are evil from the start; nor will I ever again strike down all living beings, as I have done. As long as the earth lasts, seedtime and harvest, cold and heat, Summer and winter, and day and night shall not cease." (Gen. 8:21).

So how did Noah do? He couldn't even maintain holiness for a short while. Here's what happened not long after he got off the ark. *Noah began to be a farmer, and he planted a vineyard. Then he drank of the wine and was drunk, and became uncovered in his tent* (Gen. 9:20,21). Verses 22 and 23 go on to describe this as a calamity for his sons, so much so that they walked in backwards so as to not see his nakedness. This shows that it is God's desire for us to be modest.

Nevertheless, God allows the world to go on and repopulate. But then God sees that a large group of people is capable of unified unholiness. So this is how He responds: *And they said, "Come, let us build ourselves a city, and a tower whose top is in the heavens; let us make a name for ourselves; lest we be scattered abroad over the face of the whole earth." But the LORD came down to see the city and the tower which the sons of men had built. And the LORD said: "If now, while they are one people, all speaking the same language, they have started to do this, nothing will later stop them from doing whatever they presume to do. Come let Us go down and there confuse their language, that they may not understand one another's speech." So the LORD scattered them over the face of the earth, and they ceased building the city* (Gen. 11:4-8).

By the way, herein lies another piece of evidence that God does improvise and doesn't have complete foreknowledge. Here He rejects working with one group of people. But this is something that He will do again later with the Jews. So, He changed His mind. We also just saw two other incidents where God changed His mind. He said that He regretted that He ever made man....but then He allowed man to once again populate the earth. Also, He emotionally reacted and wiped people off of the earth with a flood...but then He said that He'd never do that again. If He knew that He was going to come to this conclusion, wouldn't He have just not done it in the first place?

Those who argue in favor of predestination have used as proof Rev.13:8 (*All the inhabitants of the earth will worship it, all whose names were not written from the foundation of the world in the book of life, which belongs to the Lamb who was slain*). The key word here is "from". They say that "from" means "at" or "during". But this is incorrect. There are 5 words in Greek for "from". The one used here is "απθ". The Greek dictionary says that this word means neither "at" nor "during". Rather, it means "since". So now rereading Rev. 13:8, we can see that the names of God's people weren't written before they were born, but rather, their names have been added as they've become saved.

(Back to our story.) As the scattered peoples of the world repopulate, some groups are holier than others. But once again, it's generally a mess. Sodom and Gomorrah, which God destroyed because of their homosexuality (see Genesis 18,19:1-29) are just 2 examples.

The question now arises: can <u>any</u> group of people achieve holiness? We've had so many different types of people-groupings throughout history, and we even still have many different ones on the planet today. Yet, none of them have achieved holiness. All have had sin: greed, corruption, 'man's-inhumanity-to-man', sins of the flesh, turning away from God, idol-worship, human-worship, etc.

<u>Conclusion from Phase 4:</u> Choose* just one group of people to work with: the Jews (*hence the name: the chosen people). Give them a very strict and specific set of rules, and a sacrificial system for when they break those rules (i.e. when they break the rules, they must give up something that they value). See how this works.

Chapter 9

Phase 5

One Physical Group Of People (The Chosen People)

God has now accepted the fact that humanity can't be trusted to be holy on its own. And yet, holiness is the standard that God needs to achieve. So, God must now step in and give humanity a very complete and specific set of rules to govern their behavior....and punishments/sacrifices when they break those rules. But to do this with all people on the earth would not necessary for this phase of the experiment. So He chooses one group of people to work with: the descendants of Abraham, whom He'll make a covenant with to do this.

The new emphasis on rules will be very focused. This is definitely a step down for God and humanity, but it is better to sacrifice freedom for holiness, instead of sacrificing holiness for freedom. The reason being: when holiness is sacrificed, innocent victims are made to suffer.

So where does God start? He starts with a leader of the new chosen people. And being that this is going to be a system that is based on 'obedience to laws', many of which require trust, the new leader must be capable of the highest degree of trust. So God sets out to give Abraham one of the toughest tests of trust imaginable: He asks Him to sacrificially kill his son. You can read this story in (Gen 22:1-18), but suffice to say here: Abraham passed the test. One of the blessings that God promised to Abraham was: *"In your seed all the nations of the earth shall be blessed, because you have obeyed my voice."* (Gen. 22:18). So this shows that God did intend to eventually make a covenant with the whole human race. And He did so through one of Abraham's descendants: Jesus.

Eventually Moses became the leader of the Jewish people. And God gave Moses 613 laws (including the 10 commandments). These laws can be read in the books of Exodus, Leviticus and Deuteronomy. I heavily urge you to read these laws because it shows how far our laws today are from what God would like them to be. Most of the punishments are: death by stoning. A truly horrible way to die, but as can be imagined, must have been very effective in keeping sin to a minimum (although not totally effective, which is why a new covenant was eventually needed).

This is what God's 2-way covenant was with the Jewish people: *You shall not bow down to them* (idols or false gods) *nor serve them. For I, the LORD your God, am a jealous God, inflicting punishments for their fathers' wickedness on the children of those who hate me, down to the third and fourth generation but bestowing mercy, down to the thousandth generation, on the children of those who love me and keep my commandments* (Deut. 5:9,10). *Would that they might always be of such a mind, to fear me and to keep all my commandments! Then they and their descendants would prosper forever* (Deut. 5:29). *Now therefore, if you will indeed obey My voice and keep My covenant, then you shall be a special treasure to Me above all people, though all the earth is Mine* (Exod. 19:5). Also read Deut. 29:9-27, 30:1-31:9, and Lev. 26:3-43.

So now how and when did God decide that this 'chosen people' phase wasn't going to be sufficient enough to accomplish the holy standard He desired?

Now the LORD appeared at the tabernacle in a pillar of cloud. And the Lord said to Moses: Behold, you will rest with your fathers; and this people will rise and play the harlot with the gods of the foreigners of the land, and they will foresake Me and break My covenant which I have made with them. Then My anger shall be aroused against them in that day, and I will foresake them, and I will hide My face from them, and they shall be devoured. And many evils and troubles shall befall them, so that they will say in that day, 'have not these evils come upon us because our God is not among us?' And I will surely hide My face in that day because of all the evil which they have done, in that they have turned to other gods. Now therefore, write down this song for yourselves, and teach it to the children of Israel. When I have brought them to the land flowing with milk and honey, of which I swore to their fathers, and they have eaten and filled themselves and grown fat, then they will turn to other gods and serve them; and they will provoke Me and break My covenant. Then it shall be, when many evils and troubles have come upon them, as a witness; for it will not be forgotten in the mouths of their descendants, for I know the inclination of their behavior today, even before I have brought them to the land of which I swore to give them." (Deut. 31:15-21).

So, Moses taught them the song so that they would remember God's covenant. So what did they do? *He had them ride triumphant over the summits of the land and live off the produce of the fields* (Deut. 32:13). He made plentiful for them: honey, oil, curds, milk, fat of lambs, rams, the choicest wheat and wine...to the point where they grew to be *"covered with fat"*. Then they *"foresook God who made them, and scornfully esteemed the Rock of their salvation. They provoked Him with strange gods and angered Him with abominable idols. They offered sacrifice to demons, to "no-gods," to gods whom they had not known before, of whom their fathers had never stood in awe. You were unmindful of the Rock that begot you, You forgot the God who gave you birth. When the Lord saw this, He was filled with loathing and anger toward His sons and daughters. "I will hide my face from them," He said, and see what will then become of them. What a fickle race they are, sons with no loyalty in them! "Since they have provoked Me with their 'no-god' and angered Me with their vain idols, I will provoke them with a 'no-people'; I will spend on them woe upon woe and exhaust all My arrows against them"* (Deut. 32:15-23). (The 'no-god' philosophy should sound familiar to the current residents of the United States.) This also sounds like it could be one source of the many woes of the Jewish people throughout history. God did put a curse on the Jewish people if they didn't follow His laws: *"If you are not careful to observe every word of the law which is written in this book, and to revere the glorious and awe-some name of the Lord, your God, He will smite you and your descendants with severe and constant blows, malig-nant and lasting maladies* (Deut. 28:58,59).

Also read: Ps. 106 (e.g. Ps. 106:39,40: *They were defiled by their own works, And played the harlot by their own deeds. Therefore the wrath of the Lord was kindled against His people, so that He abhorred His own heritage.*) and Ex 32:7-14.

The Jewish people were dealt their harshest blow when the ego and greed of their main religious leaders set Jesus up to be killed (Matt. 23, 26, 27). But Jesus, knowing what was going to happen to Him, told them that because of the evil they were going to do, God was now finally going to abandon them (*Behold, your house will be aban-*

doned, desolate. Matt. 23:38), and He wouldn't return to them until His second coming as Messiah (*you shall see Me no more till you say, 'Blessed is He who comes in the name of the Lord.* Matt. 23:39). Jesus also made this gloomy prediction concerning them: *Therefore, indeed, I send you prophets, wise men and scribes; some of them you will kill and crucify, and some of them you will scourge in your synagogues and persecute from city to city, that on you may come all the righteous blood shed upon earth, from the blood of righteous Abel to the blood of Zechariah, whom you murdered between the temple and the altar. Assuredly, I say to you, all these things will come upon this generation. "O Jerusalem, Jerusalem, the one who kills the prophets and stones those who are sent to her! How often I wanted to gather your children together, as a hen gathers her chicks under her wings, but you were not willing! Behold, your house will be abandoned, desolate"* Matt. 23:34-38. And He said this concerning Jerusalem and its temple: *His disciples came to Him to show Him the buildings of the temple. And Jesus said to them, "Do you not see all these things? Assuredly, I say to you, not one stone shall be left here upon another, that shall not be thrown down"* (Matt. 24:1,2). Also once, Jesus, drawing near to Jerusalem, looked at it and wept over it, saying, *"For the days will come when your enemies will surround you, and level you, and your children within you, to the ground; and they will not leave in you one stone upon another, because you did not recognize the time of your visitation"* (Luke 19:42-44).These prophesies were fulfilled 37 years later when the Roman army completely leveled Jerusalem.

God's love/anger relationship with fickle Israel is another proof that He changes His mind. First He blesses them with a homeland and prosperity; then they sin excessively and turn their backs on Him; then He gets angry and scatters them; then He blesses them with a return to their homeland and prosperity; then they sin excessively and turn their backs on Him; then He gets angry and scatters them; then He blesses them with a return to their homeland and prosperity; then they sin excessively and turn their backs on Him; then He gets angry and scatters them; etc. (God, who, in the Bible, says He hates divorce, really shows that He practices what He preaches in His loyalty to Israel, which He even still maintains).

For example: in Ezek. 36:19 He judges and scatters; but then, like with the reunion of two separated mates, God returns His people to their homeland (v.23,24) with gifts and great intentions of making it work this time (v.25-30). (Jer. 3:20 even describes Israel as being like an unfaithful lover). But, like with reuniting mates, to clear the slate He desires them to repent of their wrongdoings against Him (v.31,32). But then He goes back to His gift-giving (v.33-38). When reading this, you can't help but feel kind of sad for God because you know His mate is going to abuse Him again. As an earthly husband I can somewhat identify with God's feelings here. All that a mate wants is for their spouse to be holy so that they can continue to completely love them without restraint. But then a mate experiences jealousy and anger when they see their spouse getting pulled into an evil world. So husbands and wives, don't get down on yourself if you find yourself getting righteously jealous and angry. Jealousy is just the feeling that God designed in us that alerts us when the glue that bonds our marriage is being tested. You're just living out what your Creator has put in your heart - for the good purposes of maintaining your family and a standard of holiness. You were made to be that way - in God's image.

Another relationship that is analogous to this situation is: parent/child.

Judaism today

So what is the status of Jews with God today? There are a lot of things that can be said, pro and con (some of which I will soon spell out). But I think that in the final analysis, the following conclusion can be drawn: (1)the system of Judaism had proven its point, was declared to be inadequate, and was *phased* out by God. That is: sin...sacrifice...sin...sacrifice.., etc. The sacrificial system doesn't work because it doesn't stop people from sinning (which is the only acceptable objective). They just keep on sinning and become numb to the fact that they'll have to sacrifice and pay a price....a price which they eventually decide they are willing to pay. Even some of the best Jewish leaders committed some very heavy sins (e.g. David). And even today's Jews have phased out the sacrificial system (along with most of the Law). (2)On the other hand: God does still save (*some*) Jews (just like He only saves *some* who *call themselves* Christians. Once again: "You shall know them by their fruit"). I'll now make some points to support the above two assumptions.

One way that Judaism and Christianity can be seen as logically co-existing is in the idea of 'Messiah'. The Jews were looking for a <u>military</u> Messiah to save them. But did a sinning people deserve to be saved? No. Besides, God had a bigger plan. So He sent a <u>humble and submissive</u> Messiah, who would teach people that humbleness and submission are the essence of what makes a godly kingdom work, not military might. But, God does have a military phase planned to finally eliminate evil. This is what the Jews were looking for (and it's what all believers now look for). So Jews and Christians now look for the same Messiah. But why did many Jews (that is, the ones who didn't become Christians) miss this important lesson the first time around?

<u>Why the Jews don't recognize Jesus as the Messiah</u>

The Jews don't see Jesus as Messiah because they were expecting a military victor who would bring justice and peace to the world. And obviously, there has not been complete justice or peace since Jesus came. But Jesus' first coming was just the beginning of the 'Messianic Age'. The end of this age is when the military victory will happen and the justice and peace will come. But this first 2000 years of the Messianic Age has been equally important. It's where Jesus planted a seed (by setting down an example of how we're to be - submissive, not militaristic), and then allowed 2000 years for the harvesting of souls. Messiah couldn't just simply come and establish justice and peace. God already proved that that wouldn't work (that is, if free will was going to continue to be allowed <u>and</u> holiness was going to be established).

I mean, it's very ironic that most of the people in the world are following a Jewish Rabbi (Jesus) and a book that is written almost entirely by Jews (the Bible) and yet most Jews aren't even in on it. Could it be that God blinds the non-Christian Jews from seeing the truth (just like He blinded Pharaoh) because He wants to continue His relationship and covenants with the Jewish people in a specific way for a specific reason? Romans 11:7,8 says that this is the case: *"What then? Israel has not obtained what it seeks; but the elect have obtained it, and the rest were hardened. Just as it is written: God has given them a spirit of deep sleep, eyes that should not see and ears that should not hear, down to this very day."* (Also, read John 12:40 and 2Cor. 3:13-16).

Jewish leader, Rabbi Lapide, acknowledged the legitimacy of Jesus by saying that Jesus was probably sent by God to bring the Gentiles back into the fold. So obviously, he sees Christianity and Judaism logically co-existing, both under the same God. What God did set up with the Jews was complete (if only they would have followed the Law). Actually, I would love it if this nation's laws were to be the Mosaic Laws. *Happy those who do not follow the counsel of the wicked, Nor go the way of sinners, nor sit in company with scoffers. But his delight is in the law of the Lord, and in his law he meditates day and night.* (Ps 1:1,2). *Happy those whose way is blameless, who walk by the teaching of the Lord. Happy those who observe God's decrees, who seek the Lord with all their heart* (Ps. 119:1,2).

The bottom-line here is that the only way for a Jewish person to determine if they need to accept Jesus in order to be saved...or if they are still just under the old covenant is for each Jewish person to look deep into their heart and answer this question for themselves.

But, there are many Jews (who often call themselves "completed Jews") who are Christians (not to mention that most of the first Christians were Jews. Even in the first century, Christianity wasn't called Christianity by most of the world...it was called the New Judaism). And many Jewish Christians have been very strong influences in the Christian community. Besides St. Paul (who emphasized that the new covenant was both for Jew and gentile, but first for the Jew) and the other New Testament writers (one of whom was the first pope: Peter), today there are: Jews For Jesus, Jay Sekulow (leading lawyer for the ACLJ, the leading legal arm of the Christian community in its fights against anti-Christian laws and unholy laws in the U.S.), Zola Levitt, etc. Also, in the entertainment industry there's: Kathy Lee Gifford, Diane Cannon, Bob Dylan, etc.

Other points that show how some of today's Jews will be saved: (1)God made covenants with and promises to the Jewish people that He won't break. (2)Rev. 7:4 says that there will be 144,000 from the 12 tribes of Israel who will be spared from "the great day of wrath". (3)There are many Jews today (who haven't become Christians) who still show a great love for and interest in God, and who defend God and godliness in the public forums (e.g. movie critic Michael Medved and talk show host Dennis Prager, and also a great number of Orthodox Jews). (4)*Those things which are revealed belong to us and our children <u>forever</u>, that we may do all the words of this law* (Deut. 29:29). (5)There are Jews in heaven: *There will be weeping and gnashing of teeth, when you see Abraham, Isaac, and Jacob and all the prophets in the kingdom of God and you yourselves cast out* (Luke 13:28). (6)A main focus in the end times is Jerusalem. (7)God has set a standard by which Jews will be judged: *"as many as have sinned <u>under the law</u> will be judged by the law"* (Rom. 2:12).

But if your flesh has a Jewish heritage, this won't be enough...you must be a spiritual Jew: *For he is not a Jew who is one outwardly, nor is that circumcision which is outward in the flesh; but he is a Jew who is one inwardly, and circumcision is of the heart, in the spirit, not the letter* (Rom. 2:28-29).

St. Paul says: *I say then, has God rejected His people? Certainly not! For I also am an Israelite, of the seed of Abraham, of the tribe of Benjamin. God has not rejected His people whom He foreknew. I say then, have they stum-*

*bled that they should fall? Certainly not! But through their
fall, salvation has come to the Gentiles. For if their rejection is the reconciliation of the world, what will their
acceptance be but life from the dead? I do not desire,
brethren, that you should be ignorant of this mystery, lest
you should be wise in your own opinion, a hardening has
in part happened to Israel until the full number of the
Gentiles comes in, and so all Israel will be saved, as it is
written: "The deliverer will come out of Zion and He will
turn away ungodliness from Jacob; for this is my covenant
with them when I take away their sins." Concerning the
gospel, they are enemies for your sake, but concerning the
election, they are beloved for the sake of the patriarchs.
For the gifts and the calling of God are <u>irrevocable</u>. For as
you were once disobedient to God, yet have now obtained
mercy through their disobedience, even so these also have
now been disobedient, that through the mercy shown you,
they also may obtain mercy. For God has committed them
all to disobedience, that He might have mercy on all* (Rom.
11:1,2,11,15,25-32).

<u>Orthodox, Conservative or Reformed?</u>

      Just like in the Christian community, there are
denominational differences in the Jewish community. But
let me point to a scripture that repudiates the basic tenant
of the Conservative and Reformed movements in Judaism
(which says that what the Bible says can be modified to fit
modern times): *You shall not add to the word which I command you, nor subtract anything from it* (Deut. 4:2). And
remember, this is a quote from the Jewish Bible. Within
Judaism, there was no reason to have changed how God
wants Jewish priests to conduct themselves. And, regarding the law: murder is murder, adultery is adultery, theft is

theft, etc. Why should God's expressed wishes for their punishments (in the laws He gave to Moses) be changed? (I wonder how many of today's Jews are for capital punishment, censorship, etc.). And (if you don't accept Jesus as the final sacrifice) why should the need to 'sacrifice for our sins' be changed?

Talk show host Dennis Prager (who is Jewish) once made a great point. He said in essence that there are Jews...and then there are Jews. That is, the term "Jew" relates to a nationality <u>and</u> a religion. He said that a lot of seriously religious Jews are hurt by the fact that they are lumped in with a lot of (e.g.) 'Steinbergs and Epsteins' who call themselves "Jews" but who are very anti what Judaism stands for. *Not all who are Israelites are true Israelites, nor are they all children of Abraham because they are his descendants* (Rom. 9:6,7). (Of course, Christians have a similar problem in that many who call themselves Christians are living lives that have a lot of unholiness in them, and they are consumers of a lot of the unholiness that is in the public markets and supporters of a lot of the unholiness that is in the public forums). A big point that I'm trying to make here is: it's not Jews vs. Christians vs. Muslims vs. etc. It's: the true children of God vs. the satanic world.

<u>Conclusion from Phase 5</u>: A group of people, who God works with closely and who are given a very complete and specific set of laws that could create a holy environment, is not able to completely submit to God and be holy. Therefore, God's covenant had to change from being one with a group of people to being one that is with individuals. It had to go from one that is based on 'strict adherence to laws' to one that is based on a '<u>spirit</u> of not wanting to break the law....out of free will, and out of love'.

Chapter 10

Phase 6

One Spiritual Group Of People
(The Final Sacrifice: Jesus)

Alas, free will beings have failed in being able to accomplish 'continual holiness' in any type of setting. So this brings us to the phase we are now in: the Christian era.

Premise (hypothesis) for Phase 6 - the best that a free-will being is able to do is: (1)make their #1 desire be 'wanting to do the right thing', (2)know what the right thing is (God's holy standards), (3)heart-bond to God, giving their allegiance to Him (instead of 'the world'), and (4)then spend the rest of their life trying their best to bridle and transform their flesh, surrender to agape, bear the sins of the world without participating in them, and obeying God's commandments.

Based on this premise, God made a new covenant with people. And He enacted this new covenant through the life and ministry of Jesus. The fact that a new covenant was established through Jesus, and that it was a fulfillment of <u>many</u> (113) Old Testament prophesies, is well documented in many books (including the Bible). I'll leave it to the reader to pursue this reading. A good place to start would be the book of Hebrews, and a New Testament word study on "the Law". Also there are many very obvious prophesies about Jesus' life in Isaiah 49-57.

A number of other things were accomplished in Jesus' life and ministry.

First, Jesus was a living, uncompromising, open and honest example of how God wants us all to be. And through His life and teachings, He showed and told us very specifically how God wants us to be. The Law emphasized how our actions should be, while Jesus emphasized how our attitudes should be.

Secondly, God showed just how much He cares about us and how fair He is by coming down and experiencing the same human and earthly settings that we have to experience. And because He allowed Himself to suffer more than any of us ever will, He showed how absolutely necessary this life on planet earth is (including its suffering) in order for us to realize that multi-sovereignty doesn't work. [That Jesus <u>is</u> God is stated in the following verses: *In the beginning was the Word, and the Word was with God, and the Word was God. He was in the beginning with God. All things were made through Him, and without Him nothing was made* (John 1:1-3). (If you continue reading this chapter you'll see that there's no doubt that "He" is Jesus). *Then God said, "Let <u>Us</u> make man in <u>Our</u> image, after <u>Our</u> likeness"* (Gen. 1:26). *"The <u>author of life</u> you put to death, but God raised Him from the dead; of this we are witnesses"* (Acts 3:15). *"I came down from heaven"* (John 6:38,41,51). *Believe me that I am in the Father and the Father is in me, or else, believe because of the works themselves* (John 14:11). *"Works"*: the miracles He performed.]

Thirdly, Jesus' ministry concluded in a blood sacrifice of Himself, finalizing the transition out of the (blood) sacrificial system. The idea here is: only a sinless person could truly make what could be considered a sacrifice (because they don't deserve any punishment). A sinner's death would not be considered to be a sacrifice being that, in God's eyes, a sinner (which all have been) deserves death anyway. Heb. 10:1-3 describes why the sacrificial system didn't work and a new covenant was needed: *the law ..can never with these same sacrifices, which they offer continually year by year, make those who approach perfect. For then would they not have ceased to be offered? For the worshippers, once cleansed, would have no more consciousness of sins. But in those sacrifices there is a reminder of sins every year.*

The reason that God would have liked for a whole group of people to have accepted His laws is because the problems of free will only show up when there is interaction between people and they have dependent need of one another. Therefore, if an individual is holy, but those who they're tied to aren't, holiness is not established (but victimization of these holy individuals usually is). Therefore, God must move throughout the entire world and harvest individuals who are devoted to Him and then reassemble them in heaven. This is where He can have His group. (Also, at times, we can experience holiness on earth via: church, the family, service to God, holy friendships, holy media, and in our fellowship with God).

Conclusion from Phase 6: The only workable covenant between God and free will beings is one that is based on the earlier premise which stated: "The best that a free will being can do is to align with God and then try their best to obey Him". The new covenant becomes: anyone who (1)surveys all of life and recognizes that Jesus' ways surpass all other ways, (2)freely chooses Him and His ways over all else (surrendering their life and sovereignty to Him as their Lord), and (3)tries their best to obey His and the rest of the Bible's teachings and submit to the Holy Spirit; they can then (4)also accept His gift of being their savior (making them eligible to be closer to God, now and in heaven).

'Having a good spirit in what we do' is much more desirable than 'begrudgingly obeying a strict set of laws'. We can easily <u>feel</u> this reality by asking ourselves which of these two approaches would we rather the people in our life take (family, friends, coworkers, etc.).

This 'good spirit' is really what God has been after all along. Therefore, in the new covenant, He now will just focus on our spirit because: if a person's spirit is right (and they have a knowledge of God's laws) they will automatically do right (and will be nice to be around). Therefore, in the new covenant, God released us from <u>bondage</u> to the law. *But if you are led by the Spirit, you are not under the law* (Gal. 5:18).

The gift of the Holy Spirit

Being that God was now going to deal with human beings on an individual level, He gave us a super bonus with this new covenant....individual instruction, guidance and vision within each one of our hearts, via: the Holy Spirit. (The fact that God gave us a Helper in this new covenant to 'aid us in being successful in our new circumstances' might mean that something similar will happen to help us be successful in an even more demanding setting: a perfectly holy heaven. As you'll see later, this is the case).

As Christians, we sometimes are dumfounded that so many people in the world 'don't get it'. That is, it seems like it should be very obvious to all that 'God and His Bible are good' and 'the basic world philosophy is evil'. 2Cor. 4:3-4 shows two factors why many people aren't seeing these things: (1)they are being blinded by the rampant darkness; and (2)the gospel is slightly "veiled" to cause us to have to dig for the truth, so that only sincere seekers will find it. My son Timmy made this analogy: it's like looking at a goldmine. At first glance it looks like an ordinary bunch of rocks and dirt. But if you dig enough, you find treasures. John 14:16-17 also shows why we shouldn't be astonished that so many aren't getting it: *And I will pray the Father, and He will give you another Helper, that He may abide with you forever, even the Spirit of truth, whom the world cannot accept, because it neither <u>sees</u> Him nor <u>knows</u> Him; But you know Him, for He dwells with you, and will be <u>in</u> you.*

And what a tremendous gift the Holy Spirit is. He lets us understand scripture; He gives us very pleasurable feelings (e.g. love, highness, knowing, comfort and peace); He gives us vision, clarity, insight, in*spir*ation, and guidance; He keeps the darkness from blinding our eyes (1John 2:11); He is the One who puts the messages in our truth channel; He gives us 'spiritual gifts'.....that is, spiritual talents so we can serve the body of Christ (the Church) and the world; He is our umbilical cord to God (1Cor. 2:10); He presents our prayers to God, first putting them in a presentable form (Rom. 8:26); and when it is said that God authored the Bible, He did so via the Holy Spirit putting words in the human writers' minds (2Tim. 3:16).

How to choose Jesus as your Lord

There are two good ways to tune in to Jesus. (1)Read His words for yourself. You'll see that He's truly coming from a higher place. And His words will excite your mind and elevate your spirit. (2)Watch "The Greatest Story Ever Told", a movie about His life, death, and resurrection. Then decide...whose side are you on (I mean, we usually do pick sides in a movie). So, whose side are you on...the evil Pharisees' (the world), or Jesus' (the Kingdom of God)? Now if you rooted for Jesus, you're half way there. The other half is this: do you feel such an empathy for Jesus that you want to truly and completely be on His side? If you do, you're going to at some point recognize that besides your love and exuberance for Jesus and the Kingdom of God, you also have *within your flesh* a side that tends to do, say and think unholy things..as well as the fact that you've done unholy things throughout your life. The way to handle this problem is this: tell Jesus that you are very sorry and ashamed that you committed these sins in the past, and that you will sincerely try your very hardest to never sin again, so that you can feel worthy to be counted as one of His followers. Then ask Jesus to forgive your sins...and help you to sin no more. If you said this prayer...Amen...and welcome to the greatest of all Kingdoms on this earth. And it is one that will continue after this life...in a much more glorious form.

But know that in the Kingdom of God there are many responsibilities. If you don't try your hardest to meet those responsibilities, then you're not truly in the Kingdom of God, *"If you love Me, you will keep My commandments"* (John 14:15). The kingdom of the world gives the <u>illusion</u> that 'things are o.k'. but that's just so Satan can trick people into his sinful webs. And it is Satan who is the master of this kingdom, otherwise he wouldn't have been able to offer it to Jesus (*Then the devil, taking Him up on a high mountain, showed Him all the kingdoms of the world in a moment of time. And the devil said to Him, "All this authority I will give You, and their glory; for it has been handed over to me, and I give it to whomever I wish. Therefore, if You worship me, all will be Yours"* Luke 4:5-7; *Jesus answered, "My kingdom is not of this world. If My kingdom were of this world, My servants would fight so that I should not be delivered to the Jews; But now My kingdom is not from here."* John 18:36). When I say the 'kingdom of the world', I don't mean the physical world...I'm speaking of a spiritual world. And I'm speaking about the one that is glorified in the 'secular church' (television), the media, the entertainment industry, the government, and the education system. And Satan is the spirit behind all of these. I mean, how often do you hear God mentioned in any of them? It's almost like it's taboo to talk about Him in these forums. So obviously, these are not His domains.

Another way to discern the difference between the Kingdom of God and the kingdom of the world is by the spirit of its citizens, media, entertainment industry, and the popular activities in it. The Bible clearly delineates between what good spiritual attributes are, and what bad ones are.

Now the works of the flesh are obvious: immorality, impurity, sensuality, idolatry, sorcery, hatreds, rivalry, jealousy, outbursts of fury, acts of selfishness, dissensions, factions, occasions of envy, drinking bouts, orgies, and the like. I warn you, as I warned you before, that those who do such things will not inherit the kingdom of God. In contrast, the fruit of the Spirit is love, joy, peace, patience, kindness, generosity, faithfulness, gentleness, self-control. (Gal. 5:19)

Here are some other verses that point out what love is and what love isn't. (1Cor. 13:4-8) *"Love is patient, love is kind, and is not jealous. Love does not brag, and is not arrogant. Love does not act unbecomingly. It does not seek it's own, is not provoked, does not take into account a wrong suffered, does not rejoice in unrighteousness, but rejoices with the truth. Love bears all things, hopes all things, endures all things. Love never fails".* (Gal. 5:26) *"Let us not become boastful, challenging one another, envying one another".*

(Excerpts from Matthew 5:3-16) *"Love mourns, is gentle, hungers and thirsts for righteousness, is merciful, is pure in heart, is peacemaking, is persecuted for the sake of righteousness, is the salt of the earth, is the light of the world, produces good works."*

The following checklist further spells out some ways that love is and isn't. Can you think of any more that can be added to this list?

IS	ISN'T
Patient	Envying
Kind	Boasting
Rejoices in truth	Rude
Protective	Quick-tempered
Trusting	Holding grudges
Hopeful	Provoked
Persevering	Impatient
Positive	Offensive
Growing	Worrying
Bearing	Cynical
Responsible	Negative
Giving	Arrogant
Knowing God	Tense
A gift from God	Critical
Reverent	Demanding
Seeing everyone as equal	Nagging
Hungering for truth	Irritable
Productive	Resentful
Perfect order	Money-loving
Sensitive	Conceited
Compassionate	Complaining
Considerate	Pessimistic
Grieved by evil	Selfish
Harmonious	Whining
Relaxed	Conniving
Contributing	Boisterous
Constructive	Argumentative
Creative	Greedy
Submissive	Taking advantage

IS	ISN'T
Uplifting	Destructive
Helpful	Frantic
Forgiving	Critical of goodness
Caring	Delighting in evil
Humble	Stubborn
Modest	Insensitive
Gentle	Hateful
Cooperative	Revengeful
Self-sacrificing	Encouraging others to do wrong
Meek	Hyper
Glass 1/2 full	Glass 1/2 empty
Polite	Overbearing

Another good thing this list can do is, after we evaluate our own self in terms of it, we can see that we've got a lifetime worth of work to do just on ourselves, without having to worry so much about what others are doing. (*Why do you notice the splinter in your brother's eye, but do not perceive the wooden beam in your own eye? How can you say to your brother, 'Let me remove that splinter from your eye,' while the wooden beam is in your eye? You hypocrite, remove the wooden beam from your eye first; then you will see clearly to remove the splinter from your brother's eye. Matt. 7:3-5*).

A very comforting passage in the Bible is where Jesus tells us (amidst our self-work) to <u>be anxious for nothing</u> in Matt 6:25-32. This is then capped off by the tremendous verse in which Jesus makes life so simple: *Seek first the kingdom of God and His righteousness, and all these things shall be added to you* (Matt. 6:33). This lightens our load tremendously. Our focus in life all boils down to <u>just one</u> basic thing. All of this shows that 'just living life in the light of being clean and acceptable to God' would be enough to completely fill our life and give it a great sense of good purpose.

The image of Jesus

Obviously people can't see Jesus today. And there are no videos, photographs or cassette series. But what is a cassette? It is: words...delivered with a flow of feelings. So then we do have something very close to a cassette: Jesus' words in the Bible....delivered by His Spirit within us.

But what about those who are insensitive to God's Spirit? How are they to know the true Jesus? One way is for them to read His words in the Bible. But people are often very busy and/or distracted these days. So then what is more immediately visible that could motivate them to take the time to read His words? There are only 4 things left: preachers, media, other Christians, and visuals.

Christian media contains a mixed bag of good and bad examples of Christianity, but is not nearly as visible as the mainstream. The general state of 'preachers' and churches also gets a mixed review. And like with the Bible, people are less and less taking the time to go to them.

As for 'other Christians', well, sometimes it's hard to tell who they are. And once this ice has been broken it's still mostly a one on one situation. This leads me to the last category, about which I have a lot to say: visuals.

I've already spoken (in Chapter 1) about how Jesus' image in the world has been tarnished recently by the bad fruit and scandals of many of the more visible (so-called) Christian preachers. So then what else is easily visible about Jesus by which people can make an evaluation about Him? Well, there are many physical images around us of Jesus: paintings, statues and crucifixes. The fact that they all look so different says that He probably looked like none of them. The 'Shroud of Turin' has the best chance of being authentic because of its scientific and historic plausibility, and because it fits what the Bible says. A person's appearance has two aspects to it: the physical look, and the vibe emitted. Jesus' vibe was: submissive, strong, centered, grieved, loving and purposeful. He wasn't hyper, jivy or syrupy. As for His physical look, here's what the Bible has to say: *There was in Him no stately bearing to make us look at Him, nor appearance that would attract us to Him.* (Is. 53:2).

Physical appearance is not important to God (*For the Lord does not see as man sees; For man looks at the outward appearance, but the Lord looks at the heart.* 1Sam 16:7), nor to Jesus (*Jesus answered, "My Kingdom is not of this world."* John 18:36). If Jesus would've been handsome this would've detracted from His message, which was all about inner beauty. But the world has lost a reverence for inner beauty, and just worships and elevates those who possess outer beauty.

In my younger years I was told that I was physically attractive. But what good did this do? It incited a lot of opportunities for adultery, out of which came a lot of harm. And to maintain this level of attractiveness I had to spend a lot of time dieting (which has left physical damage), lifting weights, exercising, and being very clothes-and-hair conscious. But what a vain and wasteful way to spend my time. Plus it does nothing good for what really matters: the Kingdom of God, others' well-being, my eternity, and my life here on earth. I had an important decision to make: was I going to devote my time to 'looking good'...or 'being good'?

If people are going to truly achieve happiness in this society, it would be very helpful if it traded in its 'nordic track' and 'abs' mentality for a 'Bible, holiness and love' mentality. (*Charm is deceptive and beauty is vain* Prov. 31:30). People should look at their motives for vanity and see if they're healthy and holy. And if they aren't healthy and are based on insecurities, peer pressure, lust or ego, they should free themselves from their slavery to these problems and transfer their energy to 'working on these inner problems' (for which the Bible is the best resource available).

When a person judges a book by its cover, they risk getting bad contents. Now Jesus, who has the greatest content ever, doesn't need to be <u>sold</u> with a 'worldly' physical appearance. Actually, it's a distraction and can hurt His image with sincere seekers...making Him look shallow.

The perfectly coiffed and syrupy 'Welcome to Disneyland' look..or the spacy 'Isn't this LSD great?' look...or the 'leading men of Hollywood step aside' look..all are gross misrepresentations of the true Jesus. These are all projections of human artists' spiritually limited and immature concepts of how <u>they'd</u> like Jesus to look.

I would very much like the Shroud of Turin to be true, because I would like to think that Jesus anticipated that people would misrepresent His physical image, and therefore He'd need to leave something behind to set the record straight. This is important because there is so much that is communicated in a face. Misrepresentation here even clouds how His message is perceived.

And have you ever noticed how each image of Jesus is usually the same nationality as the artist? Voltaire had a great thing to say about this: God made man in His image, and ever since, man has been returning the favor.

Also, don't be confused by the many 'images' of God, the saints, Satan, angels, the apostles, Moses and other Bible people. Remember, <u>these aren't photographs</u>. They are artists' renderings.

The Oxford Illustrated History Of Christianity states: "The Roman Church, like its rivals, tried to use the Bible as a control of aesthetic inspiration. The Council of Trent wanted New Testament incidents depicted with no other details than the gospels supplied". This is still carried on by some Protestant sects. I say amen to this because in nearly all of the religious artwork I've seen, there are sinful misinterpretations of the truth, holiness and spirit of God.

Bible verses that support the point I'm making: *"You shall not make for yourself an idol, or any likeness of what is in heaven above or on the earth..You shall not worship them."* (Deut. 5:8,9). And God makes it clear that it's even Himself He's talking about *"So, watch yourselves carefully, since you did not see any form on the day the Lord spoke to you at Horeb from the midst of the fire, lest you act corruptly and make a graven image for yourselves"* (Deut. 4:15,16). God doesn't want us to relate to Him second-hand, via an image based on an artist's presumed form of Him. He wants us to relate to Him directly, *"in Spirit and in truth"* (John 4:23,24).

When focusing on Jesus, we shouldn't have a pictorial image in our mind (He's no longer a human being). We should just focus on His essence (love), His mind (scripture), His character (holy), His purpose (to bring human beings into His Kingdom of beautiful love and perfect holiness), His position (liaison to human beings), and his being (God).

The earlier quote from Isaiah also says to me: if the goal is to be Christlike, we shouldn't do things that draw attention to our physical selves, and therefore away from love and God's message (like so many of today's so-called religious leaders do). I mean, are the wigs, extravagant make-up, expensive clothes, bombastic personalities and jewelry really necessary? We should be setting a standard that brings people into love and holiness, not lust, boisterousness and opulence.

Jesus' impact on human history

God and Jesus have been nearly kicked out of the American society (i.e. you rarely hear them mentioned on mainstream television, in the media, in the education system, in the entertainment industry, in government - except in court battles aimed at suppressing any expressions in public about them). But this is just a recent occurrence (which says volumes about whether we are in the end times or not). Most of human history has had God as its central and primary focus. And as for the impact of Jesus, consider this: although His public ministry was <u>only 3 years</u>, these 3 years have been pointed to as the greatest event in human history. And this impact has maintained even for the 2000 years since. Even today, most polls around the world show the Pope as being the most admired living person.

Jesus' impact was so great that even the counting of time was stopped...and then started up again with the year of His birth as the new year 1, with the tag put on it: A.D. (Anno Domini: in the year of our Lord). If for no other reason than this, there should be an extremely high public interest in Jesus. Yet, amazingly, <u>He is not even allowed in today's history textbooks...in spite of the fact that He is the most popular and influential person in history</u>.

If people would just read the wise things He said - especially in this very wisdom-starved time - they would elevate Him back to the top. This is how I ended up elevating Him to the top of my life. This is how He became the One who I hold in the highest esteem. I developed a great respect for Him when I saw how much more advanced He was than anything I had encountered in the fields I was pursuing: psychology, philosophy and the-art-of-living.

But there is this bizarre censorship in the public forums of things about Jesus. But I guess it's understandable when you consider what's been written in this book about free-will and the demonic spiritual underground. Nevertheless, it is all very insane and intolerable, which now leads us to the next chapter....the end of the world.

Chapter 11

Phase 7

The End of the Human Experiment (The End Times)

One day, after working on this book and getting in a peaceful, godly state, I took a break, got something to eat and turned on the television. Having become very peaceful, relaxed and uplifted (which is what usually happens when you focus on God's world), what I experienced from the television was literal, physical shock (in my stomach). I had forgotten how great, how deep and how many were the world's problems....and how unwise it is in seeing these problems and solving them.

First, I turned on the news to see that a cute young boy had been assaulted, dismembered, and when an attempted cremation didn't work, shoved into a refrigerator. And they showed a picture of his cute, smiling and innocent face, which made this all the more heart-wrenching. And yet there are many people who still argue against capital punishment (which the Bible commands: *"Whoever kills any human being shall surely be put to death"* Lev. 24:17. And this is one of the laws that God made for people, not Himself, to carry out).

Where is the compassion for this victim and his

family (who will suffer in anonimity for the rest of their lives)? Where is the compassion for future victims? Where is the respect for God's law?

In repulsion, I turned the channel...only to see 3 more murders on the news. My peace was already shattered, but I kept turning the channel. Next I saw angry liberals screaming to continue partial-birth abortions. I turned the channel again, this time to a religious station where I'd (hopefully) feel safe. They were debating about welfare, and concluding that it should be expanded even more. But they knew nothing about how most welfare recipients were stealing from the government (which actually is: stealing from the honest, hard workers of this country). And I'm sure they don't realize that the Bible is anti-welfare for most cases in this country (*"For you yourselves know how you ought to imitate us. For we were not disorderly among you; nor did we eat anyone's bread <u>free</u> of charge, but worked in toil and drudgery, night and day, that we might not be a burden to any of you, not because we do not have authority, but to make ourselves an example of how you should follow us. For even when we were with you, we commanded you this: <u>if anyone was unwilling to work, neither should that one eat</u>"* 2Ths. 3:7-10). Now Paul is saying here that, in addition to his ministry, he's working a regular job (and very hard work at that) even though he knows that he doesn't have to. But <u>just</u> because this point is so important, he's willing to sacrifice a good part of his time every working day.

I then turned the channel to "I Love Lucy", where everybody was continually yelling. Having just had the very high and pleasurable experience of the Kingdom of God, I could now see that much of this world has become so numb and callous to the shocking dysfunction that dominates television, they don't see the grossness of it anymore (this also happens to me if I don't stay focused on God's Kingdom). And, as a result, they've forgotten the beauty of God's kingdom (or maybe they've never known it....or have lost hope for trying to make it happen in their lives).

I finally turned the television off, my peace having been diminished, and went back to writing (actually, to write what you're reading now).

I have a very strong desire to help solve the world's problems. But this experience of turning on the television left me with a feeling that the number and severity of the problems in this world might be past the point of solution (by humans).

Now this 'TV shock' is just one of <u>many</u> such experiences that I've had. And they always manage to bring me down from high, godly experiences and into the more numb, blind, entangled, compromising level of the world. But how is God (whose essence is unchangeable) viewing this? How is He viewing these horrifying results that are happening in His creation? With grief....and anger. Do you think that He wants to see this go on forever? And, given His past ways of responding to wayward societies, do you think that He's going to let it go on forever? Hardly. So then, what would a perfect God's plan be for doing something about all of this suffering and dysfunction?

The plan for the end of the human experiment

Like with all plans, this one too has a logical end. This planet could have been used as a factory to continual- ly screen and train new souls. But God has determined that at a certain point, enough suffering is enough, and enough souls are enough. Now He wants to raise the quality.

He's made His points with each phase, and has

overall proven that: free will beings, given their own (albeit limited) sovereignty, cannot create an all-pervading peaceful, loving, and just social system. Therefore, He's proven that we need a God who has a perfect plan (for taming evil and creating peace, love and justice) to be exclusively sovereign, and with all of His subjects respectfully bowing to His sovereignty. But first He needs to clean up this mess....and then prepare what's to come.

The events of the end times

I started out here with the intention of spelling out the events of the end times in a neat little chronological package (being the leave-no-stone-unturned scientist that I am). But (groan) what a can of worms that approach turned out to be, being that I started with the basic Protestant story that I have been carrying for some time. When I went to back it up with scripture I found some *interesting* verses that didn't quite agree with each other ("let the eschatological games begin!"). I then started laboring quite painstakingly to come up with a scenario that would fit all scriptures *literally* (you should see how I'm guffawing now).

To make a long, laborious story short, I soon turned to other *scholars* (I just started guffawing again) to see what they had come up with and how they backed it up. Well, each version would sound good for awhile, but then I'd find flaws. I soon found that there were many different positions, from denomination to denomination, and even from preacher to preacher. There's pretrib, posttrib, midtrib, partial-rapture, no-rapture, premillennial, amillennial, postmillennial, who's going to heaven (and when, and in what form); who's going to hell (and why); the events of the end and their exact order; (groan). It is a very difficult, mind-bending task to try on each of these positions (and all of their possible relational combinations) and then read <u>all</u> of the pertinent scriptures to see if the position fits.

I soon found that in order to adequately understand Biblical prophesies and apocalyptic writings, you must also study (1)many other early Hebrew writings, (2)the idioms of the day, and (3)the styles of ancient Hebrew poetry.

But before we get into the specifics of the end times and afterlife, I want to make a point. I realized that I had been living as a Christian all of these years with the semi-vague story that I'd been carrying about end times, and you know, it wasn't that important to know if all of the details were absolutely right. My life was still very rich and full. It was just important to know the basic generalities of what was going to happen: that God was going to put an end to the evil world systems; that Satan, the demons, wicked people and wickedness would not spend eternity with *us*; that there is a perfect heaven; and that people will be rewarded and penalized for their actions on earth.

Knowing for sure all of the exact whats and whens of the end times doesn't change the facts of our daily obligations to be in love and to be holy. In fact, it some-times has the opposite effect in that I've seen some very heated, insulting and divisive "debates" over end times (*"Avoid foolish and ignorant debates, for you know that they breed quarrels"*" whereas *"A slave of the Lord should not quarrel, but should be gentle with <u>everyone</u>, able to teach, tolerant, correcting opponents with kindness"*. 2Tim. 2:23-25). The good that 'knowing what's going to happen' does is that it helps us to feel that maintaining holiness in our lives, and bearing the unholiness in the world, is not in vain. So I'll now try to present (like Sgt. Friday on "Dragnet" used to say:) "Just the facts ma'am!"

According to my calculations: Jesus will return in

1999, because 999 is 666 upside-down. I'm just kidding, but this is like what has been going on for 2000 years. But I do understand the feelings that create these eager theories because I'm also very eager for Jesus to return, given what I see on TV and in life, and given the greatness that He possesses and represents. But I moreso trust things to happen just as God has them planned. In the meantime I will patiently endure the offness of this world, wake up each morning with a positive attitude, knowing that there is plenty of work to be done (both on myself and in the world), and there is still much in God's creation to enjoy.

The simple story of end times is this: (1)there will be specific signs that the end is coming (and they will come like "birth pangs".....that is, with increasing frequency leading to a big, intense final event); (2)during this time will be the tribulation...a time of terror on the earth when Satan has no restraints, and *"It shall be a time unsurpassed in distress since nations began until that time"* (Dan. 12:1), culminating in a final "Armaggedon" in which Jesus and the angels will destroy all of the evil on earth; (3)Jesus will first gather His people; (4)the old heavens and earth will be done away with; (5)all that will be left will be a great White Throne judgment, in which all the dead of all time will be made to account for their lives; (6)evil and evildoers who haven't surrendered their lives to God will be cast into hell; and (7)a new heaven and earth will be made in which God will dwell with the human race forever in perfect holiness and love. So now, let's start spelling out some of the specifics of the individual parts of this story.

The signs....the birth pangs of the end times

There have been many times throughout history that people could easily have thought that the end was near (and they did). There have been many intense periods that included (some of) what the Bible says will be signs of the end times: Roman persecution of early Christians, Adolph Hitler, atheistic Communism, etc.

But none of these could have been the 'beginning of the end' because the Bible's 'first sign of the end' had not yet happened: the Jewish people regathering as a nation on the land God had once given them. Luke 21:24*"They will fall by the edge of the sword and be taken as captives to all the Gentiles; and Jerusalem will be trampled under-foot by the Gentiles until the times of the Gentiles be ful-filled."* The first part of this happened in 70 A.D., when Jerusalem was destroyed by the Roman army and 1.1 million Jews were killed. *"Until"*: being that Israel is now back together, the times in which God completes His mission with the Gentiles are being fulfilled. They'll be finished at the *"harvest"* at *"the end of the age"* (Matt. 13:39).

I have given the command to sift the house of Israel among all the nations (that is, return the scattered Jews to their homeland). *I will bring back the captives of my people Israel; I will plant them in their land; and no longer shall they be pulled up from the land I have given them, says the LORD your God* (Amos 9:9,14,15). This last line means that these prophesies have to be pertaining to this day and age. Also proof of this is the fact that James refers to this verse in Acts 15:15. And with the recent migration of the Russian Jews (*"from the land of the north"* Jer. 3:17), this task is nearly completed. And, the Ethiopian Jews said that they would never return to Israel until the hour that the Messiah is to come. They just started returning in the last few years. These are the African Jews that you see in Israel on the news.

Plus, another possible tie here is 'the parable of the fig tree'. In Joel 1:7 and Hosea 9:10 Israel is referred to as a fig tree. Well, in Matt. 24:32-4 it says that when the fig tree's branch becomes tender and sprouts leaves (which could mean the rebirth of Israel), you know Jesus' return is near. Then Jesus goes on to say that the generation that sees this will also witness His second coming.

More signs

(Matt. 24:4-14): *Jesus...said to them, "Take heed that no one deceives you. For many will come in My name, saying, 'I am the Christ,'* (When I first heard this I thought "Now how is anybody going to have the audacity to say that? This sign is going to be a tough one to see fulfilled." Well, the other day on television I saw and heard Louis Farrakhan say: "The Old Testament closes saying 'Elijah is coming. God is coming'. So who is Jesus, who is Elijah? Jesus and Elijah are one and the same. I am that Elijah. He [Jesus] wasn't born in Bethlehem of Judea. He was born in Sandersville, Georgia", Farrakhan's birthplace.), *and will deceive many* (e.g. the million man march). *You will hear of wars and rumors of wars; see that you are not troubled, for all these things must come to pass, but the end is not yet. For nation will rise against nation, and kingdom against kingdom. And there will be famines and plagues and earthquakes.* (All of these have been fairly common-place since Jesus' time, except the increase in earthquakes. Between 30 A.D. and 1900 there reportedly were 31 major earthquakes in the world. Between 1900 and 1990 there have been 58. The reason that this is significant is because Jesus wouldn't have mentioned earthquakes as a sign unless He meant: an increase in frequency of earthquakes....something out of the ordinary. The above figures are from an eschatologist who didn't list his sources, but we all have seen in the last 10 years a great increase in frequency of major earthquakes. As for plagues, today we have an increase in super-viruses, ebola, meningitis, CFS, a return of old diseases that we thought we had conquered, and AIDS. Speaking of AIDS, the Bible prophesied that AIDS would happen when it said: *and the males likewise gave up natural relations with females and burned with lust for one another. Males did shameful things with males and thus received in their own persons the due penalty for their perversity. They know the just decree of God that all who practice such things deserve death.* Rom. 1:27,32). *All these are the beginning of the labor pains. Then they will hand you over to persecution, and they will kill you.* (This has unfortunately been a regular occurrence in the communist countries). *You will be hated by all nations because of my name.* (These times are the first in the last 1700 years in which Christianity is no longer mainstream) *And then many will be led into sin; they will betray and hate one another. Many false prophets will rise up and deceive many;* (a lot of the new age, tabloids, false religions, false Christians, astrologers, psychics, etc.) *and because lawlessness will abound, the love of many will grow cold.* (This is the callousness and numbness that I've talked about. Having grown up in the 1950s I know that people used to have a lot more love back then. And my mother says that it was even better before that. Consider that the divorce rate in 1900 was 0.5%...whereas it's been over 50% for a while now. In our world, love has been replaced by hyperness, jivyness, insults, depression, fear, anger, lying, drunkenness, drugged states, rivalry, etc. Even churches have grown colder. They aren't the close, vibrant, loving, godly communities that they once were). *But the one who perseveres to the end will be saved.* (An obvious statement that a person can lose their salvation). *And this gospel of the kingdom will be preached throughout the world as a witness to all nations* (many are working hard at this and it's almost completed)..*and then the end will come.*

What will people be like in "the last days"?

"But understand this: there will be terrifying times in the last days. People will be self-centered and lovers of money, proud, arrogant, abusive, disobedient to their parents, ungrateful, irreligious, callous, implacable, malicious gossips, licentious, brutal, hating what is good, traitors, reckless, conceited, lovers of pleasure rather than lovers of God, as they make a pretense of religion but deny its power. Reject them" 2Tim3:1-5. These all are commonplace today, especially in the media. But having grown up in the 1950s, I can assure you that most of these were looked down on then....even by the media.

God's present warning/promise to the world

By your stubbornness and impenitent heart, you are storing up wrath for yourself for the day of wrath and revelation of the just judgment of God, who will repay everyone according to their works: eternal life to those who seek glory, honor, and immortality through perseverance in good works, but wrath and fury to those who selfishly disobey the truth and obey wickedness. Yes, affliction and distress will come upon every human being who does evil (Rom. 2:5-9). Also, what a person publicly stands for and how they vote can lead to their condemnation: *"that all who have not believed the truth but have* approved *wrongdoing may be condemned"* (2Ths. 2:12). Also, those who argue in favor of and defend sinful things (pornography, homosexuality, sex outside of marriage, idolizing human beings, etc.) not only will not inherit the Kingdom of God and Christ, but they will also bring God's wrath down on themselves (Eph. 5:5-6). This would include those who get defensive (instead of repentant) when confronted with their personal sin. And how we spend our time is important: *"Beware that your hearts do not become <u>drowsy</u>"* (i.e. spiritually asleep, dulled) *"from <u>indulgence</u> and <u>drunken-ness</u> and the <u>worries of daily life</u>, and that day catch you by surprise like a trap"* (Luke 21:34). These are the very common things in the world today that take our focus away from God. And, it is good to recognize that television can be a form of drunkenness.

How are Christians to be during the end times?
Read 1Thes. 5:4-22; 2Thes. 2:1-3,15; Rev. 22:11; and Matt. 25:34-40. And, love God with all your heart, mind and soul, keep His commandments, and love your neighbor as yourself. In other words, Christian business as usual. (There will be many times in this chapter that scriptures won't be spelled out and you'll need to look them up. So have a Bible handy as you go through this chapter).

2000?
A question that is often pondered is: <u>when</u> will this end take place? A reply that's often given is a quote from Jesus: *"But of that day and hour no one knows, neither the angels of heaven, nor the Son, but the Father alone"* Matt. 24:36. (Of course my son Timmy is quick to point out that this doesn't say anything about the year.) So then, do we have any clues as to what the year might be?
Jesus said (in Luke 21:32) that the generation that is present when the first signs take place *"will by no mean*

pass away until all things are fulfilled" (with "all things" being the other signs mentioned in Luke 21, as well as anything else that is prophesied in the Bible as happening in this end time period). And in the parable of the fig tree, it is reaffirmed that the generation that sees the first signs will see all of the signs: *"Now learn this parable from the fig tree: when its branch has already become tender and puts forth leaves, you know that summer is near. In the same way, when you see all these things, know that He is near, at the gates. Amen, I say to you, this generation will by no means pass away until all these things have taken place"* (Matt. 24:32-34).

Now, if we're to guesstimate when the end will approximately be, we'll need to extract 2 numbers from these verses: (1)the year that Israel restarted, and (2)how long a generation is.

Israel became a nation again on May 14, 1948. (But some say that the year that should be used here is 1967, when they regained all of their land). The next piece of data needed is: how long was a generation when these words were spoken? Matt. 1:17 says that there were 42 generations between Abraham and Jesus. It has been calculated that Abraham was born in 2166 B.C. This means that a generation was considered to be 51.57 years, or 51 years, 7 months. With these numbers, this would place the end very near New Year's Eve, 2000. (What a way to bring in the new millennium!). If this and the other figures are true, we should start seeing the Antichrist around mid 1996 (just a few months after this writing). (Of course, If I'm going to be very scientific about this, there are many possibilities with the numbers used here. For example, there are questions about the exact birth years of Jesus and Abraham. And are the 42 months in Rev. 13:5 really 42 months?).

Nevertheless, the reader should still consider all of the signs that I mentioned and ask themselves "Does this sound like the time that we're in now?" Add to this (1)if the description I gave of what people will be like in the last days sounds familiar, and (2)the fact that nearly all cultures who have had prophesies point to around the year 2000 as being the end of the world.

Those who've predicted the year 2000 include: Judaism, many modern Christians, some early Christian church leaders, Muslims (Mohammed), Nostradamus, the Mayan culture, astrologers, and in the pyramid of Cheops in Egypt it was predicted to happen on (Timmy's 13th birthday): 5/5/2000.

So what are these signs all leading up to? The apostasy, the Antichrist, the false peace, the rapture, Jesus' second coming, God's wrath and vengeance, Armaggedon, the destruction of earth, the White Throne judgment, and the new heaven and earth. I'll describe each of these in order.

The Apostasy

2 Thes. 2 says that before Jesus' second coming, an apostasy must come first...and the lawless one (the Antichrist) must be revealed. "Apostasy" means 'a falling away from the Church'. And when you fall away from one thing you must fall into something else. Therefore, people will be leaving the Church and sound Christianity, and taking on new religions/philosophies and/or distorted versions of Christianity.

When you really study scripture, you realize that both of these are very much happening today. I've made many points in this book (and will continue to in this and the next chapter) showing how what the Bible says is being distorted in many churches today. This is one form of the apostasy. Another form is in 'the new age movement', in which people are not only distorting the Bible, but they are also courting demonic spirits in disguised form (1Tim. 4:1-3), and practicing <u>many</u> of the things that the Bible forbids. The final form is the religion/philosophy of 'secular humanism', where humans are elevated to the highest positions of worship, respect and guidance instead of God.

Other evidence that we are in the apostasy now: God is more unpopular now than ever before in human history; a lot of the new-age says that "we are God" (does 'Satan' ring a bell? Also, I'd like to see them prove it by making a universe); instead of the Bible, people now turn to psychologists, psychics and new-age teachers for advice: *For the time will come when people will not tolerate sound doctrine but, following their own desires and insatiable curiosity, will accumulate teachers and will stop listening to the truth and will be diverted to myths* (2Tim. 4:3).

The Antichrist

The Bible says that before Jesus' second coming, there will be the rise of an evil Antichrist to the power of being the main world leader. What circumstances would let the world allow this?

First of all, the Bible says that Satan can come on like an angel of light. And given the current world's numbness to evil, the Antichrist won't even appear to be evil...except to those who haven't grown numb and lowered their standards, and therefore can still see.

Much of the world is being run under the dysfunctional philosophy and religion of 'secular humanism'. And because of this, evil and human misery continue to grow. One day it will reach a crisis point on the mass level (it already is at a crisis point on many individual levels).

When it does, this religion will look for its 'savior'...its 'messiah'. Enter: the Antichrist. He will appear to have the solutions to peoples' crises....or at least, he will be able to deceive people into voting for him.

2Ths. 2:6,7: *And now you know what is restraining, that he may be revealed in his own time. For the mystery of lawlessness is* already *at work. But the one who restrains is to do so only for the present, until he is taken out of the way.* The restrainer is the angel in Rev. 20: 1-3. Then Satan will have unrestrained access to planet earth. But only for a short time.

What else does the Bible say about the Antichrist? 2Ths. 2:3,4 *the man of sin is revealed, the son of perdition, who opposes and exalts himself above all that is called god or that is worshipped, so* as *to seat himself in the temple of God, claiming that he is a god.* He could speculatively be any one of a number of public figures...or maybe he hasn't fully emerged yet. In a way, we are like the people in the Old Testament times who were awaiting the Messiah. For many, only in hindsight were they able to single out all of the scriptures that identified Jesus as the Messiah. Two of His disciples didn't even realize that He was resurrecting in fulfillment of scripture (see John 20:9).

The Antichrist will perform false signs and wonders....and will spring from the power of Satan (2Ths. 2:9). In fact, if you read all of the verses about the Antichrist (1John 2:18,22; 4:3; 2John 1:7; 2Thes. 2:3,4,9,10), you'll see that 'antichrist' really is the spirit of the Satanic philosophy (which is anti Christ), which in the end times will become an embodiment of Satan...a person. But this spirit has been around since Jesus physically left (1John 2:18).

After studying the end times and prophesy, I concur with what has been the sound thinking about it through the centuries, and still is the teaching of the Roman Catholic Church, the English and Eastern Orthodox churches. That is: many of the Old Testament and Revelations prophesies have already been fulfilled in: B.C. Israel, the 70 A.D. destruction of Jerusalem, and the Roman persecution of Christians. The many theories regarding end times that circulate today were put into perspective by St. Paul's statement in 2Ths. 2:1-3: *Now, brethren, concerning the coming of our Lord Jesus Christ and our gathering together to Him, we ask you, not to be shaken out of your minds suddenly, or to be alarmed either by a "spirit," or by an oral statement, or by a letter allegedly from us to the effect that the day of the Lord is at hand. Let no one deceive you in any way.* " I once saw a funny commentary that said that the solutions to the riddle of 666 amounted to almost as many.

One of the main causes of confusion and erroneous theories in eschatology is the fact that the nation of Israel has had 3 nearly identical scenarios in history. (A)Exile: (1)Egypt, (2)Babylon (586 B.C), (3)the 70 A.D. scattering amongst the nations; and (B)Returning to their homeland: (1)"the promised land", (2)post-Babylon Israel (538 B.C.), (3)1948. Also, A2 and A3 were both punishments because of sin, and B1, B2 and B3 were all blessings. And, Israel has been attacked, conquered and ruled-over a number of other times. The problem here is that one war could be mistaken for another war; one judgment could be mistaken for another judgment; one blessing could be mistaken for another blessing; one exile for another; one homecoming for another; etc. That is, prophesies that were meant for one time period can be mistakenly applied to end times.

Sure it would be chilling and nice to be able to say that (e.g.) in 3-1/2 years all unsaved sinners will be doomed. And I have seen people scared by this tactic. But I haven't seen any of them saved. Only when a person truly sees enough of the beauty of God's Kingdom that they want to be a part of it, and/or they are convicted about the ugliness of sin (both in themselves and in the world), and they then reach out to God for an escape from it, do they get saved. People get scared because they deep-down know that they are in bad shape with God because of their sin. But, for whatever reason, they usually still don't want to give their sin up. Anyway, Jesus does often say to beware and be on guard, for <u>any moment</u> the end might happen. Isn't that chilling enough?

Other verses about the Antichrist: Rev. 13 (the beast is anti-God, anti-Church, boastful, the '#1 political leader in the world' and/or 'the #1 philosophy: secular humanism'), Rev. 19:20, 11:7, 16:13-14, 17:8,12,16; 2Ths. 2:8: *And then the lawless one will be revealed, whom the Lord [Jesus] will kill with the breath of his mouth and destroy with the brightness of His coming.* The beast and false prophet live for 3 1/2 years (Rev. 13:5) and then are destroyed in Armaggedon (Rev. 19:20).

<u>What is 'the rapture'?</u>

Jesus said that at some point He will come back. He's coming for 2 reasons: (1)to harvest those who believe in Him and bring them to heaven, and (2)to take vengeance against and destroy the evil world. And His vengeance is described as being very intense, traumatic and bloody. Now being that Jesus promised to spare His followers from this trauma (1Thes. 5:9, Rev. 3:10, 1Thes. 1:10, 2Thes. 1:7), it appears that He has a logistics problem. That is: there will be many saved people who will be alive at the time of the beginning of the terror. So how does He keep them from it? He simply and instantly removes them from the planet. 1Cor. 15:51,52: *Behold, I tell you a mystery: we shall not all sleep, but we shall all be changed - in a moment, in the twinkling of an eye;* 1Ths. 5:2: *the day of the Lord will come like a thief at night.* And how will this appear to those who are left? *Two men will be in the field: one will be taken and the other left. Two women will be grinding at the mill; one will be taken and the other left* (Matt. 24:40-41). This taking away is called 'the rapture'. And just how much of the coming trauma will those who belong to Jesus be spared? Almost all of it (except for some of the birth pangs). The general mood on the earth will be "peace and safety". 1Ths. 5:3 *For when they say, "Peace and safety," then sudden destruction comes upon them, as labor pains upon a pregnant woman. And they shall not escape.* The actions on the earth will be business-as-usual: *For as it was in the days of Noah, so it will be at the coming of the Son of Man. For as in the days before the flood, they were eating and drinking, marrying and giving in marriage...and did not know until the flood came and took them all away* (Matt. 24:37-39).

Other verses that speak about the rapture: *Then we who are alive, who are left, shall be caught up together with them in the clouds to meet the Lord in the air* (1Ths. 4:17). Jesus harvests the saved (Rev. 14:14-16) <u>before</u> God's wrath is poured out (Rev. 14:17-20); He will give rest to those who have suffered for His Kingdom (2Thes. 1:4-10); (Rev. 11:12 - I'll explain this later in this chapter); the destruction at the end (1Cor. 15:24) happens <u>after</u> the rapture (1Cor. 15:23); Luke 21:36 says that those who are vigilantly holy and unsinful will *"escape the tribulations"*; Rev. 6:4 says that peace will be taken from the earth. This could mean the removal of *"the salt of the earth"* (God's holy people) and the Holy Spirit: *and then He will send out the angels and gather [His] elect from the four winds, from the end of the earth to the end of the sky* (Mark 13:27); *"At that time your people shall escape"* (Dan. 12:1).

What will Jesus' second coming look like? *For just as lightning comes from the east and is seen as far as the west, so will the coming of the Son of Man be* (Matt 24:27); *Behold, He is coming amid the clouds, and every eye will see Him, even of those who pierced Him. All the peoples of the earth will lament Him. Yes. Amen* (Rev. 1:7).

The fall of the great Babylon

Revelations 17 and 18 talk about the fall of a place in the end times called "Babylon". Babylon is described in Rev. 17:5 as *"Babylon the great, the mother of harlots and of the abominations of the earth."* And Rev. 17:2 says that *"the inhabitants of the earth became drunk on the wine of her harlotry."* Rev. 17:1 says that it is *"the great harlot who lives near the many waters"*. But Rev. 17:15 says that *"The waters that you saw where the harlot lives represent large numbers of peoples, nations, and tongues"*. Therefore it must be a melting-pot type of place. Rev. 18:3 says that *"the merchants of the earth grew rich from her drive for luxury"*. Sound familiar? If not, let me explain. Who could the harlot be....the one who spreads immorality all around the world? Well if this time were to be the end times who would that be? Most definitely: Hollywood. I once heard a very appropriate saying: "If God allows San Francisco and Los Angeles to go on much longer, He owes Sodom and Gomorrah an apology". And hasn't there been an unbelievable number of natural disasters in these 2 places in the last 10 years? Babylon is referred to as "the great city". Therefore, it could just be L.A., or the whole

U.S., or a group of evil cities: L.A., S.F., D.C., N.Y., etc. And which 'melting-pot' country is the biggest consumer of luxury items in the world? The United States.

Here is what the Bible says will happen to the great Babylon. *"I heard another voice from heaven say "Depart from her, my people, so as not to take part in her sins and receive a share in her plagues, for <u>her sins are piled up to the sky,</u> and God remembers her crimes.* Rev. 18:4, 5. *"her plagues will come in one day - death and mourning and famine. And she will be utterly burned with fire. For strong is the Lord God who judges her"* Rev. 18:8.

And how will heaven react to her destruction? *"After these things I heard a loud voice of a great multitude in heaven, saying, Alleluia! Salvation and glory and honor and power to the Lord our God! For true and righteous are His judgments, because He has judged the great harlot who corrupted the earth with her harlotry. He has avenged on her the blood of His servants"* Rev 19:1, 2.

The rest of the world will observe the destruction of Babylon with great sorrow, but mainly out of greed, because they'll lose her as a market (Rev. 18:11-16). But then in Rev. 19 & 20:9-11the rest of the world is destroyed.

<u>Judgment day</u>

Then the old heavens and earth will be done away with (Matt. 24:35, Rev. 21:1) because they have been greatly polluted with evil and therefore are not fit for the standard of perfect cleanliness in the new world. All that will be left will be a great White Throne judgment, in which all the unsaved dead of all time will be made to account for their lives. *Then I saw a great white throne and Him who sat on it, from whose face the earth and heaven fled away. And I saw the dead, small and great, standing before God, and books were opened. And another book was opened, which is the book of life. And the dead were judged according to their works, by the things which were written in the books. Anyone not found written in the book of life was cast into the lake of fire* (Rev. 20:11,12,15).

Those who were in the first resurrection will not have to go through this judgment (Rev. 20:6). They were judged when they died. Their sins were covered by Jesus' blood (Rom. 3:25; 4:7, 8; 5:9; 1John 4:10; Rev. 1:5; 2Cor. 5:19), their bad deeds were burnt as hay (1Cor. 3:12-13), and their good deeds were rewarded (1Cor. 3:8, 12-14, Matt. 16:27, Luke 6:23, Col. 3:24, Rev. 22:12).

Evil is eliminated forever

"But the cowardly, unbelieving, abominable, murderers, sexually immoral, sorcerers, idol-worshippers, and deceivers of every sort, shall have their part in the lake which burns with fire and brimstone" Rev. 21:8. ("Cowards" are people who are afraid to stand up for God in public because of anticipated rejection or ridicule. *"Everyone who acknowledges Me before others I will acknowledge before My heavenly Father. But whoever denies Me before others, I will deny before My heavenly Father"* Matt. 10:32,33; *"For whoever is ashamed of Me and My words in this adulterous and sinful generation, of him the Son of Man will also be ashamed when He comes in the glory of His Father with the holy angels"* Mark 8:38). "sexually immoral" means: engaging in sexual activities that are condemned by the Bible, which are all of them except within-a-heterosexual-marriage. "Sorcerers"; the original Greek word here is φαρμακος; pharmakos, from which we get 'pharmacist'. The definition is "user of spell-giving potions". Therefore, the modern meaning here

is "drug users". Also included in this word is: anyone who practices magic, sorcery, witchcraft, etc. "Idol-worshippers" just doesn't mean worshipping idols, it means a person giving their worship to others, not God: e.g. movie stars, media figures, music stars, political figures, sports stars, mates, friends, organizations, etc.) Rev. 22:15 *and all who love and practice deceit.* (And this "deceit" is "*of every sort*": in family relationships, in business, in friendships, with the government, with the world in general, with God, and even with ourselves.) Now obviously this doesn't mean 'everyone who's done any of these things' because that would include all of us. It means those who have chosen these as part of their lifestyle (over being holy); who don't repent of these evil deeds; and who haven't given their lives to God.

Not only are evil people eliminated, but also evil spirits are eliminated (Rev. 20:10, Matt. 25:41), and the facilities that have held evil beings are eliminated: Hades, death, the abyss, Tartarus, and earth (Rev. 20:14, 21:1).

Can a Christian lose their salvation and end up in hell?

A warning to Christians: *You are forewarned, beloved brothers. Be on guard lest you be led astray by the error of the wicked, and <u>forfeit the security</u> you enjoy*" (2Peter 3:17).

(Read each of the following verses first, which are all quotes of Jesus, then look at my comments). Matt 24:13 (only "*the one who perseveres to the end will be saved.*"); Matt 24:42 (why would we be warned to be watchful if there was no risk?); Matt. 24:44-51 (only the *servant* who is "*faithful and prudent*" at the end will avoid hell); Matt. 25:1-13 (we wouldn't be warned to stay awake on a daily and hourly basis if there was no risk); Matt. 25:14-30 (even those who call Jesus "Master" and "Lord" will not go to heaven if they haven't exercised their spiritual gifts or used their resources - financial and otherwise - in service to God. This could put a damper on the idea that non-church-goers can be saved. Even if _you think_ all churches are polluted, then <u>you</u> jump in and make a difference.); <u>Matt. 25:34-46</u> (only those who did -or supported those who did- certain works will be accepted into the Kingdom of God). I think these parables not only mean for us to be prepared for Jesus' second coming, but also for the moment of our individual physical deaths, which can take us by surprise, which is why there's a sense of urgency in the parables.

And then there's the question of who really is a Christian. Many rightly say that Christians are saved by "faith", not by works. But how do you know if someone <u>really</u> has faith, or if they are just saying it? The Bible tells us how we can know: _Whoever says, "I know Him," but does not keep His commandments is a liar, and the truth is not in him_ (1John 2:4); _For just as a body without a spirit is dead, so also faith without works is dead_ (James 2:26).

How else can you tell who is a Christian? _For those who live according to the flesh set their minds on the things of the flesh, but those who live according to the spirit, the things of the spirit_ (Rom. 8:5). As for what is of the flesh and what is of the Spirit, read: Gal. 5:19 - 6:1, and 1Cor. 6:9-10. Also, Christians are generally just not whole-heartedly interested in earthly things (Col. 3:1-2).

Someone asked Him, "Lord, will only a few people be saved?" He answered them, "Enter through the narrow gate; for the gate is wide and the road broad that leads to destruction, and those who enter through it are many. How narrow the gate and constricted the road that leads to life. And those who find it are few (Luke 13:23, Matt. 7:13-4).

By the parables in Matt. 24 & 25, you can see now how the gates could end up being narrow in a country where 96% say they believe in God, and with most of them professing to be Christian. Surprisingly, in a *Christianity Today* survey of people in the main Protestant churches, 51-95% said that they didn't believe what the Bible had to say about various truths (e.g. the virgin birth, creation events, hell, inerrancy of scripture, etc.). And I've seen similar surveys of Catholics.

It is hard for me to communicate these truths because it means that many will perish. And I'm sure it is also hard for God who wishes that none should perish: *The Lord...is patient with you, not wishing that any should perish but that all should come to repentance* (2Pet. 3:9).

The standards for getting into heaven, presented by Jesus in Matthew 24 and 25, I'm sure will come as a surprise to many (given how erroneously easy that many, including in churches, make it seem these days). And these standards might even make you question your own salvation state. On the other hand, this could prompt (even push, frighten or shake) you into finding the much more rewarding, fulfilling, functional, clean, loving and peaceful-with-your-conscience life with God, Jesus, the Holy Spirit, the angels, the saints, the Bible and God's Church.

It seems that the bottom-line questions to ask yourself are: Do you feel close to God (e.g. do you sincerely pray)? Do you feel a friendship with God? Is God the One you lean on? Do you look up to God, Jesus and the Holy Spirit? Do you believe and read God's word? Are you a member of His Church (His family)? Do you reflect God in the world? Do you value God above all else? Is it critically important to you that you obey His laws? Do you stand up for God's principles? If you can answer yes to these questions, the Bible says you can feel assured of making it through the narrow gate. If you can't answer yes, if I were you I would be worried. My feeling in writing this book was not to make anybody worry.....but then again, maybe the reason that the gate is narrow is because (even) churches are presenting such a light, sugar-coated, easy way to salvation, lulling people into a false security, which allows them to be side-tracked into worldly activities, bonds, habits, a passive condoning-of-evil, and away from a true and active relationship with God. Remember: *Do you not know that to be a lover of the world means enmity with God? Therefore, whoever wants to be a lover of the world makes himself an enemy of God* (James 4:4).

Perhaps, for some, this is a harsh test for their comfort zone. But, consider God's perspective.....would you let someone move into your home, for eternity, who wasn't close with you or who wasn't your good friend, who didn't have a loving relationship with you, and who didn't meet certain standards for good behavior?

Of course, the overwhelmingly hopeful note here is that if you are still around to be able to read this, you can still do what it takes to be saved. *Draw near to God, and He will draw near to you. Cleanse your hands, you sinners, and purify your hearts, you of two minds. Humble yourselves in the sight of the Lord, and He will lift you up* (James 4:8,10). (I give even more proof of how a Christian can lose their salvation in the next chapter.)

A new heaven and earth
And I saw a new heaven and a new earth, for the first heaven and the first earth had passed away. And I heard a loud voice from heaven saying, "Behold, God's dwelling is with the human race. And He will dwell with

them, and they shall be His people....And God will wipe
every tear from their eyes; and there shall be no more
death or mourning, wailing or pain, [for] the old order has
passed away." Then He who sat on the throne said,
"Behold, I make all things <u>*new*</u>*." I will give of the fountain*
of the water of life freely to him who thirsts. Nothing
accursed will be found there anymore. Night will be no
more, nor will they need light from lamp or sun, for the
Lord God shall give them light, and they shall reign forever
and ever (Rev. 21:1,3-5,6, 22:5). (For a slight glimpse of
how great the visuals will be there, read Rev 21 and 22).
<u>*New*</u>: not 'νεος' (neos), which would mean 'a new, fresh
version of the <u>same</u> kind'; but rather 'καινος' (kainos),
which is 'new of a <u>different</u> kind'. Also, nothing material
will ever decay there (Rom. 8:19-21).

It is possible that those on the new earth will get a
new body. Why? So that they can have a vehicle with
which to partake of the earthly pleasures that God has
invented (e.g. Rev. 22:2). (This could possibly satisfy the
theory that says there will also be a mass 'resurrection of
bodies' at the end of time.) This is also where the nation of
Israel could possibly have many of the *poetic* prophesies
made about it fulfilled. I showed in Chapter 9 how (some)
Jews will be saved. In the next chapter I'll talk about how
other non-Christians can be saved. But of course the surest
way that I know of is to become a Christian.

<u>An argument against a millennium after the last days</u>

Being that I come from a Protestant background
(which is where I learned a lot of my Bible basics), and
being that I've since discovered how many of the popular
Protestant beliefs are not true and are not based on solid
logic, scripture knowledge or accurate interpretation

(where great liberties have been taken...and as a result, the love has not only grown cold, but has turned to: anger, syrupyness, hyper-excitement, vanity, worldliness, false condemnation, egotism, judgment, paranoia, etc.), I wanted to spend a little time here explaining why this is all true, and to try to right some of the wrongs.

The Rev. 20 reign started with Jesus' resurrection. Proof: (at the last supper) *"I tell you, from now on I shall not drink this fruit of the vine until the day when I drink it with you new in the reign of my Father"* (Matt. 26:29). Well, that day came after His resurrection and before His Ascension: *"...not to all the people, but to us, the witnesses chosen by God in advance, who ate and drank with Him after He rose from the dead"* (Acts 10:41). Christ's present reign is also referred to in 1Cor. 15:25.

This also shows how our resurrection body doesn't have to be like Jesus' earthly one was, which is the proof that many use to say that we will be eating in heaven (this never did sound right to me). The proof that His earthly resurrection body was different than His heavenly one is further substantiated when He is transformed into a more glorious body when He appeared with Moses and Elijah in front of Peter, John and James (Matt. 17:2). But the proof that it will be like neither of these is that John, who saw both of these bodies, told us that neither of them were like our resurrection body: *Beloved, we are God's children now; what we shall be has not yet been revealed. We do know that when it is revealed we shall be like Him, for we shall see Him as He is* (1John 3:2).

Also, the apostle John wouldn't contradict himself. Yet, if Rev. 20 is literally true, then John 14:1-3 couldn't be, in that Jesus made a place for us in heaven, not on earth. That is: how are we going to be with Him there if

He's going to go down to earth for a thousand years? So now which one would you choose: a literal quote from Jesus, or an apocalyptic dream (from a book that's filled with metaphors)? Plus, 1Peter 1:4 says our inheritance is <u>in heaven</u>, not on earth. Our dwelling is <u>in heaven</u> (2Cor 5:1*"For we know that if our earthly house, this tent, is destroyed, we have a building from God, a house not made with hands, **eternal** in heaven"*), where we go <u>immediately</u> after death (2Cor 5:2,3 *"For in this tent we groan, longing to be further clothed with our heavenly habitation if indeed, when we have taken it off, we shall not be found naked"*) and where we stay <u>forever</u> (2Cor 5:1, 2Peter 1:11). And Jesus says that we will reign with Him in heaven after we die (2Tim. 2:12*"if we persevere we shall also reign with him"*). This is what is meant in Rev. 20:4,6.

It is not easy to detect <u>at first</u> what John really means in Rev. 20. But we do know that whatever he meant, it would not be in disharmony with the rest of scripture. Why? Because the book of Revelations was the last book of scripture that was written. Therefore, he knew what was written in the rest of scripture....and, being an apostle, he knew it very well. So then why would he contradict any of it? This is also true for Paul, who wrote some of the key passages having to do with the end times and the afterlife (1Thes. 4, 1Cor 15, 2Thes.2, etc.), and who also was a great scripture scholar (Old and New Testaments). So, why would he write things that would contradict other things he wrote? Yet, many modern interpretations of his writings definitely would contradict some of his other writings (e.g. spirit resurrection bodies vs. physical resurrection bodies, eternal heaven vs. millennium).

The purpose of (the often misunderstood) 1Thes. 4:13-18 was for Paul to assure the Thessalonians that they would not have to wait until the second coming to rise from the dead...as the thief on the cross didn't. And 'the resurrection of the body' finds its inspiration in Paul's recognition of the need to resolve the problem of 'the corrupted state of the flesh' (see Rom. 8:23). And 'a glorified spirit body' does satisfy this concern..regardless of how Paul's grammar and metaphors have been misinterpreted (see 1Cor. 15:42-44). The fact that our resurrection body is spiritual and not physical is further substantiated by Paul: *So also is the resurrection of the dead. It is sown a natural body; it is raised a spiritual body. But the spiritual was not first; rather the natural and then the spiritual. The first man was of the earth, made of dust; the second man, from heaven. As was the earthly one, so also are the earthly, and as is the heavenly one, so also are the heavenly. Just as we have borne the image of the earthly one, we shall also bear the image of the heavenly one. This I declare, brothers: flesh and blood cannot inherit the kingdom of God* (1Cor. 15:42,44,46,47-50).

    What can make this confusing is the fact that 'death and resurrection' is used in describing: baptism, Jesus' death, physical death, Jesus' second coming....body, spirit...past, present and future. For example, Rom. 8:11 is often used in reference to 'resurrection of the body at the second coming'. But if you read Rom. 8:1-11, you'll see that he is talking about 'baptism in the Spirit'. That is: the mortal body that we are presently in (which is 'dead', v.10) comes to life <u>through</u> the Spirit dwelling in you <u>now</u> (v.9). By the way, my personal salvation testimony includes a confirmation that Rom. 8:1-11 is true. When I finally bowed to Jesus as my Lord (in late 1982), a new strength-over-sin did come in me. My flesh no longer had the <u>power</u> to force me to sin. I now <u>felt</u> like I didn't have to sin. My flesh would still suggest to me sinful things to do, but for the first time I could with strength say no. There were no residual 'troubled or urging' feelings in my soul. Instead there was a good feeling (for doing the right thing). This fact was just another piece of evidence to me that the Bible is true, and Rom. 8:1-11 is accurate. The new Spirit in me was more powerful than the flesh I was in.

Paul also equates baptism with resurrection in Rom. 6:4-14 and Col. 3:1-3.

Another dilemma for those who adhere to a literal interpretation of prophesies and apocalyptic writing is in Isaiah 65:17-25. These verses, some of which are often used to support the millennium theory, don't agree with other prophetic scriptures. For example: Rev. 21:4 says "there shall be no more death". But Is. 65:20 says that there will be people who will die in the new heavens and new earth. Also, literalists are quick to take 'a thousand years' in Rev. 20 literally, yet they take liberties with other prophetic numbered measurements (e.g. the "weeks" in Daniel 9, the "hour" in John 4:23, the "day" in 2Thes. 2:2) to fit the explanations they've conceived.

Riddle: When is a thousand not a thousand?
Answer: When it's an idiom from 2,000 years ago.

If I were to write that I got "a ton of responses" or that "I've done that a million of times" or "this job took forever", you would know what I meant. But would someone 2000 years from now, or even someone today who speaks another language, know? No. They'd probably take it literally, and then scratch their heads (just like I initially did in my studies of some of the prophetic scriptures). And just like "the day of God's wrath" and the 70 weeks in Daniel are not meant literally, also in those days: 'a thousand years' meant 'a long time'. Even in 2Peter 3:7 & 8, the <u>day</u> of judgment is referred to as taking 'a thousand years'. Other *number metaphors* in those days: 4 signified the world; 7, perfection; and 6, imperfection (ergo 666).

Also, if you're going to take the literal approach, you have a very long wait for the millennium: approximately 47,500 years. Why? Because in Psalms 105:8 it says:*"He remembers forever His covenant, the pact imposed for a thousand generations"*, and Deut. 7:9 says:*"the faithful God who keeps His merciful covenant down to the thousandth generation"*. Now being that a generation then was 51.57 years, and the covenant was made in 2166 B.C., this means the millennium couldn't happen for <u>at least</u> 47,500 years. And this couldn't mean 'a covenant in heaven' because there will be no marriages in heaven (Matt. 22:30) and therefore no generating.

Also, there were many numbers assigned to the length of the millennium by B.C. rabbis; from 40 to 7,000 years. And being that they didn't recognize Jesus as Messiah, these numbers wouldn't change.

The only explanation I can see that would fit all of scripture is this: Jesus' reign started with His Resurrection, and the "thousand years" is the time period between His Resurrection and second coming. When you see the phrase "the dead in Christ shall rise first", it means: "as they individually die", not all at once as a group. And "in the clouds" and "in the air" means 'in heaven', where end-time believers will 'meet the dead in Christ and Christ Himself'. Once again, when Rev. 20 talks about those who will reign with Christ, it means: "as they individually die".

The <u>first death</u> is: physical death. The <u>first resurrection</u> is: the saved going to heaven immediately after the first death. The <u>second resurrection</u> is the unsaved going from Hades (not Hell) to the White Throne Judgment. The second death is: destruction in Hell.

Also when Rev. 20 talks about Satan being chained, it means: restricted from being able to win over us. But it doesn't mean that he won't be in the picture or have any influence. The proof of this comes from our daily lives. That is, he can tempt us, but he has no power over us unless we give it to him. *So submit yourselves to God. Resist the devil, and he will flee from you* (James 4:7).

More logical points against the millennium: Why would those in heaven want to take a demotion and come to an earth where they will again have to experience sin and Satanic attacks? In his commentary on Revelations, Robert Mounce says something funny about the folly of assuming a post-2nd-coming millennium that would include a time of trouble: "Apparently a thousand years of confinement does not alter Satan's plans, nor does a thousand years of freedom from the influence of wickedness change man's basic tendency to rebel against his creator." It appears that there can only be one time of trouble, and that is when Satan regains his full power in the tribulation. Also, why would God rego through a phase (as described in this book) that He's already gone through? That wouldn't make any sense or progress. Plus, those who preach the millennium (which will have sin in it, according to Rev. 20) also preach the resurrection of an eternally perfect body. Obviously these 2 ideas can't logically coexist.

Regarding the 'mark on the forehead and hand', once again, this is a metaphor used in various other places in the Bible that figuratively means: who your mental allegiance is tied to (forehead), and who your actions and works are for (hand). See Exod. 13:9, 16 and Rev. 22:4.

Also, I must say that those who *sell* the millennium

theory (whom I've seen) usually have some sort of 'fruit' problem, i.e. yelling, hyped-syrupyness, uptightness, etc. Remember that Jesus said that we will know the false teachers "by their fruit". You can also scripturally know that they are delivering false teachings (which is further attested to by the fact that they don't even agree with each other). But also, a sign of whether a person is being moved by the Holy Spirit is if they act with the fruits of the Spirit: peace, patience, gentleness and love. Any other fruit says that they're acting on their own. And 'body language' says that if they can't say what they have to say in peace, they themselves are not confident of what they are saying and are deep down running from a knowledge of their error.

Re: our approach to the Bible

       Jesus: "one of you will betray me."

       Judas: "Surely it is not I, Rabbi?"

       Jesus: "You have said so." (Matt. 26:21,25)

We know the truth of this story, that Judas did betray Him. But would you know that if you just saw these 3 lines? No. You would think the opposite. There are so many ways in how people communicated millenniums ago that we just don't see. Therefore it is not wise to 'foolishly speculate' about those passages in the Bible in which it is not readily obvious as to what they mean, or where there are a number of possibilities. And because of the above scriptural example, it is especially unwise to take every verse literally.

     As we can see, Jesus sometimes spoke in mysterious ways. Another example: if we were to take Mark 13:35 & 36 literally, it seems like Jesus is asking us to either sleep in the daytime or not sleep at all. But we know that Jesus was just poetically embellishing the message that we should always stay spiritually alert. And I presume that the purpose for the embellishments was to emphasize the point that we <u>never</u> should lapse into such a sleep. Therefore, we should be careful as to what we take literally.

Some modern examples of 'poetic embellishment': "it was raining cats and dogs"; "their eyes popped out"; "she was on pins and needles"; "good grief"; "a hot potato"; "they were miles apart"; "she went off the deep end", etc. And many of our idioms today actually come from the Bible: "a drop in the bucket"; "all hell broke loose"; "see eye to eye"; "the fat of the land"; "the apple of his eye"; "the skin of my teeth"; "the blind leading the blind"; etc.

These idioms are in everyday speech, but in writing, public speaking, and songwriting, an artist takes a special pleasure in using metaphor to emphasize and dramatize how serious they think something is. For example, in a 1970s song, the singer says that he was born in a crossfire hurricane and that he howled at his ma in the driving rain. Obviously, this is not to be taken literally. Rather, it is to convey that his childhood was so traumatic that he <u>felt</u> like he was howling through crossfire hurricanes and driving rains. Taking 'poetic license' in the lyrics is a much better way to convey how he felt, rather than just saying how he felt. I know that in my own songwriting I've taken great pleasure in using metaphor. And I've taken special pleasure in nesting wisdom within mysterious lyrics because I know that it will give the listener a thrill (and/or chill) when they uncover the secrets, knowing that it takes a certain level of wisdom to do so. I'm sure that many of the prophets had this in mind when they made their prophesies (there was no media back then. Story-telling was the only source of these experiences). The good here is that in the process of digging, you end up really getting it. And only those who care enough to dig are going to have access to

these pearls. And Jesus was, in a sense, in performance situations often when He spoke because He knew that His
words would be read billions of times throughout history.

What makes metaphor mysterious and tricky (and
fun) is that each metaphor has a number of possible explanations as to what it could mean. (And when you're dealing with a whole Bible and many metaphors, the challenge
is to tie them all together.) For example, 'Satan being
chained in the abyss' could mean: 'evil is restrained',
'Satan himself is limited', 'Jesus has the last word'; 'Satan
has no power over Christians', etc., etc. But we know that
it isn't to be taken literally because: you can't put a chain
on a spirit. Other Revelations metaphors: nobody fights
wars with horses anymore (Rev. 19); and if there's no
moon or sun, there won't be day or night (Rev. 20:10).

Another thing to consider is that, in trying to dig for
fine points and hidden meanings in scripture, we are playing 'microscopic verbal gymnastics' with <u>a translation</u>.
That is, we're not even working with the languages that
they were originally written in: Greek, Hebrew and
Aramaic. Not to mention the fact that we don't have anywhere near the command of these languages that we do
with English, let alone millenniums-old versions of these
languages, complete with the idioms of those times. So it
wouldn't be so surprising if some of our microscopic
analyses were incorrect. And, to be a <u>perfect</u> translator, you
must be reading, writing, thinking, learning and living in
<u>both</u> languages...which is not possible being that you're
dealing with two different time periods. Therefore, to draw
<u>absolute conclusions</u> would be an extremely difficult, if not
impossible, task of research. And, it is a contradiction of
the term 'microscopic' to subject <u>imperfect</u> translations to
<u>microscopic</u> analysis. Because of all of this, I think that my

'logic first' approach has helped me weed through some of the linguistic problems.

But, an important point here is this: There is so much in the Bible that is obvious, we don't need to waste our time trying to present speculations as fact (*do not...be false to the truth. Wisdom of this kind does not come down from above but is earthly, unspiritual, demonic.* James 3:14,15). Within the obvious is everything we need to know in order to live a full, rich, godly life. Even just in the short span of my lifetime, the way that people communicate has changed very much. For example, in the '40s and '50s there was a greater affinity for metaphor, double entendres, and clever speech. Whereas now, it is more popular (at least in the media) to be emotional, cutting and direct. Also, humor has changed. Grossness and shock-value are more predominant today; intelligent insights before that; and slapstick before that.

In interpreting metaphorical scripture it would be easy to anxiously jump on what would tickle people's ears, what would entertain, what you know people would like to hear, and what would create the effect you'd like to create (e.g. fear, hope, etc.). But it is much better to be patient and really come upon the truth. At first I thought that I was taking a step down when I realized that the Bible was much less literal and much more metaphorical than I had been lead to believe. But after a while, I realized that I had instead taken two steps up in that there were many valuable pearls mysteriously waiting to be uncovered.

Revelations 11 - an overture of all Christian era events?

In Rev. 9:17, John says that 'he' is having a vision: "*in my vision*". Therefore, the metaphors in the book of Revelations are akin to the ones we have in our dreams (and nightmares). That is, these metaphors have no 'literal' connection to reality. And like in 'dream analysis', the 'emotion', 'drama specifics' and 'what the metaphors represent' are where the connections to reality lie.

Also, the book of Revelations is not one sequential chronology of events. This can be evidenced by the fact that a sequence of events is laid out in a chapter, but then one of the early events in this sequence is talked about again in a future chapter, where it is a part of another sequence being laid out. Some examples of this: Babylon is announced as having been destroyed in 3 different chapters (Rev. 18:8, Rev. 14:8, Rev. 16:19); the dead are judged (Rev. 11:18 and Rev. 20:12); Satan released (Rev. 11:7 and Rev. 20:3); hunger, thirst and sun attacks (Rev. 7:16, Rev. 16:bowls 2, 3 and 4; Rev. 6:seal 3); "wipe away every tear" (Rev. 7:17 and Rev. 21:4); "spring of life-giving water" (Rev. 7:17 and Rev. 21:6); etc. Each chapter (or group of chapters) appears to contain some or all of the Christian era within it (them). John doesn't say "then what happened", he always says "then I saw". This means he's sequentially moving from vision to vision, not moving along in time.

The book of Revelations is laid out kind of like a CD. That is, it contains a number of complete-within-themselves stories (chapters/songs), which are all different angles of one theme. With a music recording this one theme is the artist's philosophy/lifestyle, or 'a feel'. With the book of Revelations the one theme is 'future events'.

With these understandings of the dream-like-metaphor, non-sequential-chronology, and non-literal-numerical qualities of the book of Revelations, I reread it. I found Chapter 11 to be particularly interesting. This is how I saw it (first read the entire chapter, then read the verses along with my commentary):

• The 2 witnesses are 2 modern-day representations of the churches in Rev. 2 & 3. This is because they are referred to as "two lampstands" (v.4). And they witness for God to the world under His protection. This witnessing will go on until "the times of the Gentiles be fulfilled".

• (v.7) Satan is released "for a short time" and 'atheistic secular humanism' defeats 'Christianity' in that it is elevated to being the #1 philosophy in the world.

• (v.8) "The great city" is Babylon (Rev. 18), which is the U.S. or L.A. or a group of cities out of which great evil is marketed. "Sodom": Los Angeles or San Francisco.

• (v.9) Christianity is conquered and rendered impotent in the world....but it is not buried altogether.

• (v.10)The world sees religion as a harassment (of its evil).

• (v.11) After "3 1/2 days" God revives His Church.

• (v.12) The rapture of the Church.

• (v.13) A violent earthquake in L.A. (or this could be the "big one" predicted by scientists on the San Andreas fault that connects L.A. and S.F.). 7,000 people are killed, and 1/10 of the city is in ruins. It also appears here that there will be people saved after the rapture.

• (v.15-19) A song about the rest of the future: the day of wrath (v.14 - the 3rd woe), judgment, rewards for God's people, and God's triumph. Rev. 10:7 says that the 7th trumpet announces the completion of God's plan.

Heaven

(Couldn't ask for a better 'happy ending to a story' than this). The Bible says that at the moment of death we go right to heaven. In Luke 23:43, Jesus said to the criminal on the cross next to Him *"Amen, I say to you, today you will be with me in Paradise."* Also, in 2Cor. 5:3 it says that *"when we have taken it* (our mortal body) *off, we shall not be found naked"*, we will be in heaven. Read 2Cor. 5:1-4 to get the full metaphorical meaning of this. Also, Paul, in 2Cor. 5:8, says that when we are absent from the body, we are present with the Lord. In Phil. 1:23 he says that if he were to depart from this life, he'd be with Christ.

And Jesus made this great statement in John 14:1-3 *"Let not your heart be troubled. You have faith in God; have faith also in Me. In My Father's house are many mansions; if it were not so, I would have told you. I go to prepare a place for you. And if I go and prepare a place for you, I will come again and receive you to Myself; that where I am, there you may be also"*.

The many 'near death experiences', where people find themselves instantly in the presence of a great, loving, totally peaceful light, could also be offered as proof of this.

Heaven is our real 'home'

The Bible says that heaven is our true home (2Cor. 5:8). Why? Because this is where: our Father is (Matt. 6:9), our Savior is (Heb. 9:24), our brothers and sisters in the faith are (Heb. 12:23) (and think about what a great family this is, being that it includes: God, Jesus, the Holy Spirit, the angels, all the apostles, Moses, all of the Old and New Testament saints, the prophets, multitudes of saved people and servants of every type of people on earth and throughout the ages) It is where: our name is (Luke 10:20), our inheritance is (1Peter 1:4), our citizenship is (Phil. 3:20), we will have rewards that are so great that we should even now be rejoicing and be glad (Matt. 5:12), our Master is (Eph. 6:9), our treasures are (Matt. 6:19-21), the Holy Spirit is (Rev. 22:17) and angels are (Rev. 5:11).

This is why the Bible says that we are sojourners,

travelers, strangers, pilgrims, aliens here on earth (1Peter 2:11). (And don't you especially feel that way when you turn on the television?) *Do not love the world or the things in the world. If anyone loves the world, the love of the Father is not in him* (1John 2:15).

And we know that we are already loved there [God loves us: *God our Father, who has loved us and given us everlasting encouragement and good hope through His grace* (2Ths. 2:16), and has proven His love in a very painful action (Rom. 5:8, John 3:16); Jesus loves us (John 14:21); and there was much joy in heaven when we got saved: *"there is joy in the presence of the angels of God over one sinner who repents"* (Luke 15:10).

Other facts about Heaven

Heaven is a place. It is the home of God (Gen. 28:17), Jesus (John 3:13), the Holy Spirit (Rev. 22:17), and the angels (Mark 13:32).

We will experience joy (Matt. 25:31). We will differ from one another (1Cor. 15:41-2). We have a promise of a glorious afterlife as a reward for our suffering: *For our light affliction, which is but for a moment, is working for us a far more exceeding and eternal weight of glory* (2Cor. 4:17). We will 'know' God, Jesus, those in heaven, and the full truth about heaven and life: *At present we see indistinctly, as in a mirror, but then face to face. At present I know partially; then I shall know fully, as I am fully known* (1Cor. 13:12). What will we be like in heaven? Not like great, important people: *But many who are first will be last, and the last will be first* (Matt. 19:30), but like little children (Matt. 18:1-3, 19:14). And as God's children, we are also, with His son Jesus, His heirs (Rom. 8:16-17). Jesus is God's only son, but through Jesus, we've become

God's adopted children (Eph. 1:5). The following verses give us a glimpse of how Jesus feels about us.

He's going to acknowledge us in the presence of His Father and the angels (Rev. 3:5). *Father, they are your gift to Me. I wish that where I am they also may be with Me, that they may see My glory that you gave Me* (John 17:24). I hope I'm not stretching it here, but this sounds like a child going to his father who is excited about his new friends coming to stay at his house and wanting to share his toys (well the Bible does say that we will be like little children in heaven). And to show how much He loves us, in this same prayer He very painfully accepted that He would have to die a torturous death so *"that they may be brought to perfection as one"* (John 17:23) and therefore be acceptable to be adopted into God's house, *"so that they may share My joy completely"* (John 17:13). Our job now on earth is to be as faithful to Jesus as He's been to us: *As You sent Me into the world, I also have sent them into the world* (John 17:18). And Jesus is also praying for the many generations of people who will hear the words of His Christians: *"I do not pray for these alone, but also for those who will believe in Me through their word"* (John 17:20). And those who reach back to God's reaching out to them will be aided by the angels: *Are they not all ministering spirits sent forth to minister for those who will inherit salvation?* (Hebr. 1:14).

What will our new bodies be like in heaven? *"Incorruptible"* and *"immortal"* (1Cor. 15:53). Our heavenly body is a spiritual one (1Cor. 15:44), like Jesus' spiritual body (1Cor. 15:45,49), maybe a glowing white like in "Close Encounters Of The Third Kind" (1Cor. 15:41a,b). Also, those who've had near-death experiences always see a light at the end of the tunnel. And angels are always described as angels of <u>light</u>. We'll be able to tell one another apart (1Cor. 15:41). We'll be like Jesus (1John 3:2).

<u>More on our new, heavenly bodies</u>

You bury a mere seed, and it comes up a much more impressive fruit tree, vegetable patch, stalk, etc. Similarly, 1Cor. 15:42-44 says: *So also is the resurrection of the dead. The body is sown corruptible; it is raised incorruptible. It is sown in dishonor; it is raised in glory. It is sown weak; it is raised powerful. It is sown a natural body; it is raised a <u>spiritual</u> body.* As to how glorious our resurrection body will be compared to our earthly one, consider how much more glorious what a seed produces is than the seed itself (e.g. trees, watermelons, corn).

<u>What will we do in heaven?</u>

The Bible says that those in heaven spend much time singing to God and worshipping Him (Rev. 7:9-15; 15:3-4; 19:6). And I'm sure that the sounds are new and thrilling, as can be glimpsed in Rev. 19:6. And consider how great what they're seeing and hearing must be in order to inspire them to sing and worship *"day and night"*. Being that heaven is perfect, their singing and worshipping are real, genuinely inspired responses to the degree of beauty and greatness that they're encountering. (Consider that 'duration of applause' varies from performance to performance, and even from moment to moment within a performance. So "day and night" is quite a response.)

Let's look at some other reactions from people who have had a glimpse of heaven. In 2Cor. 12:4 Paul says that he *was caught up into Paradise and heard ineffable things, which no one may utter.* That is, what goes on in heaven is so great it can't even be described by a human being.

Webster's Dictionary defines "ineffable" as: "(1)too over-whelming to be expressed or described in words; (2)too awesome to be spoken". Also, in 1Cor. 2:9 Paul says that no one has ever seen anything so great, heard anything so great, or even imagined anything so great as what we'll encounter in heaven: *Eye has not seen, and ear has not heard, nor has it entered the human heart, what God has prepared for those who love Him.*

In my visual, audio and heart meditations, I believe that I've gotten a glimpse of these things. At least I know that in them I've had visual, audio and feeling experiences that have topped anything I've experienced in the world.

Also, in 1Cor. 2:7 it talks about how those who love God receive a glorious, hidden wisdom in their spirit. Amen, I can testify to that. When I've gone deep into a truth channel meditation, the feelings I felt were the most beautiful, pleasurable and peaceful I've ever experienced. Ecstacy. Plus, wisdoms came at me quickly in visions. And I knew that I knew that what was being given to me was the clearest I'd ever seen myself or life. My biggest problem had always been that I was too much into 'controlling' (my being and my life) and not enough into 'surrendering' (to how God wanted to move me). And I would get caught in the tangled web of the life I had mapped out for myself. Not a very good approach to life. Only when we're relaxed and surrendered do we see life clearly.

I believe that I can, on the basis of my meditation experiences, relate at least somewhat to what those in heaven are experiencing. I've come out of these high experiences with very strong "Wow!" and "You wouldn't believe...." feelings in my heart. Other things that have made me say "Wow!" and "You wouldn't believe...." are: discovering God (amidst trying to tie my allegiance to and

look up to something in this very spiritually polluted, dysfunctional and unwise world); and discovering the Bible
(and how great it is for our heart <u>and</u> mind, and how it
totally completes life). I've tried hard to be in and communicate these things to others (obviously I'm still doing it
with this book, the writing and presenting of which is the
greatest inspiration of my life). Only the pragmatic problems of life have brought me down. But in heaven, we
won't have these problems (not even from our own bodies)
and we'll be able to stay at a high level. That alone is cause
for us to give thanks to God. Another reason is called: the
'Beatific vision'. *For now we see in a mirror, dimly, but
then we shall see face to face* (1Cor. 13:12). And when we
see God, it will be such a tremendous, crowning vision that
it will inspire and energize our singing and worship to the
degree that is described in the Bible.

And when people (in the Bible) have encountered
God, they've reacted by immediately falling on their faces
(Gen. 17:3, Ezek. 1:28). This says a lot about the greatness
of who and what they've seen.

And the many who have had near-death experiences nearly always say that what they saw was so beautiful and peaceful and loving that they didn't want to come
back...and that the only reason that they did come back is
to communicate the beauty of what they saw, out of compassion for those who don't realize the reality of the Bible
and the situation that they're in. (By the way, there are
those who've said they went to Hades and have come back
with an equally inspired, very chilling warning; e.g. in the
book "Beyond The Darkness" by Angie Fenimore). People
who have had near death experiences often say things that
relate to some of my deepest feelings and insights....things
that I don't see expressed anywhere else. This lets me

know that they've experienced some of the same beautiful visions that I've had (of aspects of God). The real proof is not in the lip service though, but in the fact that their lives and the things that are really important to them were drastically altered, and are now holy, not worldly.

We will have jobs in heaven (Rev. 7:15, 22:3). We will be in charge of important things (Matt. 25:23) (the reason that I think that this parable applies to 'heaven' is because the 3rd servant was sent to Hades).

Completing the transformation to perfection before heaven
The Bible says *"as it is written: There is no one just, not one. All have gone astray"* (Rom. 3:10,12), except Jesus. Now being that heaven is a place of perfect holiness, and being that there are saved people who are bound for heaven who haven't achieved perfect holiness, how does God make them perfectly holy? And we know that they are holy, both in heaven (2Peter 1:4, Rom. 8:29), and in the new heavens and earth (*...but nothing unclean will enter it, nor any [one] who does abominable things or tells lies* Rev. 21:27). And how does He ensure that they won't fall away like other free-will beings who were once with Him in heaven (Satan and the angels who became demons)?

Well we do know that this will be accomplished because in Hebr. 12:23 it says in heaven there will be *"the assembly of the firstborn enrolled in heaven, and the spirits of the just made perfect"*. And in 1John 3:2 it says: *"what we shall be has not yet been revealed. We do know that when it is revealed we shall be like Him"* (Jesus). Therefore we will be perfectly holy in our new state. And being that our new bodies are *"incorruptible"*, this means that they are not even capable of possessing corruption (1Cor. 15:53. Actually, read all of 1Cor. 15:42-54).

That accounts for our body, which is good because our "flesh" was a major source of unholiness. But what about our will? How will any residual tendencies to sin be erased? We do know that God has overcome this hurdle with the angels: 2Pet. 2:11 *"whereas angels, who are greater in power and might, do not bring a reviling accusation against them before the Lord"*.

The Catholic Church maintains the traditional doctrine of Purgatory. This can be read in "The Catholic Catechism" pp. 268,9; #s 1030-2, and in the Council of Trent (whose purpose was to try to bring order back to rebelling elements of the Church, in one way by restating oral traditions going back to the time of Jesus) Canon XXX Session VI, Session XXV, Session XIV Canons 12-15, Chapter IX Session XIV. This includes the tradition of praying for the dead (which is still done in today's masses). This was a Jewish tradition (as was expressed in 2Macc. 12:46) that never left the Church. This practice is supported by 2Ths. 2:15 *"Therefore, brothers, stand firm and hold fast to the traditions that you were taught, either <u>by an oral statement</u> or by a letter of ours"*. Other scriptural bases for Purgatory: 1Cor. 3:13-5 *"the work of each will come to light, for the Day will disclose it. It will be revealed with fire, and the fire [itself] will test the quality of each one's work. If the work stands that someone built upon the foundation, that person will receive a wage. But if someone's work is burned up, that one will suffer loss; the person will be saved, <u>but only as through fire</u>."*; and Matt. 12:32 *"And whoever speaks a word against the Son of Man will be forgiven; but whoever speaks against the holy Spirit will not be forgiven, either in this age <u>or</u> in the age to come."* , and Dan. 12:10 *"Many shall be refined, purified, and tested"*.

Now there is still 1 more piece to this puzzle: hell.

Hell

    I always had a hard time (logically) with the notion that there would be an *eternal* hell. I mean, if God has deemed certain souls to not be worthy of His heaven, <u>why</u> would He keep them around suffering <u>forever</u>? That seemed to be logically imperfect.

    Then I did a Bible study on 'hell' and found that the scriptures could be interpreted as meaning: not a hell that will go on for *eternity*, but rather, a hell that has *eternal* consequences. And I still could present this case.

    For example, passages about hell usually refer to people being <u>destroyed</u> in hell...which is <u>final</u>, not prolonged. And, 2Thes.1:7,9 mentions *"eternal destruction"*. Now the only way that destruction could be eternal is in the sense that it can't be reversed. Otherwise, this is an oxymoron. And in Jude 7, Sodom and Gomorrah are said to have been destroyed by *"eternal fire"*. Well, they're still not burning are they?

    Also, the Greek word for hell is "Gehenna" - which is different from "Hades", the place of the dead. Gehenna was the eternally burning fire outside of town that was used as the dumps...where things considered to be trash had their existence terminated. But then I ran into a scripture that gave a good logical reason for a hell that could go on for *eternity*, (Rev. 14:11,12): *"And the smoke of their torment ascends forever and ever; and they have no rest day or night..." <u>Here is what sustains the holy ones</u> who keep God's commandments and their faith in Jesus.* But when I looked at this passage a second time, I saw a way that hell still doesn't have to be eternal. That is: the smoke is what's eternal, not hell (and this could just mean that the *effect* of the smoke would be eternal, given my earlier argument re: *eternal,* eternally viewed in a heavenly video format). And this would be all that is necessary to remind those in heaven of the danger of sin. The *"no relief"* could mean 'just while they're going through the trauma'.

Also, God keeping us in the dark about this helps people implement a 'fear of hell' to keep themselves straight in their lives now. I mean, would you want to risk eternal suffering....or any suffering at all for that matter? Of course, most Protestants have diminished this by erroneously saying that you can't lose your salvation. But as I pointed out earlier, this is not what the Bible says.

Another <u>good</u> reason for God to invent suffering is: to show that there <u>have to be</u> consequences for sin, as part of a complete plan to eradicate sin. That's how serious sin is. Those who can see, know this. But it's obvious (by what is condoned in and purchased from the media and entertainment industries - especially in regards to marriage, sex and violence) that most in this world can't see.

An overall look at the dark side of afterlife: (1)There is the 'institution of death', i.e. physical death. (2)There is a dark netherworld. In the Old Testament it is called "Sheol", in the New Testament it is called "Hades". This place is not to be confused with Hell, which is a separate place. Hades/Sheol is the holding tank for all unsaved who are awaiting their trial at the White Throne Judgment. (3)Hell, which doesn't yet exist. It'll come into being at the end as God's incinerator of all that is evil (Rev 20:14).

If the Lazarus parable (Luke 16:19-31) is to be taken literally, then there is a "torment side" of Hades, which is the holding tank I mentioned earlier, and the "comfort side", which is where those who are destined to go to heaven go. (This could also possibly be the location of Purgatory). Then Rev. 20:13 says that there is a separate place called "death". This is probably where those throughout the ages, who were not worthy of heaven are. Those who are in 'soul sleep'....who returned to *"the dust"*. The logical argument that could be made for 'soul sleep' is the fact that we have proof every night that life can go on without our awareness: sleep. Also, the man who recently awoke from a 7 1/2 year coma was not aware that any time had elapsed. And in Deut. 31:16 and Job 7:21 death is referred to as *"sleep"*. The Hebrew word is "shakab". This is the same word used for 'nightly sleep', as in Gen. 28:16. The Old Testament concept of death being referred to as sleep is also stated as such in 1Cor. 15:20, where this sleep is said to have been conquered by Jesus, who is the <u>first</u> to do so. The Greek word (κοιμαω, koimao) also means both slumber and death. And in Dan. 12:2 it says that *"Many of those who sleep in the dust of the earth shall awake"*.

On the angelic side, there is the abode of Satan and his demons, the abyss; and there is the prison for fallen angels: Tartarus (2Pet. 2:4). When Rev.20:13 mentions *"the sea"*, it could be referring to the abyss, which is possibly referenced as 'the sea' in Rev. 13:1. Another reason for making this conclusion is: even though *"death and Hades"* are destroyed (after giving up their inhabitants), nowhere is there a mention of *"the abyss"* being destroyed except possibly in Rev. 21:1, where 'the sea' is said to be no more. And, on the logical side, why else would there be a differentiation between the dead in the sea......and in death? (Author's disclaimer: nothing that I present in this book regarding the book of Revelations is being presented as absolute gospel. I'm only making my best attempt to interpret it. I am neither *"adding"* nor *"subtracting"* anything. If you want to know why I wrote this, see Rev. 22:18,19. My purpose here is to present the reader with the most popular theories given to date, and to give my opinion of what the soundest interpretations would be. But it still is nebulous as to what <u>exactly</u> is going to happen. Only God and the future know the exact answers. To you, and my fellow theologians, it would be wise if we were to never present the nebulous as absolute facts: *"Paul..wrote you...letters. In which are some things hard to understand, which those who are <u>ignorant</u> and <u>unstable</u> <u>twist</u> to their own <u>destruction</u>, <u>as they do also the rest of the scriptures</u>. You are forewarned, beloved brothers. Be on guard lest you be led astray by the error of the wicked, and <u>forfeit the security</u> you enjoy"* (2Peter 3:15-17). And wouldn't a person who presents inaccurate descriptions of the future be accurately classified as a "false prophet"? Therefore, the reader is encouraged to do their own studies on these matters which, if nothing else, will give them good reason to do a lot of Bible studying, which is good.)

So, in God's final clean-up: *"death"* (i.e. the institution of death) and Hades will be cast into hell (Rev. 20:14). Therefore, there will be no more death. This is an obvious sign that God will emerge triumphant in His plan to eliminate the 'problem of free-will' (which manifested in Satan, fallen angels, Adam and Eve, and human history). What goes on at that point will be so good that it will go on for eternity. It's an exciting thing to be a part of...and it feels good and clean down to the very depths of our soul.

Now the only thing left is "What to do until the Messiah gets here" (which was a great book title from the early 1970s). If you're not sure that you're saved, I hope this book has put the greatness and importance of being in God's Kingdom on your heart and will prompt you to action. If you are saved, I hope that you've seen the importance of always being holy and being in God's heart. With this thought we will now move on to the next chapter.

Chapter 12

Applying God's Solution To Our Lives

We joyfully look forward to heaven. But even though this world is imperfect, we as Christians do live in the Kingdom of God now: *You are fellow citizens with the saints and members of the household of God, having been built upon the foundation of the apostles and prophets, with Christ Jesus Himself being the chief cornerstone* (Eph. 2:19, 20); *For many walk, of whom I have told you often, and now tell you even weeping, that they are the enemies of the cross of Christ: whose end is destruction, whose god is their belly, and whose glory is in their shame - who set their mind on earthly things. But our citizenship is in heaven* (Phil. 3:18-20). This is where we find our true citizenship. But like God, Jesus, the Holy Spirit, the angels and the saints, we have important work to do while here on earth; both on ourselves, and in the world.

We are involved in a sanctification process of retraining and restraining ourselves to not sin, from which we'll learn a lot for our preparation for heaven.

The following are some random thoughts that can help us apply God's solution to the free will problem to some of the more difficult aspects of life.

The wisest approach to life

The wisest, most bottom-line approach to life, that would cover all possible situations, can be simplified into just one focus: *"Seek first the Kingdom of God and His righteousness, and"* [then] *"all these things"* [that you need] *"shall be added to you"* (Matt. 6:33. Actually read all of Matt. 6:25-34). This is wise also because once you get the things you need (such as: a marriage, a church, a job, children, a ministry, etc.) you will be capable of living with them in a functional (not dysfunctional) way because you will be obeying the correct rules that make these work (which you seek and find in the Kingdom of God).

So then how do we seek the Kingdom of God? Sincere prayer, Bible study, belonging to a church, yielding to the Holy Spirit, and limiting our words, thoughts and deeds to being only those which are holy. And as an encouragement, keep in mind that nothing you go through is in vain. Everything that a child of God does is working towards a good end: *We know that all things work together for good to those who love God, to those who are called according to His purpose* (Rom. 8:28). And know that all good will be rewarded in the afterlife and all evil punished.

If God was to give you everything you needed without you having connected with Him, you would proba-bly be lulled into a complacent comfort zone and would miss the main thing that you need to accomplish in your lifetime: making yourself eligible for a peaceful, eternal afterlife in heaven (by connecting to Him, understanding Him, making peace with Him, and surrendering to Him).

Faith

It is good to recognize how faith works. For one: faith (that secure feeling in your heart) is a gift from God

(Eph. 2:8 *For by grace you have been saved through faith, and this is not from you; it is the gift of God*). That is, we can't will the feeling of faith into existence. The most we can do with our will is believe in God and pursue His righteousness. And we do so because we know that this is the optimum approach to life. And then we should never take God's response (a feeling of faith in our heart) for granted. We should thank Him for this very valuable gift. And to let us know that it is a gift, He will sometimes take it back (to some degree...hopefully small).

And, it is important and comforting to recognize that even in what feels like dark and uncomfortable times, there are good reasons for them to be happening (Rom. 8:28, Heb. 12:3-13, 2Cor. 1:7, 1Pet. 4:12-14). Purification can sometimes be unpleasant...but it has a good end: we are able to live life in a more functional and less dysfunctional vehicle. Plus, it's good for others. Gain through pain.

But of course, we would like to minimize the unpleasant times in our lives as much as possible. The way to do this is: while in your time of trial, look intently for the lesson that God is trying to teach you and discipline you into. Then flow with the desired good result. Don't cling to sin-habits. And, remember the 23rd Psalm.

Ultimately, the effect that I've desired to create in the reader is 'faith'. And then secondly, the wisdom and knowledge of how to live out a faithful life. And some degree of faith is necessary. I mean, I can't show you news footage of Jesus' miracles and resurrection, or video footage of heaven. Therefore, we need to have faith that God and Jesus are who the Bible says they are, that this life works as the Bible says, and that there's a glorious afterlife for those who maintain faith, as it says. But like I said earlier in this book, my allegiance to and belief in God and the

Bible will never change because of my investigations, which I shared with you. Nevertheless: *For by grace you have been saved through faith, and this is not from you; it is the gift of God; it is not from works, so no one may boast* (Eph. 2:8,9). Faith is a validating feeling that He rewards our heart with as a response to our trust and belief in Him, our allegiance to Him, our reaching out to fellowship with Him, our desire and efforts to serve and glorify Him...and one more way to prove that He's real. And this great feeling should be at the top of the list of what we value in this life. (Bible verses on faith: there are so many, so I'll just refer you to a concordance, or the 15 pages of verses on *faith* and *faithfulness* in Nave's Topical Bible). But beyond faith, Jerry Falwell once said "Even if there was no God..or heaven or hell..I'd still live according to the Bible". Why? Because its approach feels good and it works.

The paradox of fear

         The Bible says that *"The fear of the Lord is the beginning of wisdom"* (Prov. 9:10. Also: Heb. 10:31, Matt. 10:28). But it also says that *"For God has not given us a spirit of fear, but rather of power and love and self-control"* (2Tim. 1:7. Also, Rom. 8:15, Ps. 91:5,6,9). So now how can these two approaches to fear coexist?

         Think of your Christian life as being in a bubble. Inside the bubble is: faith, hope, love, joy, holiness and the Holy Spirit. Outside the bubble is: sin and judgment (and all of the negative emotions that go along with them). It is therefore healthy and wise to experience fear when we are starting to leave the bubble (kind of like our brake sensors that squeal to warn us that our brakes need to be fixed). We especially need the feeling of fear to alert us if we are completely outside of the bubble.

But when we're inside this bubble, we have no need to fear God (Is. 12:2). When we live sinlessly, we can enjoy its comfort and pleasures (1John 4:18: *There is no fear in love; but perfect love casts out fear, because fear involves torment. But he who fears is not yet perfect in love*). And there will be people and situations that will test our ability to stay in the bubble. But we just work at weathering these storms in the ways the Bible instructs us to, and cling to staying in the bubble as best we can.

The cycle of injury/pain/anger/forgiveness

A big problem in life is that many people are carrying a lot of anger. It's not that <u>they</u> <u>are</u> angry....it's that there is anger existing within their *body* . Kind of like when you have the flu, you (the *spirit*) are not sick...rather, your body is suffering with a reaction to a germ and is passing this suffering on to you via your indelible attachment to your body while here on earth. And the anger in the body comes from one of 3 sources: (1)anger from an unresolved past injury caused us, (2)a subconscious knee-jerk angry reaction based on stances against those who have attributes similar to the people who have harmed us or who are harming us now, and (3)anger towards a current real or *perceived* harm being done.

So, just like analyzing a physical sickness so as to assess its cause and what can be done for it, let's analyze 'anger sickness'.

But first let me say that anger will happen within us whether actual harm is being done, or whether we are *inaccurately perceiving* that harm is being done. Source #2 (mentioned a couple of paragraphs ago) is an example of the latter. Also, sources #1 and #3 can include inaccurate perceptions. But, we won't deal with 'inaccurate perceptions' here. They are another kind of problem, which doesn't fit the natural workings of anger. Rather, when a person with an inaccurate perception deeply looks within themselves, they will see a guilt feeling, as well as a lack of support from the truth channel. It is best for them to respect these inner reactions and proceed to solve their problem by analyzing and working on their tendency to have inaccurate perceptions. We will only be dealing here with 'natural, justified anger'. So now on with the analysis.

What causes anger? Anger is a reaction that we have when we've been harmed (e.g. physical, emotional, relational, business, property, etc.) or when we see another person unjustifiably harmed.

Why did God invent anger? To push us to emphatically communicate, in an unpleasant way to an injurer, that they've unjustifiably caused an injury. And, if they don't respond, anger will energize us to see that justice is carried out against them (in most cases).

Potential problems here though can be that many injurers: (1)don't care about the fact that they are creating victims, (2)don't <u>see</u> that they have 'forms of injuring others' as deeply-ingrained, subconscious habits, and (3)are carrying a lot of unresolved anger themselves.

And, if you've been habitually abused for years (mainly as children - which is why teenagers are so attracted to media, entertainment and lifestyles that include anger), you can carry anger for a long time, and in a chronic way. Why? Because you never were able to fulfill the natural function of 'getting it through to your injurer how they injured you'. As you can see by this last statement: <u>a natural purpose of anger is to stop injurers from committing further injury</u>. The next natural step in the process, if they don't listen, is to formally bring them to justice, either through the courts, through the church, through others, or through loss of relationship with you. And if these don't work, you can take solace in the fact that God sees every-thing (*"For He looks to the ends of the earth, and sees all that is under the heavens."* Job 28:24; *Can a man hide in secret without My seeing him? says the LORD.* Jer. 23:24; *"There is nothing concealed that will not be revealed, nor secret that will not be known.* Also see Luke 12:2). And all injurers will find their just punishments (or lack of rewards) with God. *"Vengeance is mine, I will repay, says the Lord."* (Rom. 12:19). And those who do right and have to bear injustices will receive rewards: *Surely there is a reward for the righteous; there is a God who judges the earth!"* (Psalms 58:11); *"you shall rise for your reward at the end of days."* (Dan. 12:13); *"Rejoice and be exceeding-ly glad, for great is your reward in heaven."* (Matt. 5:12); *Your Father who sees in secret will repay you* (Matt. 6:4); *He is a rewarder of those who diligently seek Him."* (Heb. 11:6), *For we must all appear before the judgment seat of Christ, so that each one may receive...according to what he did in the body, whether good or evil* (2Cor. 5:10).

What, if anything, can be done to prevent the unpleasant-to-excruciating experience of having anger? Well, actual (not mis-perceived) anger is always triggered by sin. Therefore, the more a society's laws, media and philosophies stand for holiness, the better off its citizens are going to be. Unfortunately, our society is very deficient in this regard, which was a big motivating factor for me to write this book. I want to try to make those who are in a position to influence our laws, media and policies aware of why we need only policies that are pro-holiness and anti-sin. This goal is also helped as citizens (sometimes moti-vated by anger*) become enlightened, which then leads them to be inspired to put pressure on policy makers.....and vote only for those who stand for holiness...and who stand against sin. (*This is why Rush Limbaugh is so popular.)

This is what we can do on a society level. But what can we do on a personal level? Well, first of all, avoid contact with a person who is prone to being an injurer. *"Make no friendship with an angry man, and with a furious man do not go, lest you learn his ways, and find a snare for yourself"* (Prov. 22:24,25).

But what about the anger that we already carry, from past injuries......or from current entanglements (like: anger at the media, entertainment industries, corrupt politicians, bad mates, bad business associates, etc.)? Well, for one, give yourself permission to let the anger or pain come on when it is pushing on your psyche. Don't bring it on...or *voluntarily* feed it. But also don't suppress it ('suppression' can bring on a whole different set of problems). Anger is part of a God-invented process you may not be able to avoid. Even though the feeling might sometimes be unpleasant, allow it to run its natural course, keeping in mind that its natural purposes are: (1)communication*, i.e. to try to get the injurer to stop their injurious ways; (2)to push you to do the things that will ensure that justice will be carried out; (3)to energize you to try to influence changes in unholy public, family, business, and personal policies; and (4)to draw you closer to and endear you more to a clean God amidst a dirty world. (*By the way, isn't it great how a sincere "I'm sorry" can magically free us from having to suffer anger, as well as somewhat free the injurer from suffering guilt? This is also God's pattern for restoration of peace after sin: first repentance, then forgiveness)

And of course, this God has as central to His advice to us: forgiveness. Why? *"Then Jesus said, 'Father, forgive them, for they know not what they do.'"* (Luke 23:34); *"Judge not, and you shall not be judged. Condemn not, and you shall not be condemned. Forgive, and you will be forgiven."* (Luke 6:37); *"And be kind to one another, tender hearted, forgiving one another, just as God and Christ also forgave you. (Eph. 4:32); "as Christ forgave you, so must you also do".* (Col. 3:13).

But, we should try to limit our contact with other people to being: just with those who only exhibit healthy behavior. But, being that no one is perfect, we will need to extend our definition to include: those who are growing and who sincerely want to cleanse themselves of sinful and injurious tendencies. The "I'm sorry"s will allow these relationships to carry on in a clean way. Of course, it is optimum to just associate with people who subscribe to the phrase: it is good to be sorry...but it is better to be careful. (Do you remember the phrase: to err is human...but why must you be so human?). And definitely try to avoid those who are inclined to be defensive and arrogant, lest they give you a ball and chain of anger that could rob your peace, clarity, and bring you suffering for a long time.

And foremost, make sure you work on getting rid of all injurious tendencies in yourself....for the sake of others, to glorify God's love....and to enjoy the experience of having a clean conscience. And do continually work on enlightening yourself, because you diffuse a great amount of the injuriousness of another person's actions when you can <u>see</u> how and why that person is not doing anything <u>personally</u> against you. It's usually just that they've been injured, and also have not been enlightened as to how to handle their anger (once again: *"Forgive them Father for they know not what they do"*). But now on to something nicer and lighter.

Happiness, Sweetness and Love

Happiness, sweetness and love are some of the most valuable things we can have in this life. But those who don't have them often try to ridicule and hurt the feelings of those who do, trying to cause them to stop having these positive feelings ("misery loves company"). This is especially so with young children (schoolyard intimidation). But where it starts is: the perpetrating children have been subjected to relatives and friends who are prone to being harsh, insensitive and unloving. So they either end up *imprinting* them....or they become caved-in by their injurious traits. So now, out of their anger, pain and jealousy (of the *healthy* kids), and the fact that they are hyped up (because they are trying to avoid the unpleasantness of these emotions), they try to suppress the happiness, sweetness and love in others. And this is possible because, unlike anger and harshness, which can be energetic, strong and intimidating.....happiness, sweetness and love are tender, sensitive and delicate....like fragile fine art treasures.

But, like with fine art treasures, we should protect and defend happiness, sweetness and love, and make sure that they are preserved in safe environments. And because happiness, sweetness and love are even more valuable than fine art treasures, a school teacher's highest priority should be to make sure that they are preserved in their students (which is not the case in many of our schools today).

Children have a great natural abundance of happiness, sweetness and love. But sadly it is often gradually eroded away by mean parents and siblings, unkind school mates, 'bad' neighborhood kids, first girl/boy friends, etc. And then add to all of this a constant bombardment by a media that is greatly devoid of happiness, sweetness and love. The music industry rarely produces a sweet song anymore (whereas they were the norm in the '40s and '50s); sports figures often lower themselves to 'trash talking' and fighting; the movie industry is filled with violence; and television has as its main feelings: insulting, hyperness, jivyness, ridiculing, whining, etc., and all of which are deemed to be 'cool'. (By the way, 'cool' is a 1950s jazz term that comes from 'cool, calm and collected'. So in this light, none of these current "vibes" in the media are cool).

So, what is a godly person's protection from all of this? What is our armor against the sicknesses of the world? It is: strong, loving, gentle families.....who restrain their harsh words.....the Bible, the Holy Spirit, and the fact that the greatest power in the universe is on our side (and on our insides). Also: knowing that God is building us towards a heaven that will be devoid of all of these sicknesses. And remember (when you think you are being pressured to be cool or adultlike), an essence of what Jesus says our ultimate spirit will be like in heaven is: like a child. *He [Jesus] rejoiced [in] the holy Spirit and said, "I give you praise, Father, Lord of heaven and earth, for although you have hidden these things from the wise and the learned you have revealed them to the childlike* (Luke 10:20,21). So just enjoy the sweetness and innocence of being childlike; observe, be with, and support sweet children; and don't be intimidated by the world.

Manners and politeness

Manners and politeness are the social lubricants that make life smooth and keep it nice experientially. And there is no circumstance, when dealing with nice people, where we should lose our manners and politeness, even if we are suffering or upset. It's okay to let out our anger, but not on an innocent person, thereby alienating a potential sympathetic ally. That is: it's okay to shoot arrows, but not <u>at</u> somebody. Shoot them at what, not who, has made you upset. Also, *whining* isn't a polite form of communication.

Our ability to have manners and be polite can be greatly aided by the following well-known Bible *verses:* *"Love thy neighbor as thyself"; "Do unto others as you would have them do unto you"; "The one who is least among you, this one is great"; "Blessed are the meek and the humble";* and *"It is better to give than receive".*

<u>Narcissism</u>

'Narcissism' is: a concern for only one's own interests, whims, needs and desires. Narcissists are not only insensitive to others, but they usually are not even *really* aware that others exist...at least as 'feeling beings'. 'Others' are seen either as obstacles or beings that can be utilized in the narcissist being able to fulfill their interests, whims, needs and desires.

And we currently live in an 'age of narcissism' (abortion, divorce, greed, rivalry, irresponsibility, crime, drugs, sexual irresponsibility, etc.). The narcissist gropes for the quick fix...instead of the responsible solution.

A Christian is just the opposite. A Christian thinks mostly about (and does) what's best for others: their family, their ministry, their job, their church, God, etc. *Love does not seek its own interests* (1Cor. 13:4,5).

My son Timmy is at a certain crossroad in his life that touches on narcissism and is basic to the theme of this book: do we always act on how we feel each moment of life...and if we don't, why not?

It would be nice if we could live life <u>exactly</u> how we <u>feel</u> to. But that approach doesn't always work well with other human beings....or even with our own body.

Therefore, as an important part of our approach to life, we must at times accept doing things that we don't feel like doing, and we must stop ourselves from doing things that we do feel.

This fact of life can be perceived as a bitter pill to swallow, but this pill is really good medicine if we see all of the great things that can happen when we live life this way: It allows us to be able to peacefully and pleasurably enjoy the company of other free-will beings; and it gives us the great feeling of high self-esteem. And, in regards to our body, we are able to go through life in a vehicle that functions well and gives us good feelings (instead of bad ones). Therefore, in the challenge of self-control, it is very helpful for us to 'see the good reasons for self-restraint and sacrificial-giving', and to see how these are also good for us.

Some examples from Timmy's life: brushing our teeth daily = no painful dental problems now or later in life; politeness = a good feeling among people, no hurt feelings, and developing an attitude of submission; doing homework = an ability to make a good wage as an adult, which is very important for being able to have a good adult life; holiness = making God, your parents and other people happy. More examples from other lives would be: no gluttony = a better feeling body to go through life with; sexual restraint = no disease, guilt, or spiritual crime of bringing a helpless, sensitive human being into the world without having prepared a proper nest; work = the guiltless feeling of knowing that we're doing our share, and that we're contributing to the common good, not stealing from it.

And it is good to recognize that life is a 2-way street. That is: we wouldn't want others to ignore the negative effects that their actions might have on us. Therefore, this whole process is undergirded by: *"Do unto others as you would have them do unto you"*, and *"Love your neigh-bor as yourself"*.

In Jesus' examples of washing His disciples' feet and dying on the cross, He's saying that even all-powerful God can't co-exist nicely with other beings without 'giv-ing'. And when we live life right, God supports this approach by rewarding us with good feelings.

So, the choice is clear: Option 1 - always get your way, but miss out in a lot of other ways and suffer a lot of problems in life; or Option 2 - learn the sacrifices of 'disci-pline and giving', and then enjoy the resulting benefits (as well as freedom from the problems that occur when you take the other approach). By the way, can you see how the 'Option 1' approach is the seed for crime?

The Bible's superiority over psychology

Psychology's biggest failing comes from the fact that it mostly dwells on 'what's wrong' (and how, why and where things went wrong). And often, while in the depths of analysis, a patient is overtaken by depression and other bad feelings ("paralysis from analysis").

But at the end of the analysis (although I don't think it ever does reach an end), a person is still faced with the same challenge they were faced with in the beginning: discovering what is right, and then retraining themselves to only act within its guidelines. But this can be a hard thing to do in a society that is so tolerant of wrong. And, ironi-cally, the psychology community is one of the leading branches of society that is expanding and perpetuating this tolerance.

Unlike psychology, the Bible's approach is simple: know what's right...and do what's right. Also, know what's wrong and don't do it.

We shouldn't ever have to focus on the ugliness of wrong. It's specifics should be embarrassing and troubling (as they naturally are). God tried to spare us this 'knowledge of good and evil', but Adam and Eve proved that we couldn't handle this luxurious position.

A case example here would be: a person has problems in life because they're narcissistic. Psychology's approach would be to have them spend (expensive) years analyzing how, why, where and when they got this way (and debate if this is even a problem at all). Whereas they simply need to learn: manners, politeness, giving, humbleness, religion, and taking joy in submitting to and fulfilling their responsibilities in life. Doing these will restore good feeling to their lives, as well as take away the bad feelings.

But if people are basically selfish, what would be their motivation to do these things? It would be because they love God, and would feel good about themselves if they were a <u>contributor</u> to the emotional and functional beauty of His kingdom (instead of being a detractor and a leech). (By the way, can you now see one place where 'self-esteem' problems might come from?)

This 'doing-out-of-love-for-God' could solve all personal and societal problems. Why? Because each person would be carrying within them an 'inner police' that would keep them from doing wrong. (This could be one of the things that makes heaven work.)

<u>How to live spiritually</u>

Many people (even some who say they are Christians), are not having a relationship with the real God, Jesus, Holy Spirit or Bible. They are just having a relationship with the God of their mind, the Jesus of their mind, the Bible of their mind, and the Church of their mind (i.e.

how they've conceptualized these), while they continue to bow to 'the world', their impulses, and other people.

When you pray, pray sincerely, with all your heart, to the real God. When you have questions, immediately go to the Bible, don't <u>think</u> about them or ask others. Submit to others in your duties, but bow only to God, Jesus and the Holy Spirit. Always be with God in your heart. Doing these things is having a real relationship with God.

<u>The true Christian spirit</u>

I saw a TV show recently on EWTN about a new feminist uprising in the Catholic Church. It was said that these feminists were complaining about the fact that the Pope, cardinals, bishops and priests were all men....and that God was referred to as "He", etc.

My immediate response was that these women are not having a true Christian <u>experience</u> and don't really know God or understand Christianity. To make this a focus in their lives, they must be very unhappy, embittered, self-absorbed souls who would rather be enslaved to their egos and bitterness, than to love God and His Church.

I mean, it wouldn't matter to me if the entire hierarchy of the Church were women....or 1/2 women, 1/2 men... or 72% women, 28% men...etc. All that matters to me is to <u>follow</u> (not lead) the will of God. It just so happens that the Bible says that the primary leaders of the Church should be men. But really, what's the difference? It wouldn't change <u>our position</u> as Christians no matter what gender roles are prescribed in the Bible, which is: submission....to holiness.. in love. This is the true Christian experience, the fulfillment of God's plan for us, and why we are here.

On this TV show, after the long list of feminist complaints were read off, the cardinal who hosted the show had just one response: "With all due respect, It just sounds like 'whining' to me". That is, instead of initially dealing with the specific issues being complained about, He went right to the <u>heart</u> of the matter: these complaints weren't emanating out of a Christian spirit.

But those who do have the true Christian spirit (submission to holiness and love)....male or female...have a reward that is invaluable: the deep inner peace of knowing that you're doing the right thing. Therefore, my advice to these women who are presently calling themselves feminists is: let go and let God. Only in surrendering to God and His holiness will you find true liberation and peace.

<u>What about devout religious people who never heard of Jesus or the Bible?</u>

Another important question to pose here would be: do people who have never seen a Bible or heard of Jesus have a chance?

A Bible phrase that is often ungently delivered by Protestants when this question comes up is a quote by Jesus: *"I am the way, the truth, and the life. No one comes to the Father except through Me"* (John 14:6). But then the other side will say: "How can a loving God condemn people - whom He's made - who show a great love for Him, a devotion to Him, and who are so moved to work on cleaning up their lives?" I have an answer that will satisfy both of these positions. Jesus was in a human body for only 33 years. The rest of the time He's been a spirit. Therefore, He can manifest anywhere in the world in any way or form that He pleases.....and save whoever He wants to and in whatever way He wants to. And He has at His disposal all that is available in heaven. This concept satisfies both of the positions described above.

This concept also finds support in Rev. 5:6: *I saw standing in the midst of the throne and the four living creatures and..the elders...a Lamb as though it had been slain, having seven horns and seven eyes, which are the seven spirits of God sent out into <u>all</u> of the earth.*

Another verse that supports what I've said here is: *I have other sheep that do not belong to this fold. These also I must lead, and they will hear my voice* (John 10:16).

I mean, what <u>other</u> sheep was He talking about? It has been said that He meant the Gentiles. But being that He didn't specifically say this, the phrase has the possibility of meaning the whole world.

And we can see that other people in the world are showing some good fruit and doing good...even much better than the western nations. Many of them place a high priority on spirituality, politeness, holiness and personal growth....much moreso than western nations. Where is their inspiration to do so coming from? If the above verses are to be believed, then we have to assume that it is the Holy Spirit that is moving them. Good fruit means a good tree. How can western countries, which show much worse fruit, logically conclude that God is only on their side? If God's purpose is to teach free-will beings submission..well then there are many very religiously submissive people in other cultures and religions. Where do they get their motivation if not from God within them?

There are even many stories of devotees who have submissively worked very hard for their masters for many years <u>just</u> in the hope that at the end of years of labor, they would receive the knowledge of God and life from them. Do you think that God is going to turn His back on them? Especially when the book that gives that knowledge (the Bible) is more and more being shunned in the western societies. (Kind of brings to mind the Bible verse that speaks about "casting pearls at swine").

In his letter to the Romans, Paul explains how Christians, Jews and non-Christian Gentiles will be judged, and how they all have a chance for salvation or condemnation. *There will be glory, honor, and peace for everyone who does good....There is no partiality with God. All who sin outside the law will also perish without reference to it, and all who sin under the law will be judged in accordance with it. For not the hearers of the law are just in the sight of God, rather, but the doers of the law will be justified; For when Gentiles, who do not have the law, by nature do the things contained in the law, these, although not having the law, are a law to themselves, who show that the demands of the law are written in their hearts, their conscience also bearing witness and their thoughts accusing or else <u>excusing them</u> on the day when God will judge people's secrets through Christ Jesus, according to my gospel* (Rom. 2:10,11-16).

(Now whether a person believes all of this is true or not is not important because, as long as there is a strong <u>possibility</u> that it could be true [and I've just pointed out how, in this case, there Biblically and logically is], we shouldn't make a condemning judgment of others. It is an arrogant and negative waste of time which could be spent on positive pursuits. We should just be concerned about "lighting candles" and judging real, obvious sin; not speculatively judging others' candles.)

Actually, I very much wish that the western societies had some of the eastern ways. Before I received "the knowledge" (and it really was a tremendous knowledge), I had to go through a period of being an "aspirant" (i.e. *aspiring* to receive the knowledge). I went to "satsang" every night in which I heard stories from other people on how their lives were being *bliss*fully* elevated by this knowledge. It was very exciting. I was being shown a door of hope that would take me from a world that my sensitive side had become very repulsed and injured by, to a beautiful world of a perfect God who lived within me. (*The greeting of the "premies" [which is Indian for "lovers of God"] to each other was: "Ja Satchit Anand", which means "Truth is the consciousness of bliss").

Every once in a while, a "Mahatma" would come through town and would meet individually with the aspirants to see if they were ready to receive the knowledge. They would ask you questions and look at your vibe. They did this because they knew that if they cast the pearls at you and you were still swine....well....what purpose does a pig have with pearls? And that's how this very subtle knowledge would look to a person who wasn't ready...like pearls do to a pig. For example, nearly every western house has a great pearl in it - the Bible - and yet look at how much unholiness goes on in these houses.

So if the Mahatmas didn't feel that you were ready to receive knowledge, they would say to you "You need more satsang....then come back and see me or another Mahatma again". This would give a person something to look forward to...and also a sense that God was very special....as opposed to the many emotionalistic alter calls in which people feel like they've been saved, and that this means they don't have to worry about their salvation for the rest of their lives. But this is not a Biblical position, as can be seen in Hebrews 3:12,14,10,11,4:6:

Beware, brethren, lest there be in any of you an evil and unfaithful heart, so as to fall away from the living God. We have become partners of Christ only if we hold the *beginning of our confidence steadfast <u>to the end</u>. I (God) said, "They always go astray in their heart, and they have not known my ways." So I swore in my wrath, <u>They shall not enter into my rest</u>." Therefore, since it remains that some will enter into it, and <u>those who formerly received the good news did not enter</u> because of disobedience.*

Also, in Col. 1:22,3: *In the body of His flesh through death, to present you holy, and blameless, and irreproachable in His sight - <u>provided that</u> you persevere in the faith, firmly grounded, stable, and <u>not shifting</u> from the hope of the gospel that you heard, which was preached to every creature under heaven, of which I, Paul, became a minister.*

Yes, a person can lose their salvation (which might even mean they never really had it in the first place).

Another good line out of this verse that could support my conclusion earlier about God having other criteria for relating to and judging other people: *"the gospel that you heard, <u>which was preached to every creature under heaven"</u>* .

Another thing that I liked about the eastern way, was that there were "ashrams", which were either all-male or all-female households where those living there would live a monastic lifestyle. Being that it's sometimes very difficult to stay living in your current home when you suddenly want to make a religious conversion in an unimpeded way, having these ashrams are very helpful to cement your conversion deeply into your being, and give you some distance from unholy habits and people who support and would even push these habits. Also, while in these ashrams, people could even see if they are called and gifted to commit to a celibate lifetime as God's servant.

I also liked the visuals (cloth patterns), the incense,

the music, and the food. But most of all, I liked the high reverence for God and spirituality within our everyday lives....the sense that our every moment was a spiritual workshop and an opportunity to get higher and closer to God.....as opposed to surrendering to the television and other crude, unspiritual and unholy western habits.

A good habit that I developed while I was a premie was "inner pranaming". "Pranaming" is the act of bowing down in a prayerful position, or with arms outstretched and face down. You've seen many Muslims do this, especially in Mecca. What I extracted from this was: every time I find myself getting uptight, confused, arrogant, or any other negative feeling, I simply (in my mind) pranam to God or Jesus or the Holy Spirit or other people. This either totally washes away the negative feeling, or greatly reduces it.

But, like I mentioned earlier in this book, as beautiful as this all sounds, the reason that it failed was because it didn't understand the specific mechanics of holiness in our everyday lives (as described in the Bible).....especially in the area of male/female relationships. So, what good is it to become <u>very</u> sensitive (through meditation and a religious lifestyle) when you're just going to get painfully shocked by the sin and dysfunction of your (no-guarantee-it's-for-a-lifetime) mate, who might be toying with the nouveau idea of 'free love' (which the Pope said is neither free nor love)? Therefore, most who were involved in this and other higher-consciousness movements abandoned this sensitivity training for the more (seemingly) practical western, callous-building, shock-absorbing approaches of: alcohol, television, etc. For this reason, the true gateway to establishing sensitivity and love in a society is for that society to more and more instate God's laws as their laws.

A proof of this to me comes from the work I've

done to make a living: music. My work recently has included incorporating in my live performance repertoire a group of very sweet songs from the 1950s and early 1960s, for example: Stranger On The Shore, Misty, Sukiyaki, etc.

While playing these songs recently, I became overwhelmed by a feeling/realization that I grew up in a different world. People were more polite, more friendly, more submissive, more religious, more holy, more family-oriented.....and, because of all of this....much happier. (For those who have exhibited an inclination to debate this last point, they simply need to compare the popular music - which is an expression of the general state of people's hearts - of today with the popular music of the '40s, '50s and early '60s.) This should be a strong motivation (especially for those of us who lived through these years and remember the general public feelings) to try to do what it would take to recapture some of these precious and very pleasurable feelings: change some of our current laws and what is and isn't acceptable in the media and entertainment industries.

The **source** of this nation's **woes** is very **simple**

People are suffering because they are:

(A)living <u>unholy lives</u> (which is reinforced by their laws);

(B)with an <u>unholy vibe</u> (which is exemplified and perpetuated by their media and entertainment industries); and all because

(C)they have **turned their backs on God** as being the central focus of their lives.

It is this simple. Any other attempts to analyze the problems or create solutions are going to fall short and be futile (the present world is proof of that). The bottom-line point to be made to those who are debaters against Christianity and who are proponents of a non-religious (in

the mainstream), secular-humanist society (which is most
of the media and entertainment industries) is this: these
kinds of societies have always failed (such as: the collapse
of nearly all of the atheistic communist countries, and the
moral/emotional state of the current United States).
Whereas, societies whose mainstream (truly) upheld
Christianity above all else have prospered (such as: the
very-low-crime/almost-non-existent-divorce-rate/healthier-
emotional-state [low fear, high happiness, abundant love]
of pre-1966 U.S.). A fact that further supports this comparison of time eras is: in the '40s and '50s most people didn't
lock their doors. Even as late as the mid '50s, some cars
didn't require keys to turn them on. Whereas today, even
with all of the locks and alarm systems, the crime rate is
much higher. Also, regarding poverty as an excuse for
crime: in the midst of the most intense state of poverty -
the depression of the 1930s - the crime statistics were
much lower than today. These facts only leave 'the religious and moral decline' as the cause of increased crime.

De-evolution
        The most critical factor in the de-evolution of the
western world in the last 30 years is: secular-humanism
replacing Christianity as the mainstream philosophy. The
second biggest factor is: the breakdown of the family. This
satanic spiritual assault was waged on 3 fronts: ease of
divorce (aided by secular-humanism's guru: psychology);
women abandoning their natural roles (feminism); and the
sexual "revolution" (aided by pornography, the pill, peer-
pressure-intimidation, the media, alcohol and drugs).
        One of the greatest indicators of the breakdown in
sexual morals is the fact that in the early '60s, if you
<u>weren't</u> a virgin it was hush-hush. Whereas in the early

'90s, if you <u>are</u> a virgin it's hush-hush. This change from '<u>submission</u> to what is good' to '<u>rebellion</u> against what is good' is probably the greatest cause of the breakdown of the institution of 'family'.

Here's how it happened: (1)'Playboy' was initially allowed into society...then it *gradually** devolved. (*Satan knows that the world won't allow big moral changes....but he still gets to the big changes via small, gradual changes). (2)Guys started patting each other on the back for conquering the *final frontier*: a girl's sacred biological trust (with God and nature), her virginity. (3)The invention of 'the pill' made it harder for girls to say 'no'. (4)'Free love' became the 'hip' thing to do. (5)Drugs and alcohol broke down natural inhibitions. (6)Women's freedom, pride, anger and independence were challenged (at the expense of holiness), and *flames* fanned (ala Satan) with feminism.

The only way out of this is for people to first look at the ruins: rampant divorce; unhappy marriages; children from broken families or 2-parent-working families turning to drugs, gangs, crime, adultery, abortion, single-parenting, suicide, etc. Then realize that in countries (including the U.S.) and times when God was more popular, these problems existed only on a very small level 'Conservatism' means: trying to 'conserve' what has worked well in the past. Whereas 'liberal' means: taking liberties to change. By the way, I'm not saying that all of the intentions of liberals are bad. I'm just saying that most of their attempts have resulted in 'the baby being thrown out with the dirty bathwater'. That is, if there are problems within families, you work at solving the problems, not at attempting to abolish or reinvent the natural, God-invented institution of heterosexual family. And yes at times these problems may appear insurmountable. But God can resolve them all. Plus, why are we here?: to learn that only submission works. Therefore, the answer is: return to God and holiness. This can, at least, be done on an individual level. If this isn't done on a mass level, this means that this is probably the end times, when God will wipe out the evil systems. (Mother Teresa said that Americans are the poorest people in the world.....not materially, but inside themselves).

How 'pride' can lead to a downfall

     I mentioned in Chapter 5 how 'pride' led to Satan's downfall (which He then passed on to Adam and Eve). Well here's another example of how 'pride' can lead to a downfall.

     I spent the first 32 years of my life in San Francisco. The San Francisco I grew up in was an all-American city.....in tune with the rest of the U.S. and basically no different: nice, normal, religious, family-oriented.

     But it did possess a unique physical charm. And it took pride in this charm. But then it started boasting about this charm and its elevated stature compared to other cities. And in its rivalry with other cities (who themselves took pride in being cultured), San Francisco, not wanting to be outdone, added 'being progressively cultured' to its pride portfolio. Enter: Satan.

     'The arts' have traditionally been breeding grounds for Satan anyway. The theatre, literature, dance, poetry, sculpture, music, photography, cinema and art have been the main places where the boundaries restraining evil are tested, broken and commercialized. The new, more evil boundaries then become the accepted norms in society (e.g. nudity, rebellion, sexual perversion, and liberal thought).

     Now if San Francisco was going to be able to maintain its 'progressive' status, it had to be the first city for any new progressive movement. Its contract with Satan became this: you just make us be first...and then we'll allow whatever you think you can get away with....and our media and people will even promote it (along with promoting our pride for being first). So, San Francisco became the first mecca for: beatniks, hippies, gays, sexual perversion, and liberals. Now San Francisco has become the most dysfunctional city there is. It has become the leading experimental center of evil and dysfunction. It manufactures the evil, and then Los Angeles markets it. The beautiful city that I grew up in is now gone.

(By the way, I'm not down on people who <u>fall</u> into the gay lifestyle. I've had many gay friends, some who've died of AIDS, which is some of the reason for my inspiration to try to do something about the evil and dysfunction in this world. I see people who fall into the gay lifestyle as being somewhat victims of permissive spiritual traps...the kind that San Francisco takes pride in allowing to happen. But I know that within the Bible is a good life for anyone, no matter what their circumstances. And there are <u>many ex</u> gays to prove this, including ex gay activist leaders. In defense of people who are in the gay lifestyle, many of them have a high degree of 'sweetness', which is an admirable and endearing quality. And, they often are interested in personal growth. They just need to take that next step now in growth by surrendering to God and following the holy standards in His Bible).

<u>The paradox of freedom</u>

The basic error in the hippie movement was in thinking that 'freedom is unlimited' (e.g. freedom to take drugs, have sex, be irresponsible, co-mingle with nature, etc.). Many tragedies later, the liberals of today somewhat carry on this same legacy, while some of us who experienced those tragedies try to warn those who are considering doing these things of their potential danger.

I also try to spread the message that the greatest freedom possible is not to be found in trying to break down every possible barrier to freedom. A person could save themselves the dangers and frustrations of this approach if they would realize that <u>total freedom is impossible</u>. We could never be free from: death, hunger, illness, sleep, etc.

So then, how free is the freest we can be? The paradox here is that we end up experiencing the greatest freedom when we give up our freedom...to God. And this includes giving up an obsession for freedom. God will take your entire burden and give you a feeling of freedom in return. And all that He asks is that you obey His laws....which anyway, are all <u>good</u>. And anything that goes against His laws, also goes against functional science (physiology, sociology, etc.). The battery might say that it wants to be free of the car, but that is impossible, because what will recharge it? (Also the battery needs to recognize that it is needed by the car).

Those who are obsessed with freedom are that way because they really don't feel free. They're usually enslaved by: anger (at their past or present); an empty God-void; and/or being tied to dysfunctional people, systems or philosophies. A person who feels free doesn't even think about freedom.

My personal testimony is: I didn't find true freedom until I submitted my life to God and Jesus as my leaders. A frustration that I feel as I look out into the world is seeing so many people looking for freedom in all the wrong places...and in the process causing a lot of damage. That's one of the reasons why I write.

Grace

Most people don't realize the position of grace that we're in (that is, until something bad happens). It is a tremendous <u>privilege</u> just to be able to wake up every morning in a relatively peaceful society, in a relatively calm environment, in a relatively healthy body, and be able to relatively do what you want. And this privilege is often wasted, taken for granted, and even used to create evil.

But the power that made and runs this universe, and that allows this privilege to continue in relative safety, could destroy us in an instant. Instead, He has decided to let us <u>choose</u> to do good and follow Him...or not. But this choice isn't extended to us forever. And this choice, that most of us have been given many years to make, will be the basis of our eternal fate when the many years are over.

Something to notice: do the more powerful beings on earth show this kind of grace to the less powerful beings? That is: parents to children, rich to poor, bosses to employees, husbands to wives, wives to husbands, bigger kids to smaller kids, teachers to students, smarter people to less smart people, the healthy to the unhealthy, the fortunate to the unfortunate, leaders to citizens, society to the unborn, stronger people to weaker people, etc.

Summary: Why We Are Here
(1) Because God finds pleasure in sharing life with us.
(2) For us to see how God has proven through history that free will beings, on their own, cannot peacefully coexist in such a way that is fair and uninjurious to all of them.
(3) To realize that the only way free will beings can peacefully coexist is for <u>all</u> of them to submit to what's best for the whole (and never submit to impulsive whims [that aren't from healthy needs] or schemes for greedy gain).

(4) To realize that we need a sovereign, perfect, all-knowing God to direct us, because we, in our own sovereignty, would continue to fail (in trying to figure out how to live life by the 'trial and error' method), and would continue to create harm for others and ourselves.

(5) To understand God's plan for resolving the problem of free will, and that He's made a way to reconcile imperfect-us to perfect-Him through perfect Jesus as our savior.

(6) To pass life's one-on-one test and enter into a sovereign-God/submissive-human relationship by making Jesus our sovereign Lord, and the Holy Spirit our closest companion (after first accepting the proof of God and the fact that He authored the Bible*). We must then try our best to fulfill what God asks of us in the Bible and through our spirit. (*Many don't need to do this because they simply look out into the universe and *know*...and they read the Bible and *know* - that is, it resonates in their spirit as being good and right, and they want to align with what is good and right.)

(7) Once we've gotten all of the above, to enjoy the great things God has made for us, and to spread the beautiful and perfectly functional information we are seeing.

The main purpose of (2)-(6) is: to make us eligible for a higher, evil-free, more pleasurable existence (heaven) and a closer relationship with God (now and in heaven).

<u>Three states to determine 'how important you are to God and humanity'</u>

(1)<u>Spiritual liability</u>: Selfish; rebellious; take-without-giving; impulsive; bad attitude; argumentative; defensive; rude; sinning; criminal activity; criticizes the Church.

(2)<u>Spiritual neutral</u>: Not religious; does nothing for the Church, humanity and others; wasted life (i.e. no spiritual activity or involvement, plus a lot of involvement in trivial, superficial, meaningless activities).

(3)<u>Spiritual asset</u>: Goes to church; witnesses; has a ministry; keeps sin in check; is holy, giving and loving; works at growing (i.e. takes on good traits, and suppresses and reprograms bad traits); submits; has a positive attitude.

<u>Highness vs. hyperness</u>

I recently went to church (unfortunately in a very underslept state) and started feeling like it was very slow, tedious and boring. At one point I even considered switching churches. I wanted to leave the service, but *something* told me to force myself to stick it out...as a matter of discipline...and respect for God and my Sunday obligation.

To make a long story short, I was very surprised when the mass was over to find myself in a <u>great</u> feeling state (I don't know why I was surprised, having had this experience many times in my life). I felt very peaceful, calm, full of love, and unbothered by my lack of sleep.

Within this experience is a very important thing to understand about life.....about boredom and stimulation; about highness vs. hyperness.

Causes of boredom: (1)unspent energy (sometimes falsely built up from allowing ourselves to get too hyped); (2)unfulfilled pressing needs (including: doing something you don't feel like doing...because you need to be doing something else); (3)being in a situation where others and/or the environment and/or the activities are unconnected.

This unconnected feeling could also happen in us if an environment is revving at a lower biorhythmic rate than where our's is at when we enter it. So, we might feel bored at first, but if we submit to the new environment we'll get transformed to a better state (e.g. church, calm music, etc).

(The way that church could never become boring is to see every second in it as an opportunity to become more focused in the Holy Spirit. It's an hour to practice having a perfect thought life, and to develop into beings that glorify God's desire of how He'd like us to be. Plus, church is a heartfelt exchange of love with God, as He looks on.)

Throughout this book, when I've criticized the hyper-unconnected-constant-excitement of TV (shows and commercials), I'm basing my criticism on 3 things: (1)long exposure to this can lead to a drained stupor, (2)it's a crazy (i.e. unnatural) energy state [and both '(1)' and '(2)' can end up being chronic]; and (3)the most pleasurable state of life is to be found in a calm, agape-filled union with God.

Once we get hyped up or drained from *spiritually saccharin* focuses, it might be difficult and uncomfortable to subject ourselves to what really will transform us to a higher, natural state (e.g. church, prayer, Bible study, etc.). But it's worth it because we end up in a much more plea-surable, peaceful, connected, no-boredom state.

So, one of the great challenges of life is: if a person wants to remain in a high, pleasurable, connected-to-God state, they need to be discriminating as to what they allow themselves to focus on...and even what they think (in 1Pet. 1:13 and 2Cor. 10:5 we are told to stand guard over our mind). This is important, because once we're in a hyped-up state: (1)it's very difficult to even see that that's what's wrong; and (2)bad things can happen (to us and others) when we're unconnected, insensitive and unable to see.

By the way, this discussion about boredom brings to mind a great benefit I've had in becoming a Christian: since I became a Christian, I've never experienced bore-dom. Whereas, before I became a Christian, the experience of boredom was sometimes a big problem for me.

Other benefits I've experienced: I lost a compulsion I had for gambling (now I couldn't even force myself to gamble); I lost my desire for drugs and alcohol; my self-esteem problem was eliminated; etc. (There are more...plus I know <u>why</u> these freedoms happened. But I'll save these long discussions for other books).

<u>Final tidbits</u>

✝ The 3 wise men had a definite star to follow...to guide their path and dictate what it was going to be. What is the star in your life? What causes you to make certain decisions...turns...and reactions to circumstances, feelings and opportunities? What goals and focuses guide your path? Is your star a holy one (God, holiness, growth, love, fulfillment of your God-given responsibilities on earth, and ministries).....or is it a carnal one (pursuit of pleasure, fame, pleasing your friends, anti-God liberal causes, etc.)?

✝ "The honors of this world are nothing but puff and emptiness and fear of falling." - *St. Augustine.* Whereas, the honors of God's Kingdom are joy, peace, fulfillment, inspiration, satisfaction, great works, love, etc.

✝ The American media: *"They are gossips and scandalmongers and they hate God"* (Rom. 1:29-30).

✝ Instead of turning to <u>prayer</u> in times of need or peril, now kids bring their hope for resolution of their and the world's problems to <u>sublimated</u> fantasies of Superman, the Incredible Hulk, and other fiction. *Fr. Joseph Neuville*

✝ When I find that peace is leaving me in a social situation (or even in my own thoughts about someone), I recall this saying from "The Imitation Of Christ": "The person who does not strive to be the least, and subject to all, cannot long remain in peace". *Thomas Á Kempis.*

✝ "Jesus Christ teaches people that there is something in them which lifts them above this life with its hurries, its pleasures and fears. Those who understand Christ's teachings feel like a bird that did not know it has wings and now suddenly realizes that it can fly, can be free and no longer needs to fear." *Tolstoy.*

✝ "I think God has planned the strength and beauty of youth to be physical. But the strength and beauty of age is spiritual. We gradually lose the strength and beauty that is temporary so we'll be sure to concentrate on the strength and beauty which is forever." *J. Robertson McQuillan.*

✝ "The fragrance always stays in the hand that gives the rose." *Hada Bejar.*

✝ "I am a little pencil in the hand of a writing God who is sending a love letter to the world." *Mother Teresa.*

<u>Our greatest hope</u>

We won't achieve a perfect environment, or even perfection ourselves, while here on earth (although we will continually strive towards these). But Jesus says that we will experience these with Him in heaven (and what a great way to end this book):

"Let not your heart be troubled; You have faith in God; have faith also in Me. In My Father's house are many mansions; If it were not so, I would have told you. I go to prepare a place for you. And if I go and prepare a place for you, I will come back again and receive you to Myself; so that where I am, there you may be also" (John 14:1-3).

Index

Bibliography

Bible. English. *New American Bible*. Kansas: Catholic Bible
    Publishers. 1970.

Bible. English. *New King James Version.*. Thomas Nelson. 1982.

Bible. English. *New American Standard*. Moody Press. 1978.

Vos, Johannes. *Religions Of The World*. Baker House Books. 1965

St. Michael And The Angels. Illinois: Tan Books. 1983.

"Scientist Stifled From Teaching Life's Origins". *The Oregonian.*.
    Stephen C. Meyer. January 4, 1994.

"Judge Makes The Case For Christianity". *The Washington Post.*
    April 10, 1996.

"How True Are The Stories In The Bible?". *Time*. Dec. 18, 1995.

The Works Of Josephus. Hendrickson Publishers. 1995.

Barnett, Lincoln. *The Universe And Dr. Einstein*. Page 95.

Freeman, Ira. *All About The Wonders Of Chemistry*. Random
    House. New York. 1954.

Exploring Our Country. California State Dept. of Education. 1956.

Kempis, Thomas Á. *The Imitation Of Christ*. New York. Catholic
    Book Publishing. 1977.

Payne, J. *Encyclopedia of Bible Prophecy*. Harper & Rowe.

Marcellino, Dennis. *Sweeping It Under The Drug*. California:
    Lighthouse Publishing. 1988.

Schouppe, Fr. F.X. *Purgatory*. Illinois: Tan Books. 1994.

Wilmington, H.L. *Book Of Bible Lists*. Illinois: Tyndale. 1987.

Mounce, Robert. *The Book Of Revelation*. Eerdmans. 1977.

MacArthur Jr., Dr. John. *Looking Toward Heaven* (audio cassette
    series). California: Word Of Grace. 1987.

Bible study tools: Concordances (English, Greek, Hebrew),
    Nave's Topical Bible, Dictionaries (English, Greek,
    Hebrew), Greek Interlinear Bible, MacBible (NAB),
    Study Bibles (NAB, KJV, NKJV, Ryrie [NAS]),
    The Catholic Encyclopedia, The Catholic Catechism,
    Commentaries (Jerome, The New Bible Commentary).

About The Author

Dennis Marcellino is 48 years old, has been married 31 years, and has 3 sons and 1 daughter. He has completed 210 units in science, engineering, theology and psychology from California State University (Northridge), Los Angeles Valley College, Logos Bible College, Wholistic Psychotherapy Institute, City College of San Francisco, Pierce College and Santa Monica College.

For 28 years he, along with his award-winning math and analytical abilities, has had deep and continual involvement in most of the major philosophies and methods of personal growth in the world, including: most of the major and experimental forms of psychology (Freudian analysis, Transactional Analysis, hypnosis, psychodrama, Primal Therapy, Rolfing, drug therapy, wholistic psychotherapy, etc.), meditation (chanting, the word, light and music), eastern religion, Utopianism, various new-age involvements, Scientology and secular-humanism. His involvement in Christianity has included: Protestant fundamentalism, Catholicism, and a thorough knowledge of the Charismatic movement. Some of his experiences in psychology, science, spirituality and Christianity are described in this book.

He's had a private counseling practice, and was a counselor at Grace Community Church in Panorama City, California, headed by popular Christian author Dr. John MacArthur, Jr.

"Why Are We Here?" is his second book. His first book: "Sweeping It Under The Drug" (subtitled:) "A complete book about 'recreational' drugs, and how to have a great life without them", was the first book on the market (early 1988) in the current wave of concern about the 'drug issue'. It received great reviews and quotes (some of which can be seen on page 303 of this book).

He's also worked in the music industry. This work gave him the free time and funding necessary to do the research that resulted in this book. This work has included: being a member of Rubicon, The Elvin Bishop Group, Sly & The Family Stone, and The Tokens (who had the hit "The Lion Sleeps Tonight"). With these groups he recorded 10 albums/CDs. As a solo artist he's had two releases: "It's Christmas" and "Daddy's Home" (which was recorded with a desire to try to fill a very needy void in today's music market: healthy romance, family and love). He has a current CD on the market called: "An Evening To Remember". It's received many quotes as being very beautiful and relaxing, including a 5-star review in Jazzscene Magazine.

Dennis Marcellino

𝕬𝕔𝕜𝕟𝕠𝕨𝕝𝕖𝕯𝕘𝕖𝕞𝕖𝕟𝕥𝕤

First and foremost I'd like to thank God....for being there, and being exactly as He is: a standard of perfection...in an imperfect world. And I'd like to thank Him for caring about us, and giving us the most valuable things on earth: the Bible and His Spirit. I'd also like to thank the Holy Spirit for taking me on this 28 year (and still continuing) journey of seeing more and more of God's truth and beauty. Although it has at times been bumpy, I know that it's partially these bumps that now allow me the privilege of seeing and being able to put down in words God's truth. And I feel honored to be able to share and pass on such clear truth in such a filled-with-untruth time as we live in now.

I'd like to thank EWTN for being a lotus flower that floats atop a very muddy television viewing selection.

Putting a project like this together is not an easy task. Therefore I want to thank those who have helped and supported me along the way: my son Timmy (and also thanks for his great analogies in this book), my wife Pat, my son Tony, Mark and Janice Stefani, Roberta and Dennis Haglund, Daryl Dixon, Ron Fry, Sally Stuart, Dan Poynter, Jan Bear and Ron Turner (the "friend" on page 121). I know there'll be more people to thank between the time this book goes to the printer and the time it gets to the readers...so I'd like to thank them here in advance. The above photo is by Melody Saunders.

"...a catalyst to turn around the lives of those currently in the grip of drug addiction. It is the dedication of people like the author that gives all of us hope for the future."

G. Albert Howenstein, Jr., Executive Director, Office Of
Criminal Justice Planning, California Governor's office

"...frank and friendly...sincere and optimistic...not only concerned with ridding people's lives of drugs, but also with leading them to a higher state of being and greater fulfillment as individuals...a sympathetic voice which will affect readers for the better...This book is personal rather than systematically therapeutic or a 'pop' treatment of a current social concern...touches upon the important factors of human life---the self, environment, relationships, mates, and others."

Corinne Buck, The Small Press Book Review ('feature' review)

"I highly recommend the reading of this book as an understanding guide for all of the 12 step recovery programs. It gave me greater insight into my need for continuous spiritual development in order to maintain quality sobriety and peace of mind."

Gloria Montgomery
Chairperson, ALL/ANON GROUP. Founder, RECOVERY SYSTEMS
Founded many alcohol & chemical dependency rehab centers
and hospital clinics throughout the U.S. & Canada
CEDARS SINAI Alcoholism Counselor. 29 years clean & sober
Personal counselor to Shelley Winters. Highly mentioned in her book.

"Your book is absolutely --WONDERFUL! I could not put it down until I had read all of it. It is one of the most fascinating books I have read in years. One thing is certain ... you are a very talented and creative writer. SWEEPING IT UNDER THE DRUG possesses huge market potential. It has all the ingredients of a best seller. In my opinion it has success written all over it."

Robert Tyre, Editor, Eclectic Press

"Very powerful material. An amazing piece of work by an amazing man."

Scott Fagan, Head of the recovery unit at Brotman Hospital
(one of Los Angeles' largest).
UCLA graduate (Drug Rehabilitation Clinic Design)
Very active leader in AA and CA (Cocaine Anonymous)

"...a carefully reasoned argument against drug use that goes further than telling people to 'just say no'--it offers real help for people who want to break free of the bondage of drugs. The book gives vivid insight into the realities of the drug culture that most of us never see."

Dr. John MacArthur Jr., a leading author in the Christian market,
Pastor, Grace Community Church, Sun Valley, CA

Order Form

Lighthouse Publishing
PO Box 40 - B
Gladstone, Oregon   97027
(503) 557-2277
E-mail: Light3740@aol.com

Telephone orders: 1-**800**-355-2776
Mail orders: Lighthouse, Box 40-B, Gladstone, OR 97027
Fax orders: (503) 557-2278
Internet: http://members.aol.com/Light3740/House.html

PRICES

"Why Are We Here?" $14.50
"Sweeping It Under The Drug" (see pages 301 & 303) $10
"The 10 Awarenesses" A solution to all non-physical problems $6
"Daddy's Home" (see p. 301)   (CD) $12; (cassette) $7
"An Evening To Remember" (see p.301) (CD)$16; (cass.) $11
"It's Christmas"   (cassette single) $2
"T.R.U.E." Newsletter   Bi-monthly; $19/year,$3.50/issue

SHIPPING

Book Rate: $2.50 for first book/CD/cassette ($3.50 for
Air Mail)...75 cents for each additional item.

PAYMENT

☐ Check/Money Order

☐ Credit Card: VISA__ MasterCard__ AMEX__ Discover_
Card number:_____
Name on card:_____Exp. date:__/__

PLEASE SEND TO

NAME:_____
ADDRESS:_____
CITY:_____ **STATE:**____ **ZIP:**_____
COUNTRY:_____ **PHONE:**_____